What Your Colleagues Are Saying . . .

"A welcome addition to the professional literature on dual language program implementation! Co-planning across instructional personnel and across languages, co-teaching, collaborative assessment, and collaborative leadership are critical to the success of dual language programs, and this volume delivers on all of those topics. Packed with useful figures, charts, and checklists and organized around catchy recurring icons that represent the overarching organizational structure for each chapter, this volume is extremely approachable, highly interactive, and well grounded in the four pillars of effective dual language programs."

—Nancy Cloud
Professor Emerita
Feinstein School of Education and Human Development, Rhode Island College

"Educators involved in dual language programs will find *Collaboration and Co-Teaching for Dual Language Learners: Transforming Programs for Multilingualism and Equity* a much-needed book that guides teachers in how to effectively plan and reflect together. The many voices represented in the book are refreshing, and the research presented is strengths based and highly relevant. This book is essential reading for teachers in two-teacher dual language programs who share students!"

—Karen Beeman
Co-Author of *Teaching for Biliteracy: Strengthening Bridges Between Languages* and Co-Founder of the Center for Teaching for Biliteracy Skokie, IL

"Successful collaboration in education has transformative power for the educators engaged in it and, most important, for the students benefiting from it. Yet, collaboration requires specific resources for success—time, intention, knowledge, and skill. *Collaboration and Co-Teaching for Dual Language Learners* is a key publication for acquiring the knowledge and skills to make collaboration successful in dual language classrooms. From a social justice perspective, it is a critical contribution to the field to bring about equity to the multilingual learners in dual language. Thank you for bringing this work to life and to our classrooms. ¡Adelante!"

—Mariana Castro
Deputy Director
Wisconsin Center for Education Research, University of Wisconsin–Madison

"In this volume, the authors offer a strong rationale and practical, research-informed guidance for teacher collaboration and co-teaching for the sake of dual language education and the support needed to effectively design, deliver, and assess engaging instruction in dual language programs. In this unique resource, you will explore the fundamentals of dual language education and how the collaborative instructional cycle—co-planning, co-teaching, co-assessment, and co-reflection—is an essential component of dual language programs. This one-of-a-kind book is a must-read for anyone who teaches or administers a dual language program!"

—**Maria G. Dove**
Professor
School of Education and Human Services, Molloy University
Rockville Centre, NY

"In this powerful and practical new resource, Joan Lachance and Andrea Honigsfeld have outlined not only why teachers should collaborate in dual language programs, but also how this collaboration can happen and what school leaders can do to support it. By integrating the collaborative cycle of co-planning, co-teaching, co-assessing, and co-reflecting within the unique dual language ecosystem, this book helps to build important connections—across languages and across disciplines—catalyzing both student learning and teacher learning."

—**Jon Nordmeyer**
International Program Director
WIDA and University of Wisconsin–Madison

"This is an invaluable resource for guiding educators who co-teach and co-plan in dual language programs. Not only is it based on theory and research but it also includes options to facilitate the process of getting started and making existing dual language programs more effective. This well-stated phrase—'Dual language is for everyone in K–12 education'—cannot be emphasized enough! Multilingualism promotes equity for all and should be the norm in all schools!"

—**Mónica Lara**
Senior Educational Consultant for Bilingualism and Biliteracy
San Antonio, TX

"At last, a book we have been waiting for—one that combines our growing interest in dual language programming with collaboration and co-teaching. Scholars Joan Lachance and Andrea Honigsfeld provide practical guidance on the laws and regulations on one hand and our professional creativity and inspiration on the other. Drawing from their kindred spirit of space adventure and exploration, each chapter takes readers to a Mission Control room to learn about key ideas, an Exploration site to try new things in our own contexts, a Captain's Log space to reflect on our learning, Navigation Systems to provide us with key information from research and the field, and much more as we prepare for takeoff to using an approach that works."

—**Debbie Zacarian**
Author of *Transforming Schools for Multilingual Learners: A Comprehensive Guide for Educators*
Zacarian and Associates

"This engaging and accessible book provides a valuable resource to catalyze teacher collaboration in dual language programs. Joan Lachance and Andrea Honigsfeld take care to present strategies across the collaborative instructional cycle—from planning to teaching to assessment to reflection. For the novice and veteran alike, this work will guide and inspire collegial partnerships that advance dynamic bilingualism."

—**Martin Scanlan**
Associate Professor at Lynch School of Education and Human Development
Campion Hall, Boston College

"This book is the professional resource we've all been waiting for! I love the structure of this book and how it's designed for an accessible book study for teams as they navigate the unique opportunities presented by co-teaching in dual language settings. I found this resource incredibly valuable for educators and leaders as it has practical tools and strategies that can equip us all to effectively collaborate with each other in our effort to better serve our dual language students!"

—**Carly Spina**
Multilingual Education Specialist
Illinois Resource Center
Arlington Heights, IL

"*Collaboration and Co-Teaching for Dual Language Learners: Transforming Programs for Multilingualism and Equity* is *the* instructional resource that our dual language programs have been waiting for. It provides coaches and teachers a dual language–specific collaborative instructional cycle that enhances teacher capacity and elevates student outcomes. Every chapter provides tips and tools for effective and practical implementation. I highly recommend it for district dual language directors, campus and district coordinators, coaches, teachers, and paraprofessionals."

—**Gloria Stewart-Kooper**
Bilingual ESL Director
Lamar Consolidated ISD
Rosenberg, TX

"Joan Lachance and Andrea Honigsfeld's text invites us to explore learning spaces where dual language programming and teacher collaboration unite, creating a schoolwide web of intentional support for multilingual learners to flourish both academically and linguistically. I can't wait to fly to the moon with this transformative lens of collaboration coupled with multilingual language development!"

—**Helen (Lannie) Simpson**
English Learner Director
Burke County Public Schools, NC

"Mission accomplished! My mind traveled through six chapters with a mission in mind: to learn, to understand, to anchor into real examples of practice and powerful strategies based on research. Strategic reflection pushes readers to pause, think, and formulate next steps to implement right away. This exceptional resource provides educators with much-needed tools to navigate, explore, and map out ways to develop higher levels of teaching in dual language programs. As a dual language instructional coach, I traverse these territories in my daily practice, and I can say I have found a focus for my upcoming year in my school with this book. *Es una combinación perfecta de teoría, práctica, y reflexión.*"

—**Gabriela Garcia-Marroquin**
Dual Language Instructional Coach
Jeffco Public Schools
Edgewater, CO

"Very few books explore the topic in a way that Joan Lachance and Andrea Honigsfeld do. This book is for anyone embarking on implementing a dual language approach or revisiting their current program. It pinpoints the key elements of collaboration and co-teaching from delivery, to assessment, to reflection. The book is unique in its format, allowing the reader the opportunity to hear from practitioners and students."

—**Barbara Tedesco**
Co-Manager
Language & Literacy Associates for Multilingual and Multicultural Education
(LLAMAME)
Colonia, NJ

"This book couldn't be more timely! Creating space for teacher and leader collaboration that is efficient and effective can make all the difference when striving for a well-articulated program where each and every dual language immersion student, teacher, and leader thrives. Thank you for this publication. It will go a long way toward helping leaders and teachers to advocate in their own districts and schools for finding space in an already busy schedule for meaningful collaboration."

—**Jon Valentine**
Director of World Languages and Dual Language Immersion
Gwinnett County (GA) Public Schools

"Joan Lachance and Andrea Honigsfeld harness their knowledge on collaborative practices to provide critical research-supported and classroom-approved recommendations for dual language educators that will maximize student growth toward bilingualism, biliteracy, and multiculturalism. This book will be a powerful and practical tool for educators to understand the how and why of collaborative practices in a dual language program."

—**Ryan Zak**
Director of Linguistic Programs
Mundelein (IL) Elementary School District 75

"This book provides a better understanding of how collaboration can move student learning, as well as strategies for additive forms of multilingualism, and presents an invaluable historical perspective addressing the dangers of a deficit approach to language pedagogy. Examples and anecdotes show how dual language programs and collaborative teaching can change dynamics and better support student learning. Not only does this book provide tools and resources; it also provides writing and discussion prompts that allow readers to process and clarify their own perspectives as they react to the content. This book really hits the mark in helping shift mindsets about dual language education."

—**Lisa Auslander**
Senior Project Direct and Principal Investigator
Bridges to Academic Success, Center for Advanced Study in Education (CASE),
Graduate Center, CUNY

"This practitioner-oriented book is a must-have for all educators—from paraprofessionals to classroom teachers to school and district leaders—who support dual language learners. It is perfectly timed for today's dual language educators who are advancing students toward multilingual language diversity. In addition to the most recent foundational research on dual language instruction, the book provides a plethora of essential tools and resources, coupled with real-world scenarios demonstrating the work necessary to implement effective dual language programs. Best practices are highlighted and showcased throughout the book through a robust array of authentic examples."

—**Ron Woo**
Executive Director
NYS Statewide Language RBERN (Regional Bilingual Education Resource Network)
Metro Center, New York University

"Our students deserve coherent, language-rich, multilingual learning, yet it's often so hard when we lack a map to guide our work. Joan Lachance and Andrea Honigsfeld remind us that our intentional planning and our collaborative conversations will ensure that our students simultaneously develop academic, linguistic, and cross-cultural skills. I'm delighted that Joan and Andrea have stepped into this unique space, and I'm anxious to share their road map with my colleagues in Tigard-Tualatin schools."

—**Tim Blackburn**
Title III Administrator
Tigard-Tualatin (OR) School District

"It is exciting to see an advance copy of this book. This book will be transformational for our practice as a group of dual language schools. The authors masterfully weave practice, practical application, pedagogy, and the multicultural multilingual voices of students and educators in schools throughout the globe. I am thrilled to have this resource for my dual language teams. It is packed with concrete examples of pedagogy manifested in the classroom, but also highlights that most important ingredient that must be baked into any dual language program—collaborative practice."

—**Stephanie Drynan**
Dual Language Coordinator
Qatar Foundation Schools

COLLABORATION and CO-TEACHING for DUAL LANGUAGE LEARNERS

COLLABORATION and CO-TEACHING for DUAL LANGUAGE LEARNERS

Transforming Programs for Multilingualism and Equity

Joan Lachance

Andrea Honigsfeld

Foreword by Margo Gottlieb

Including Illustrations by Claribel González

FOR INFORMATION:

Corwin
A SAGE Company
2455 Teller Road
Thousand Oaks, California 91320
(800) 233-9936
www.corwin.com

SAGE Publications Ltd.
1 Oliver's Yard
55 City Road
London EC1Y 1SP
United Kingdom

SAGE Publications India Pvt. Ltd.
B 1/I 1 Mohan Cooperative Industrial Area
Mathura Road, New Delhi 110 044
India

SAGE Publications Asia-Pacific Pte. Ltd.
18 Cross Street #10-10/11/12
China Square Central
Singapore 048423

President: Mike Soules
Vice President and Editorial
   Director: Monica Eckman
Program Director and Publisher: Dan Alpert
Content Development Editor: Mia Rodriguez
Editorial Assistant: Natalie Delpino
Project Editor: Amy Schroller
Copy Editor: Melinda Masson
Typesetter: C&M Digitals (P) Ltd.
Proofreader: Dennis Webb
Indexer: Judy Hunt
Cover Designer: Gail Buschman
Marketing Manager: Melissa Duclos

Copyright © 2023 by Corwin Press, Inc.

All rights reserved. Except as permitted by U.S. copyright law, no part of this work may be reproduced or distributed in any form or by any means, or stored in a database or retrieval system, without permission in writing from the publisher.

When forms and sample documents appearing in this work are intended for reproduction, they will be marked as such. Reproduction of their use is authorized for educational use by educators, local school sites, and/or noncommercial or nonprofit entities that have purchased the book.

All third-party trademarks referenced or depicted herein are included solely for the purpose of illustration and are the property of their respective owners. Reference to these trademarks in no way indicates any relationship with, or endorsement by, the trademark owner.

Printed in the United States of America

Library of Congress Cataloging-in-Publication Data

Names: Lachance, Joan, author. | Honigsfeld, Andrea, 1965- author.

Title: Collaboration and co-teaching for dual language learners : transforming programs for multilingualism / Joan R. Lachance, Andrea Honigsfeld.

Description: Thousand Oaks, California : Corwin, [2023] | Includes bibliographical references and index.

Identifiers: LCCN 2022034390 | ISBN 9781071849996 (paperback) | ISBN 9781071850039 (epub) | ISBN 9781071850022 (epub) | ISBN 9781071850015 (pdf)

Subjects: LCSH: Teaching teams—United States. | Multilingualism—United States. | School improvement programs—United States. | Language and languages—Study and teaching—United States.

Classification: LCC LB1029.T4 L33 2023 | DDC 370.117/50973—dc23/eng/20220921
LC record available at https://lccn.loc.gov/2022034390

This book is printed on acid-free paper.

23 24 25 26 10 9 8 7 6 5 4 3 2

DISCLAIMER: This book may direct you to access third-party content via Web links, QR codes, or other scannable technologies, which are provided for your reference by the author(s). Corwin makes no guarantee that such third-party content will be available for your use and encourages you to review the terms and conditions of such third-party content. Corwin takes no responsibility and assumes no liability for your use of any third-party content, nor does Corwin approve, sponsor, endorse, verify, or certify such third-party content.

Contents

Companion Website Contents	xiii
Foreword	xv
Margo Gottlieb	
Acknowledgments	xix
About the Authors	xxi
About the Illustrator	xxv
Chapter 1. Introduction	1
Chapter 2. Foundations of Dual Language Programs	27
Chapter 3. Collaborative Planning in Dual Language Programs	63
Chapter 4. Collaborative Teaching in Dual Language Programs	105
Chapter 5. Collaborative Assessment and Reflection in Dual Language Programs	139
Chapter 6. Collaborative Leadership Support for Dual Language Programs	173
References	**211**
Author Index	**217**
Subject Index	**221**

Companion Website Contents

Figure 2.7:	Questions to Begin the Conversations	58
Figure 3.2:	Co-Planning Pillars and Priorities Crosswalk Grid	75
Figure 3.4:	Integrated Focus on Planning for Dual Language Teaching	78
Figure 3.12:	Co-Planning Focus Form for Dual Language Instruction: A Week-at-a-Glance Tool	99
Figure 3.13:	Checklist for Collaboratively Planning Based on the 12 Dimensions of Scaffolding	100
Figure 5.1:	Multidimensional Assessment of Classroom Language Use in Dual Language Classrooms	147
Figure 5.2:	Integrated Focus on Assessing Your Dual Language Teaching	151
Figure 5.6:	A Collaborative Protocol of "Look Fors" in Lesson Activities	156
Figure 5.7:	A Collaborative Protocol to Co-Design Assessment Tools and Measures	157
Figure 5.8:	A Collaborative Protocol to Review Existing Assessment Results	158
Figure 5.11:	EL ESPEJO Framework Adapted for Dual Language Classrooms	168
Figure 6.4:	Discussion Prompts for Teachers' Collaborative Curricular and Instructional Decisions	184
Figure 6.7:	Collaborative Leadership Discussion Prompts	191
Figure 6.8:	The Four Pillars of Dual Language Education in Collaborative Leadership	195
Figure 6.9:	"Look Fors" in Holistic Program Evaluation	197
Figure 6.10:	Navigation System for Your Common Understandings, Shared Visions, and Shared Goals	200
Figure 6.12:	Guiding Questions for Creating and Sustaining Equitable Dual Language Programs	205

Visit the companion website for downloadable resources at
Resources.corwin.com/CollaborationandCoTeachingforDLL

Foreword

You are about to embark on an unparalleled adventure into unchartered territory. In fusing principles and practices of dual language education with those of co-teaching/collaboration, Lachance and Honigsfeld create an unrivaled rationale for propelling educators of multilingual learners into the stratosphere. This merger, exemplified by an extensive space metaphor along with iconic reminders, gives a unique perspective on how to position the four pillars of dual language education—bilingualism/biliteracy, high academic achievement, sociocultural competence, and critical consciousness—onto a foundation of collaboration. The synergy produced by this teaming, substantiated by expert testimony, literature, and research, provides a solid grounding for pairing these two educational endeavors.

Adhering to the sociocultural tenet that learning is a social activity, we see how the coupling of dual language and co-teaching can strengthen linguistic and cultural connections among teachers and between teachers and multilingual learners. Lachance and Honigsfeld thoughtfully tackle this multifaceted vision of language education. In systematically undertaking this challenge, we are made aware of the innumerable factors to be considered in collaborative dual language program design, including: (1) different configurations of teacher collaboration, (2) models of dual language education, (3) languages of instruction and groupings of multilingual learners, and (4) adherence (or not) to the stipulated time allocation assigned to each language of instruction.

Research has confirmed that dual language programs, when constructed as enhanced and accelerated experiences for all students, offer language-rich environments in multiple languages that simply cannot be replicated in monolingual classrooms. Keeping this fact in mind, we are also made keenly aware of the strength of the additive features of collaboration and co-teaching when applied to any educational initiative. The heart of the book draws on strong testimonials on the value and benefits of combining dual language with collaboration from both scholars and practitioners. The substantial body of evidence that emerges supports dual language programming throughout the collaborative instructional cycle- co-planning, co-teaching/team-teaching, co-assessment, and co-reflection.

Clearly articulated goals and outcomes of each chapter illuminate the natural interaction between collaboration and dual language that puts a premium on language-driven content in two languages. After the introduction, historical backdrop, and reasoning behind dual language education that are outlined in the first two chapters, *Collaboration and Co-Teaching for Dual Language Learners* moves into enacting each phase of the collaboration cycle through field-based examples from dual language educators and multilingual learners. Their varied perspectives lend themselves to an important philosophical shift—from embracing dual language programs as the interplay between two languages to envisioning dual language programs as an expression of multilingualism.

In Chapter 3, collaborative planning within dual language contexts, we create a vision of co-teaching as a shared experience in which partner educators work together to reinforce the values of multilingualism and multiculturalism within a robust standards-aligned academic program. Intentionality is a key ingredient to this process as teachers collaborate in weaving elements of language education unique to multilingual learners, such as metalinguistic awareness, opportunities for translanguaging, and strategies for scaffolding, into curriculum. In addition, during this initial phase, tips and co-planning tools based on the four pillars or dimensions of dual language spark engagement of co-educators.

Chapter 4 presents an array of collaborative teaching approaches for both partnership and co-teaching models as pathways that lead to equitable instructional delivery for multilingual learners in elementary and secondary settings. A rationale bolstered by real-life examples of seven approaches or collaborative models opens possibilities to the many choices for customizing co-teaching that take into account the: (1) students, (2) content, (3) types of learning activities, (4) participating teachers' preferences, (5) logistics, and (6) availability and organization of space. Additionally, the four pillars of dual language serve as the launchpad for partner or co-teachers' agreement and commitment to a set of shared premises and core beliefs for their selected model.

Collaborative assessment and reflection, the focus of Chapter 5, invites multilingual learners and their teachers to continue learning from each other through ongoing interaction and feedback. We see how three collaborative approaches—assessment as, for, and of learning- can optimize the building of relationships throughout the instructional cycle. A series of protocols and actionable steps apply these assessment approaches specifically to dual language contexts. Ultimately, the convergence and alignment of the collaborative, instructional, and assessment cycles build a strong case for creating and sustaining an equitable educational system for multilingual learners.

Continuous support from leadership, illuminated in the final chapter, is an absolute necessity for ensuring and reinforcing the success of multilingual learners in dual language programs. The presence of teacher and administrator co-leadership reinforces and makes visible collaborative planning, collaborative teaching, and collaborative assessment and reflection. What hopefully emerges from the teaming of administrators and teachers is ongoing dialog and deep conversations on issues that lead to a navigation system that consist of a common vision, shared ownership, enduring trust, and mutual respect. Joint decisions around these core values of dual language, in turn, can jumpstart curricular, instructional, and programmatic transformation.

Empowered by the opportunity to become a potential collaborator in the growing dual language network of educators, it's time to gear up for a stimulating journey. In the spirit of collaboration, this ground-breaking book is your booster rocket for rethinking and reconceptualizing the who, what, where, when, and why of dual language education. Join Lachance and Honigsfeld in counting down to an historic launch into an exciting newly configured dual language world where collaboration reigns.

—Margo Gottlieb
Co-founder of WIDA, author and consultant

Acknowledgments

We are most grateful to the many educators who shared their experience, passion for dual language education, and commitment to collaboration. Their generosity with their time and expertise as they participated in interviews, countless email exchanges, phone calls, or Zoom meetings, or as they opened their classroom or office doors to us, is deeply appreciated. We are truly honored that we are able to include both researchers' and practitioners' perspectives in this volume along with numerous classroom scenarios, collaboration tools, success stories, photographs, and other artifacts as examples of what collaboration may look like in the dual language context. A very special bilingual educator, Claribel González, served not only as our critical friend but also as the sketch note artist for the book. Her creative talents and insightful comments are invaluable additions to this volume. We are also very grateful to Alyson Mooney for her technical assistance with the manuscript preparation.

The teachers whose work informed and/or illustrated many of the points made in this book include Alejandra Aguilera, Vanessa Aspiazu, Sarah Brooks, Sami Chen, Jaclyn Ewing, Aida Alejandra Garcia, Marie Green, Liliana Grejada, Matt Hajdun, Gilliam Jackson, Sean Kennedy, Vanessa Kittilsen, Caitlyn (Kate) McNally, Kelly Murphy, Sarah Olsen, Lauren Ozimek, Susan Pryor, Sabina Rahman, Blake Ramsey, Tamara Shotts, Nidia Vaz-Correia, Brittany Welch, and María Cristina Youtsey.

The many school and district administrators, coaches, or consultants who also supported this project directly or indirectly are Sana Alavi, Dalal Ali Ahmed, Maha R. Al Romaihi, Jeremy Aldrich, Gloria Cho, Stephanie Drynan, Alexandra El Khawaja, Julianne Foster, Hartwell Francis (Unega Tsisdu), Francesco L. Fratto, Kerry A. Girod-Fedha, Erin Goldstein, Mats Haaland, Aurelia Henriquez, Rocio Hernandez, Tamara K. Hewlett, Megan Hichwa, Kellie M. Jones, Seika Kobari, Sarah LoPresti, Michelle Marrone, Carmen Melendez-Quintero, Danette Meyer, Jennifer C. Norton, Patricia Padilla, Natalie Pohl, Omar Ponce Vera, Alma G. Rocha, Carol Rodd, Michael Rodríguez, Katie Smith, Norma Villavicencio, Chelsea Wilson, Ruiyan Xiong, Jess Yáñez, Ryan Zak, and Todd Zollinger.

Researchers and nationally recognized experts who also offered their support for this book include Margarita Calderón, Virginia Collier, Maria G. Dove, Margo Gottlieb, Tan Huynh, Jon Nordmeyer, Sarah Bernadette Ottow, and Wayne Thomas.

We are most appreciative of our editor, Dan Alpert, who believes that teacher collaboration, partnership teaching, and co-teaching continue to be a critical topic and wholeheartedly supported this project! We also wish to thank the entire Corwin team, especially Lucas Schleicher and Mia Rodriguez, for their work on the manuscript preparation and production process and marketing.

We are indebted to the author of the foreword, Margo Gottlieb, as well as all our critical friends and peer reviewers—Margarita Calderón, Marialuisa DiStefano, Phyllis Hardy, Barbara Kennedy, Jon Nordmeyer, Marjorie Ringler, and Michael Rodríguez—for their recommendations and validations of our work. We also wish to acknowledge many other friends and colleagues who have encouraged us to pursue this project: You know who you are, and we love you!

About the Authors

Joan Lachance, PhD, is an associate professor of teaching English as a second language (TESL) at the University of North Carolina at Charlotte. She directs the TESL graduate programs and undergraduate TESL minor. She is the co-author of the National Dual Language Education Teacher Preparation Standards and the director of the Council for the Accreditation of Educator Preparation (CAEP) specialized professional association in dual language education called "EMMA: Education for a Multilingual Multicultural America." She received her undergraduate degree in secondary education, modern languages, and linguistics from Florida International University. With Spanish as the language of program delivery, she completed graduate coursework to earn her master's degree in school counseling from Pontifical Catholic University in Poncé, Puerto Rico. Dr. Lachance completed her doctoral work in curriculum and instruction, with an emphasis on urban education, literacy, and TESL, at the University of North Carolina at Charlotte.

Dr. Lachance's research agenda encompasses dual language teacher preparation, academic literacy development, and authentic assessment with multilingual learners and has resulted in over 25 publications including articles, book chapters, technical reports, and state-level curriculum guides since joining UNC Charlotte. She serves on several journal editorial boards and is a board member of the Multistate Association for Bilingual Education (MABE), Northeast. With the publication of this book, Dr. Lachance is specializing one aspect of her work further into collaboration and co-teaching for multilingual learners in the dual language context. She is also working to support dual language education for the preservation of Native American languages, currently and most honorably collaborating with a K–8 school serving the Eastern Band of Cherokee Indians (EBCI).

In addition to her faculty position, Dr. Lachance's service agenda has resulted in over 100 conference presentations, invited panels, keynotes, and roundtables to support the North Carolina Department of Public Instruction and the nation at large. Her service specializes in professional learning for teachers, school counselors, and school administrators. She co-created materials and professional learning institutes for myriad North Carolina state-led initiatives including *Using the WIDA Standards*, *The North Carolina Guide to the SIOP Model*, *The North Carolina Guide to ExC-ELL*, and *Dual Language/Immersion Program Support*. The presentations, webinars, and asynchronous learning opportunities share innovative practices for multilingual learner academic language development, equitable active multilingual learner engagement, dual language program development, sociocultural nuances in school counseling, and international comparative education.

For fun, Dr. Lachance enjoys camping—it's really glamping!—with her husband Carl, their son, and their two rescue dogs. She is passionate about science, astronomy, the outdoors, hiking in the Blue Ridge Mountains, and the preservation of the Appalachian Trail. While she lives and works in North Carolina, she shares her heart deeply with New Mexico and has a passion for the Native American Pueblo languages, the Pueblo ways of living, and *everything Hatch green chile*. Finally, she is a former dual language parent, who had the honor of experiencing multilingualism come to life in her own home.

Andrea Honigsfeld, EdD, is a professor in the School of Education and Human Services at Molloy University in Rockville Centre, New York, where she teaches graduate courses related to cultural and linguistic diversity. Before entering the field of teacher education, she was an English as a foreign language (EFL) teacher in Hungary (Grades 5–8 and adult) and an English as a second language (ESL) teacher in New York City (Grades K–3 and adult). She also taught Hungarian at New York University.

She was the recipient of a doctoral fellowship at St. John's University in New York, where she conducted research on individualized instruction and learning styles. She has published extensively on working with English learners and providing individualized instruction based on learning style preferences. She received a Fulbright award to lecture in Iceland in the fall of 2002. In the past 12 years, she has been presenting at conferences across the United States, Great Britain, Denmark, Sweden, the Philippines, and the United Arab Emirates. She frequently offers professional learning opportunities, primarily focusing on effective differentiated strategies and collaborative practices for English language development specialists and general education teachers. She co-authored *Differentiated Instruction for At-Risk Students* (2009) and co-edited the five-volume *Breaking the Mold of Education* series (2010–2013), published by Rowman and Littlefield. She is also the co-author of *Core Instructional Routines: Go-To Structures for Effective Literacy Teaching, K–5 and 6–12* (2014) and author of *Growing Language and Literacy* (2019), published by Heinemann. With Maria Dove, she co-edited *Co-Teaching and Other Collaborative Practices in the EFL/ESL Classroom: Rationale, Research, Reflections, and Recommendations* (2012) and *Co-Teaching for English Learners: Evidence-Based Practices and Research-Informed Outcomes* (2020). Dove and Honigsfeld also co-authored *Collaboration and Co-Teaching: Strategies for English Learners* (2010), *Common Core for the Not-So-Common Learner, Grades K–5: English Language Arts Strategies* (2013), *Common Core for the Not-So-Common Learner, Grades 6–12: English Language Arts Strategies* (2013), *Beyond Core Expectations: A Schoolwide Framework for Serving the Not-So-Common Learner* (2014), *Collaboration and Co-Teaching: A Leader's Guide* (2015), *Co-Teaching for English Learners: A Guide to Collaborative Planning, Instruction, Assessment, and Reflection* (2018), *Collaborating for English Learners: A Foundational Guide to Integrated Practices* (2019), and *Co-Planning: 5 Essential Practices to Integrate Curriculum and Instruction for English Learners* (2022). She is a contributing author of *Breaking Down the Wall: Essential Shifts for English Learner Success* (2020), *From Equity Insights to Action* (2021), and *Digital-Age Teaching for English Learners* (2022). Nine of her Corwin books are best sellers.

About the Illustrator

Claribel González is a resource specialist for the Regional Bilingual Education Resource Network (RBERN) in western New York. She supports districts in achieving academic excellence for multilingual learners through professional development, technical assistance, and instructional coaching. Her passion for language and equity started at a young age as she was raised in a bilingual home and experienced the benefits of participating in bilingual programs. As an avid doodler, she celebrates creativity and the power of sketch notes as a vehicle to synthesize information. She has illustrated *From Equity Insights to Action: Critical Strategies for Teaching Multilingual Learners* (2021) and *Co-Planning: Five Essential Practices to Integrate Curriculum and Instruction for English Learners* (2021), both published by Corwin. González has served as a bilingual classroom teacher and district instructional coach. She is currently a doctoral student in the language education and multilingualism program at the University at Buffalo. Her research interests include bilingual education, biliteracy, and assessments.

This book is dedicated to all the families, children, and educators who champion dual language education!

We also dedicate this book to our respective families who are our ongoing inspiration.

From Joan

To Carl and Manu for transforming my life by sharing yours with me.

To Ginger and Wayne for transforming dual language education by virtue of your lifelong research, courage, and dedication to programs that are best for students. I am forever grateful for your heartfelt guidance, our kindred fellowship, and our shared experiences.

To Spencer and Sami for sharing a "love for the Very Large Array" with me.

To Andrea for honoring me with your mentorship, brilliance, and sense of adventure in the co-creation of this book.

To Unega Tsisdu, Tohisgi, Alsqwetawo, Nugaltli, and Twodi for being in this time.

From Andrea

To Howie, Benjamin, Jacob, and Noah for always supporting me in all my endeavors.

Introduction 1

> *"Dual language education for multilingualism is the tool for social and educational transformation."*
>
> —Wayne Thomas and Virginia Collier

Did you know . . . ?

- There are over 350 named languages and dialects spoken in the United States.
- Almost one-quarter of U.S. children speak a language other than English at home.
- Nearly one-third of children under the age of 8 have at least one parent who speaks a language other than English at home.
- More than 10% of school-age children (about 5 million) are classified as English learners (a large percentage of whom are U.S. citizens, born in the United States).
- There are over 3,600 dual language programs across the United States (American Councils Research Center, 2021).
- The five states with the most dual language programs (over 200) are California, Texas, New York, Utah, and North Carolina.
- The top five languages in dual language instruction are Spanish, Chinese, French, Japanese, and German (closely followed by Portuguese, Hawaiian, and Korean).
- The Seal of Biliteracy is approved in 48 U.S. states.
- Multilingualism, as well as bilingualism, has significant academic, cognitive, economic, and sociocultural benefits (National Clearinghouse for English Language Acquisition, 2022).
- Students participating in dual language education, of all the program models that support language development, consistently outperform others academically.
- Multilingualism is the norm in much of the world.
- It is never too late to learn a new language.
- The most important instructional strategy for dual language learning requires students to collaborate and co-create knowledge.
- Multilingual people demonstrate increased creativity and problem-solving skills (Thomas & Collier, 2017).
- With collaboration and shared leadership, dual language programs can eliminate the need for pullout programs.

What Is Dual Language Education?

Much has been written, explored, and even debated about bilingualism and bilingual education. More specifically, there is an emerging body of research and practitioner-oriented work about dual language education and its benefits for all students. There is much less practical guidance, however, on how to infuse and sustain teacher collaboration in dual language programs. Before we offer opportunities to fill that gap in this book, let's explore a few basics.

Simply stated, dual language education is defined as programs that teach content and literacy in two languages. We begin by acknowledging there are many operational definitions of dual language education in the field. For the purposes of this book, we recognize that two-way dual language programs typically serve students from two different linguistic groups or backgrounds whereas one-way programs typically serve students from a more similar linguistic group. In dual language programs, the students participate in at least half of the instructional day in their home or primary language and the remainder of the instructional day in the program's partner language. Depending on the program's time allotments, the percentages of home/primary and partner language instruction will vary. For example, in a 90/10 program, a greater percentage of the instruction is in the program language other than English, and instruction shifts over time until reaching the minimum of 50/50 in both program languages.

Inclusive of the varying time allotment options, all dual language program types have key aspects that unify the program structure. According to the *Guiding Principles of Dual Language Education* (Howard et al., 2018),

> *dual language* refers to any program that provides literacy and content instruction to all students through two languages and that promotes bilingualism and biliteracy, grade-level academic achievement, and sociocultural competence—a term encompassing identity development, cross-cultural competence, and multicultural appreciation—for all students. Dual language programs can be either one-way or two-way depending on the student population. (p. 3)

To look a bit further—and to disrupt some common myths about dual language development and dual language instruction (Espinosa, 2013)—we offer a few additional key points about what dual language *is* and what it *is not*:

- Dual language *is* a way to promote multilingualism via content-based instruction in two languages.
- Dual language *is* for everyone in K–12 education—and beyond!
- Dual language *is* a way to advance language education.
- Dual language *is* a way to design, deliver, and assess intuitive learning across languages.

- Dual language *is* a program of acceleration.

- Dual language *is* dynamic and increases learners' cognition and metacognition.

- Dual language *is not* just for students in early grades.

- Dual language *is not* a way to promote English while learners transition away from multilingual development.

- Dual language *is not* an enrichment or gifted program for specially selected students.

- Dual language *is not* going to confuse learners, nor will it delay language development for participants.

- Dual language *is not* off-limits for students with special needs who also participate in special education programs of service.

- Dual language *is not* the same as parallel monolingual development in two languages.

A Note on Terminology

Along with so many other researchers and practitioners, we have encountered challenges when finding and using consistent terminology. "Two-way bilingual models are no different, alternatively termed two-way or dual language immersion (recalling their roots in Canadian immersion models), dual language education, two-way dual language education, two-way bilingual education, and two-way dual language bilingual education" (Hamman-Ortiz & Palmer, 2020). We wish to recognize that our readers might be using a range of different terminology. It is beyond the scope of this book to address the complex and occasionally conflicting ways dual language programs are designed, implemented, and labeled. Our goal is to acknowledge the rich diversity within the field, the well-established seminal research, and emerging ways in which dual language programs are shaping multilingualism. We use the term *dual language education* as an umbrella approach, a canopy for varying program structures. Take a moment and consider the terminology you are most familiar with when it comes to dual language program models, types, languages, and time allotments, as well as the students being served. Make a mental note of your thoughts as you continue to read the chapters.

In this book, we will refer to dual language programs that have the primary goal of fully developing students' academic and linguistic competence in two languages, whether the programs are one-way, two-way, or other program designs. We refer to the participating dual language teachers as partner teachers and their students as multilingual learners. Our goal with this type of inclusive terminology is to place an extraordinary emphasis on students' development of complex, positive academic, linguistic, and sociocultural identities. We showcase them as members of multilingual learning spaces that are jointly supported by multiple educators. At the same time, we have offered flexibility to the educators who contributed their unique examples to the book to use the terminology that best fits their own contexts.

Here are some key terms you will see throughout the chapters and a brief explanation of how we use them. We invite you to make connections to these terms as they are used in your settings, either in the same ways or with some variations.

Dual language learners and *multilingual learners*: We refer to the students enrolled in dual language programs as dual language learners and multilingual learners. Some students may be those who were referred to the program as English learners. Others may be those named as English speakers. We recognize that dual language education programs are expanding and nomenclature patterns are shifting, and as such we embrace all students' cultural and linguistic richness. Dual language programs may include learners who are becoming bilingual, those who are becoming multilingual, and those with multiple home languages, both named and unnamed.

Program languages and *partner languages*: Given the tremendous diversity in dual language programs, we refer to the two languages in the programs as either program languages or partner languages. In the U.S. context, English is most often one of the two program languages, partnered with another. We recognize, however, that in some cases English is not one of the two program languages. For example, Spanish may be partnered with an Indigenous language. In all cases, the dual language program languages must partner together.

Home language: We use this term to refer to the languages students experience and practice in their homes and communities outside of the traditional school setting. Some of these languages are named while others are not. We honor the richness and multidimensional aspects of all the home languages within dual language programs and advocate for their recognition as a critical part of multilingual engagement. When multilingual learners are afforded equitable opportunities to use what they already know from their home and community lives, they are better supported to embrace and build upon their linguistic identities.

English learner (EL), *English language development* (ELD), and *English as a second language* (ESL) *teachers* and *specialists*: We recognize and experience the varying terms in place with program teachers and specialists, in our work and yours. In some states, multilingual learners participate in programs with an EL teacher/specialist. In other states, similar programs are labeled ELD programs with ELD teachers/specialists. You may also know of states where the teachers are referred to as ESL program teachers/specialists. In any case, you will find these acronyms throughout the chapters and vignettes based on the teachers' narration contexts.

We must also recognize that there are numerous program models that support students' language and literacy development and how dual language programs fit in the larger context of language education. Figure 1.1 offers a summary of the major programs that support language and literacy development. Notice how dual language instruction is uniquely positioned to support all students and help develop academic and linguistic competencies in two languages.

Figure 1.1 Programs Supporting Language and Literacy Development

PROGRAMS	TARGET STUDENT POPULATION	PROGRAM GOALS	DESCRIPTION
Stand-alone English language development (ELD) programs	English learners (ELs), multilingual learners (MLs)	To develop English language proficiency	Classes may be organized according to ELs'/MLs' level of language proficiency or grade level. Instruction may or may not contain academic content similar to students' grade level.
Integrated ELD programs	ELs/MLs	To develop English language proficiency while also learning grade-level content	Student populations are integrated. Student support services are integrated. Classes may be co-taught or instructed by a dually certified/endorsed teacher of ELs/MLs.
Transitional bilingual education (TBE) programs	ELs/MLs	To develop academic skills in students' primary language while developing language, literacy, and academic skills in English	Student population is segregated (only ELs/MLs who speak the same primary language). TBE facilitates the transition of ELs/MLs to an all-English, monolingual instructional program, in both early and late exit structures.
Two-way dual language programs	All students (i.e., close-to-equal numbers of students who are monolingual/dominant in either of the program languages)	To develop grade-level academic skills and sociocultural competence through two languages	Literacy and content instruction is provided to all students through two languages while bilingualism and biliteracy, grade-level academic achievement, and sociocultural competence are also promoted.

PROGRAMS	TARGET STUDENT POPULATION	PROGRAM GOALS	DESCRIPTION
One-way dual language programs	Linguistically homogeneous groups of students	To develop grade-level academic skills and sociocultural competence through two languages	Students come from the same primary or home language/background and then have the opportunity to become bilingual or multilingual. One-way programs have the same goals as two-way programs while maximizing the number of ELs/MLs who participate in the program as a matter of equity and access to grade-level content/curriculum. One-way programs aim to replace the other programs of service for ELs/MLs.
Heritage language programs	Heritage language speakers (those with some language skills and/or a cultural connection to the language through family, community, or country of origin, including Indigenous peoples)	To develop language and academic skills in the home/heritage language	Heritage programs include any language development program designed to address the needs of heritage language learners/speakers at any level or setting, including community-based, K–12, and higher education. These programs allow learners to build/strengthen skills and make various connections they may have in the heritage language.
World language immersion programs	All students	To acquire complex language and literacy skills in the target language	Programs are predominantly directed toward elementary/K–8 students and are content-based.
World language programs	All students	To acquire foundational language and literacy skills in the target language	Programs predominantly serve secondary students.

As we embrace, honor, and cherish the notion that transformations in dual language education include equitable access to programs for all students, with the various program options captured in Figure 1.2, we present this mosaic of languages and cultural assets in dual language.

Figure 1.2 A Multitude of Languages Represented in Dual Language

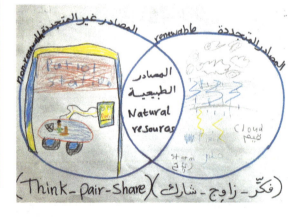

Image Sources: Rocio Hernandez, Sarah Olsen, Megan Hichwa, and Hamad Al Kurwai. Used with permission.

Why Dual Language?

For those of us who work in dual language education, this question has many answers, all of which connect to students' multilingual, multicultural development. Dual language educators across the United States and the world can easily describe, with great pride and joy, the rich and empowering environments in dual language schools. There are countless success stories where becoming multilingual transformed students' lives for the better. We feel certain you can relate to the sentiments. In addition to the linguistic, academic, and sociocultural benefits of dual language, there is research to support its role in creating equitable, effective schooling. Dual language programs are constructed to promote equity among all groups of learners and fundamentally serve to celebrate multilingualism, erasing the costly sacrifice of students' home language loss (Howard et al., 2018).

The seminal research of Virginia Collier and Wayne Thomas is a result of their combined professional and personal lives, dedicated to programmatic transformations in dual language education. Their numerous publications and presentations reveal statistical and real-world accounts of successful dual language programs with equity and equitable access to high-quality programs at the core of their work. These world-renowned scholars shared their voices with us in an interview, which we now share with you. We trust that their 40+ years of longitudinal research, inclusive of data analyses of over 8 million dual language learner outcomes in the United States (Collier & Thomas, 2007, 2009, 2018), will help motivate you to craft your own collaborative and equitable dual language experiences. In addition to their stateside research across the United States, they have worked internationally in countries such as Mexico, Canada, Scotland, and many others. The following is an excerpt from our interview:

We feel strongly that it's important to acknowledge that many immersion programs for English speakers initially had a homogeneous approach. Too often educators insisted on classes with the students all having the same language levels, and if the students didn't meet this standard, they weren't able to participate. In fact, some dual language/immersion programs have been and still are viewed as a program only for the elite. Students from diverse backgrounds have not always been welcomed. But we know, based on all our research, observations, thousands of school visits, and countless conversations with dual language educators, that heterogeneous groups are vital for multilingualism and enhanced learning.

English learners should be able to enroll at any grade level in dual language programs that teach the curriculum through their primary language and English. No more pullout for these students! And we need to avoid emphasizing low-level cognitive skills in classrooms. To address these issues, the teachers must collaborate in different and deeper ways. Heterogeneity in the classroom does powerful things for the kids to give them the skills they need to move forward to prepare for their future. Students need strong skills to work together collaboratively with other students who are very different from them, and dual language schooling is a powerful vehicle for developing these skills, thus transforming education and ultimately our society.

Why Collaboration?

Collaboration and co-teaching have been researched and practiced supporting learners of English as a foreign language (EFL), as well as a second or additional language (ESL or EAL), for over 20 years (see, for example, Dove & Honigsfeld, 2020b; Honigsfeld & Dove, 2012a; Nagle, 2013; Yoon, 2022; and the special issue of the *TESOL Journal* dedicated to collaboration and co-teaching [Honigsfeld & Dove, 2012b]). A considerable volume of research has focused on collaboration among general and special education teachers; similar attention to collaboration for the sake of English learners (ELs) and multilingual learners (MLs) is also expanding. Among others, Chris Davison (2006) extensively researched collaboration among EAL and content-area teachers with a special emphasis on the nature and challenges of developing collaborative and co-teaching relationships. She was the first to use the term *partnership teaching* (also commonly used in research and publications originating in the United Kingdom) and emphasized, "It builds on the concept of co-operative teaching by linking the work of two teachers, or indeed a whole department/year team or other partners, with plans for curriculum development and staff development across the school" (Davison, 2006, pp. 454–455).

There are growing research-based evidence (Dove & Honigsfeld, 2014; Greenberg Motamedi et al., 2019; Honigsfeld & Dove, 2017; Peercy et al., 2017), practitioner documentation (Foltos, 2018; Norton, 2016), and state and local policy initiatives (Massachusetts Department of Elementary and Secondary Education, 2019; New York State Education Department, 2018) to support teacher collaboration and integrated co-teaching services for ELs and MLs. Similarly, collaboration within dual language inclusion programs is gaining attention. For example, Diane Baker and colleagues (2018) examined the common misconception that dual language programs are not well suited for students with disabilities, including those with autism. They emphasize that multilingual classrooms offer neurodivergent students integral and unique opportunities to practice linguistic repertoires while also building social relationships. With regard to inclusion practices in dual language education, their research tells us "the philosophy of inclusive education holds that all children—regardless of disability category or learning needs—should be fully accepted and should have the opportunity to participate in the entire range of public educational opportunities" (Baker et al., 2018, p. 175). Thomas and Collier (2017) also confirm that "if the dual language program is implemented effectively, English learners are no longer isolated from their classroom peers and pull-out instruction is not needed" (p. 24). Can you imagine the successes we could offer all students by increasing collaboration in dual language education?

Building on literature reviews and our own examination of the research, several major themes have emerged that indicate the positive impact of teacher collaboration and co-teaching on the following:

1. Teacher learning and capacity building (Martin-Beltrán & Madigan Peercy, 2014)

2. Teacher relationship building and trust building (Honigsfeld & Dove, 2017; Pawan & Ortloff, 2011)

3. Shifts in instructional practices and role definition due to collaborative and co-teaching approaches to serving ELs and MLs (Davison, 2006; Martin-Beltrán & Madigan Peercy, 2012; Peercy et al., 2017)

4. Equity in education and culturally responsive teaching (Compton, 2018; Scanlan et al., 2012; Theoharis & O'Toole, 2011)

5. Teachers' professional lives through reduced professional and social isolation (Safir, 2017)

6. Programmatic cost-effectiveness (Thomas & Collier, 2017)

7. Combatting teacher shortage (Guerrero & Lachance, 2018)

8. The effectiveness of dual language education (Howard et al., 2018)

WHAT PRACTITIONERS SAY

Claribel González, the illustrator for our book, is a resource specialist for the Regional Bilingual Resource Network (RBERN) supporting bi/multilingual students in western New York. In addition to her artwork, she shares the following with us about her current role:

I have the privilege of working with dual language educators. We frequently engage in critical conversations surrounding best practices in dual language education by centering the pillars. Research has highlighted that bilingual individuals are not two monolinguals in one body. This begs the question: How do our pedagogies, perspectives, and assessments honor and reflect that? Our approaches must move beyond basic applications of translated monoglossic methods and ideologies. An integral component of amplifying our students' linguistic practices is to explore alongside them the dynamic ways they utilize their entire repertoires while simultaneously and strategically making space to question how linguistic hierarchies present themselves in and out of the classroom. As numbers of dual language programs continue to increase, we must engage and include all stakeholders in these conversations. Further, we must constantly reflect on our actions and ask: How do we continue to provide access and center the needs of the communities these programs were created for?

Keisha La Beach, language inclusion alliance coordinator, administrator, and coach at the International Education Training Center, also one of the founding faculty members of a dual language school in Shenzhen, China, recognizes the importance of teacher learning and capacity building. She shared the following with us:

Collaboration in the dual language setting where you have educators from a variety of cultural backgrounds and teacher training backgrounds must be supported. I think it's so important to have those beginning-of-year conversations.

(Continued)

(Continued)

Some might be slightly uncomfortable, but it could also be that unexpected connections will emerge and foster community. Some topics we always explore early in our grade-level and co-teaching team discussions include what we think is important for our students and what kind of climate we want to set in the classroom. As the year goes on, we further discuss what some of our strengths are and what areas we want to work on. Setting shared goals and sharing responsibility for the growth of all students help us to maintain a collaborative relationship.

How do you and your colleagues build a collaborative school culture? What is the role of school leaders?

Understanding the Collaborative Instructional Cycle

For teaching pairs, trios, or quads who are either co-teaching or partnership teaching (see Chapter 4) and collaborative teams who devise and implement instruction for dual language learners, we recommend that all members develop a clear understanding of the collaborative instructional cycle—co-planning, co-delivering instruction, co-assessing, and co-reflecting.

Co-planning is an essential activity; it provides teachers the opportunity to set general learning goals for students based on educational standards, to maintain continuity of instruction, to integrate curricula that include language and content objectives, to dialogue and discuss effective ways to differentiate instruction and assessment for students, and to co-create materials that give all students access to content while developing both their basic and disciplinary literacy. Without co-planning, there is no co-teaching or partnership teaching, the second element in the integrated instructional cycle. On the flip side, you do not have to co-deliver instruction and still can engage in co-planning.

Co-delivering instruction may take various forms and involve a range of educators in the dual language context. Co-delivery requires coordinated purpose, equal teaching partnerships, and shared responsibilities for a class community of learners who are not separated for instruction by their labels. It involves the thoughtful grouping of students for learning, a clear understanding of one's roles and responsibilities during the co-taught lesson, and the coordination of teaching efforts. It challenges teachers to remain flexible, to be open to new ideas, and to trust one another.

Co-assessing provides teaching partners with opportunities to consider their students' individual strengths and needs by reviewing available student assessment data to establish instructional goals and objectives. This practice allows teachers to decide the need to further build students' background knowledge or the requisite for re-teaching and review. Although the analysis of standardized assessment scores provides some information, in order for teaching teams to establish pertinent learning objectives the examination of additional data such as local school assessments, unit tests, writing samples, learning summaries, journal writing, student observations, and other formal and informal evaluations may best determine individual student needs and be used more effectively for planning follow-up and continued instruction.

Co-reflecting on educational practices has many aspects, and it frequently sets the parameters for the next collaborative instructional cycle. Reflection provides insight into whether strategies and resources used during lessons are affecting student learning and can be particularly useful when teaching teams want to hone their collaborative skills. Successful teaching partners often reflect on both their challenges and their successes to refine instruction. To this end, some co-teaching teams digitally record their teaching and analyze the videos to gain insight. Other teaching partners document their reflective discussions and identify next steps to meet the identified challenges. In addition to examining their teaching practices, collaborative teams reflect on their collaborative practices as well (see Figure 1.3).

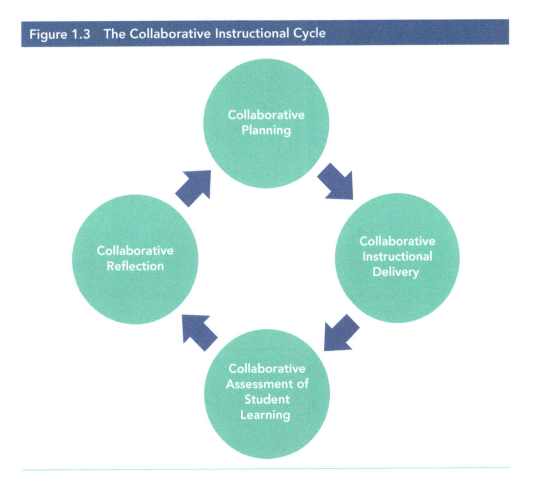

Figure 1.3 The Collaborative Instructional Cycle

WHAT THE RESEARCH SAYS

As John Hattie (2015) reminds us,

> *collaboration is based on cooperativeness, learning from errors, seeking feedback about progress and enjoying venturing into the "pit of not knowing" together with expert help that provides safety nets and, ultimately, ways out of the pit. Creative collaboration involves bringing together two or more seemingly unrelated ideas, and this highlights again the importance of having safe and trusting places to explore ideas, to make and to learn from errors and to use expertise to maximize successful learning. (p. 27)*

What does creative collaboration look like, feel like, and sound like in the dual language classroom?

Facts and Myths About Teacher Collaboration and Co-Teaching

If you are like most educators, you have had some experience with collaboration, and perhaps even with co-teaching. Consider the following statements and decide on your own—or in collaboration with your colleagues—whether you would consider them facts or myths:

- Teacher collaboration is costly.

- Teacher collaboration must be both a top-down and bottom-up process: It must be supported by leadership and fully committed to by teachers.

- Collaborating teachers must have a shared philosophy and common goals.

- Partner teachers or co-teachers must agree to use the same teaching styles.

- All teachers collaborating within a dual language program must be bilingual.

- Collaborating teachers always work with the same groups of students.

- Collaboration and co-planning is a lengthy process that can only be done in special circumstances.

- Collaboration is only for teachers who have the same number of years of experience.

- Collaboration includes shared responsibilities to promote teachers' and students' linguistic and cultural equity.

WHAT PRACTITIONERS SAY

Building on research and evidence-based practice, Francesco L. Fratto, director of world languages, language immersion, and English as a new language for Herricks Union Free School District in New Hyde Park, New York, and president of the New York State Association of World Language Administrators (NYSAWLA), has contributed to building and sustaining one of the most widely recognized and unique K–12 Spanish–English dual language programs in a predominantly Asian community with 70% Chinese speakers. The New York State Education Department (NYSED) is considering establishing this as a state-wide model for multilingual and global citizenship development (Tyrrell, 2021). Fratto shared with us that collaboration is at the core of the program's success:

> *The success of our K–12 Spanish dual language immersion (DLI) program is due to teaming. Teams of teachers meet at every level to ensure that goals are established and a plan is in place to achieve them. Our secondary DLI model is no different! The social studies and world language departments collaborate and work closely with building administrators and the district office of human resources to ensure that we attract and hire candidates that meet our criteria. Professional development and instructional coaching are provided to teachers to help them understand how to balance content and language goals to ensure continued proficiency and content acquisition. Teachers are provided with release time to work together to reflect and adjust curriculum guides and create scaffolds so that we meet the needs of students. Our program would fail if we allowed ourselves to work in a silo.*

What is your experience with working in silos? What are your own strategies to break down barriers?

Why This Book?

When implemented with intentionality, dual language works! Collaboration and co-teaching work! Let's leverage both together to maximize multilingualism within content-based instruction. Why is this important? With the wide range of dual language programs serving ELs, combined with the national shortage of bilingual teachers (Center for Applied Linguistics [CAL], 2017), we note that program configurations often call for teacher collaboration in order to sustain and expand K–12 dual language education. This practitioner-oriented book will be closely aligned to the essential concepts and practices presented in *Co-Teaching for English Learners* (Dove & Honigsfeld, 2018) and will also address how dual language educators serving students in either one- or two-way programs can effectively design, deliver, and assess engaging instruction for multilingualism and multiliteracies. With this work, we will craft a much needed resource for educators in need of guidance on how to have collaborative support to facilitate key aspects of *collaborative approaches* while working with dual language learners.

More specifically, this book is designed to support dual language teachers to collaborate with each other and with other educators outside the dual language program who work with multilingual learners (going beyond due to rich variations in available dual language program designs and structures). By addressing these concepts, we offer an expansion of viable options for schools, districts, and state education agencies to effectively support dual language education, especially in situations where administrative teams believe they are "locked in" with limited program configurations (there is a dramatic shortage of highly qualified bilingual teachers, and there is limited funding available for new program development). With this book, we aim to facilitate the process of getting started and/or becoming more effective and impactful with sustaining and expanding dual language programs through collaboration and collaborative teaching.

Why Now?

With the wide range of dual language programs serving ELs, combined with the national shortage of bilingual teachers (CAL, 2017), we note that program configurations often call for teacher collaboration to sustain and expand K–12 dual language education.

- We live in an era of momentum with the growth of dual language programs.
- There is a monumental shift in education reform recognizing the benefits of multilingualism.
- There is a continued need to interrupt English-only efforts in serving the immigrant population (as well as children of immigrants).
- Teacher collaboration and collegial support have become lifelines during the COVID-19 pandemic.
- Collective teacher efficacy and collaborative teacher expertise have been recognized as strong indicators of student success (Donohoo, 2017; Visual Learning, 2018).
- The more we collaborate, the more we can work together to strategically build middle and secondary programs.
- From the Indigenous languages viewpoint, we take the stance that many languages, both named and unnamed, are in danger of permanent disappearance and must be protected through language revitalization and reclamation programs.

The Urgency of Dual Language Education

We mention heritage programs in Figure 1.1. We want to acknowledge that some heritage programs, along with some other types of dual language programs, are intensely focused on Indigenous language preservation, revitalization, and reclamation. An example we showcase comes from the Eastern Band of Cherokee Indians (EBCI) in western North Carolina where, tragically, the language has been categorized as a critical language in grave danger of extinction. Hartwell Francis (Unega Tsisdu), curriculum director for the New Kituwah Academy, and his colleagues and EBCI community are diligently working to avoid further language loss. The collective commitments include creating pathways for collaborative teaching and learning experiences. Francis (Unega Tsisdu) leads endeavors whereby Elder Speakers, pre-K–6 classroom teachers, classroom language aides, and community members work together for the revitalization and preservation of the language and traditions, strengthening the EBCI communities. The collaborative planning, teaching, assessment, and reflection for units of instruction anchor the community's Elder Speakers in the heart of language learning. The approach is vital given that the Elders are regarded as central participants in classroom lessons, valued as precious assets for the school and the community. When asked about the importance of collaboration for the success of the program, Francis (Unega Tsisdu) shared:

> *We must include the classroom, grade-level teachers in our collaboration processes for language teaching and learning. They are the direct source of the Cherokee language for our learners, and we have to ensure they have the tools and resources they need to communicate well and promote Cherokee language development. When they work closely to review the language development units of instruction, it helps them tie the information to content and determine which curricular materials will support the development of both language and content.*

Inspired by discussion-based communication traditions of Cherokee speakers Sami Chen and Gilliam Jackson, Francis (Unega Tsisdu) worked collaboratively to create Figure 1.4 as one of the thousands of authentic examples of visual and linguistic supports the school and the community have created for collaborative use with Cherokee language development. Figure 1.4 is also significant in that it represents the richness, depth, and complexities of the Cherokee language as it indicates the *five objects categories* that shape verb usage: solid, long/rigid (L/R), flexible, animate, and liquid.

Figure 1.4 The *Five Objects Categories* in Cherokee (Tsalagi gv'di)

	ᎤᏍᏗᎰᎵ Solid	ᎦᏅᎯᏓ Long/Rigid	ᎤᎦᏛᏍᎩ Flexible	ᎡᎻᎵ Animate	ᎩᏂᏯ Liquid
Item →	ᏒᎦᏓ svgta apple	ᏗᎪᎲᏟᎶᏛᏗ digohwelododi pencil	ᎠᎾᏬ ahnawo shirt	ᎣᎦᎾ ogana groundhog	ᎠᎹ ama water
Verb Sentence ↓					
I have it.	ᎠᎩᎠ. Agiha.	ᎠᎬᏯ. Agwvya.	ᎠᎩᎾ'ᎠZ. Agina'a.	ᎠᎩᎧᎠ. Agikaha.	ᎠᎩᏁᎠ. Agineha.
Give it to me.	ᏍᎬᏏ! Sgvsi!	ᏍᎩᏗᏏ! Sgidisi!	ᏍᎩᏅᏧᏏ! Sginv'vsi!	ᏍᎩᎧᏏ! Sgikasi!	ᏍᎩᏁᎲᏏ! Sginehvsi!
Give it to her/him.	ᎲᎥᏏ! Hwihvsi!	ᎲᏗᏏ! Hwidisi!	ᎲᏅᏧᏏ! Hwinv'vsi!	ᎲᎧᏏ! Hwikasi!	ᎲᏁᎲᏏ! Hwinehvsi!

Source: Hartwell Francis (Unega Tsisdu). Used with permission.

We sincerely honor Hartwell Francis (Unega Tsisdu), his team of collaborative educators, and the EBCI community.

For Whom Is This Book?

If you are reading this book, you might be a K–12 dual language educator; a teacher educator; a school, district, and/or state-level administrator; a paraprofessional; a coach; or a preservice teacher. This book will support you as you wish to look for examples of successful, innovative instructional practices related to collaborative work with dual language learners.

Core Premises

The following premises have guided not only the writing of this book, but also our collaborative professional endeavors. We invite you to consider which of these premises are already aligned to your own beliefs and which might challenge your thinking as you embark on exploring this topic with us:

- Dual language education is for *all* students.
- Collaboration for equity is an essential stance for dual language program success.
- The four pillars serve as collaborative agreements and commitments rather than "goals" (Cervantes-Soon et al., 2017; Howard et al., 2018; Palmer et al., 2019).
- Parallel monolingualism is different from dynamic bilingualism.
- There is no one *right way* to collaborate in the dual language context.
- Co-teaching may not always be feasible, but collaboration and partnership teaching can help create a cohesive program model.
- All teachers are language teachers.

Overarching Goals

This book aims to facilitate *collaborative approaches* while working with dual language learners, transforming dual language programs for multilingualism. Each of the chapters provides essential, research-informed, evidence-based content; tools and resources for actionable transfer to practice; real-world vignettes with work samples and photos; and built-in points of reflection that allow you to make each chapter applicable to your own context. Here is a quick preview of what each subsequent chapter has to offer:

Chapter 2: Foundations of Dual Language Programs

Chapter 2 is designed to help you gain insight into some foundations of dual language as you learn more about the importance of enhancing collaboration within the dual language approach. To begin, we'll take a closer look at some history of dual language instruction, what those of us in the field are currently experiencing, where we're heading in the future, and why collaboration is so important for progress. Each part of Chapter 2 will guide you to make direct connections to collaboration in your own programs.

The fundamental goals of Chapter 2 are to:

1. Illustrate essential historical elements of dual language and bilingual education in the United States
2. Describe the role of collaboration across dual language program types and structures
3. Explore the ways in which teacher partnerships contribute to the benefits of dual language education
4. Establish a pathway to building capacity for collaboration in your dual language program

Chapter 3: Collaborative Planning in Dual Language Programs

In Chapter 3, we argue that collaborative planning is an essential component of dual language programs regardless of the model of instruction. We show how partnering teachers and other members of the school community collaborate for the sake of their multilingual learners. This chapter defines the *who*, *what*, *where*, *when*, *how*, and *why* of collaborative planning and offers actionable recommendations and tools to support co-planning in the dual language context. More specifically, the goals of Chapter 3 are to:

1. Define the essential elements of collaborative planning in the dual language classroom
2. Identify the purpose and key practices of co-planning using the four pillars of dual language instruction
3. Review and evaluate collaborative planning protocols and tools

Chapter 4: Collaborative Teaching in Dual Language Programs

Chapter 4 introduces collaborative teaching approaches as pathways to offering equitable and rigorous yet well-supported instructional delivery within the dual language context. More specifically, the goals of this chapter are to:

1. Differentiate between partnership teaching and co-teaching and define each practice in varied dual language contexts
2. Identify the place partnership teaching and co-teaching occupy within the collaborative instructional cycle

3. Explore several approaches to partnership teaching

4. Describe and evaluate seven co-teaching models

Chapter 5: Collaborative Assessment and Reflection in Dual Language Programs

Chapter 5, parallel to Chapter 3, defines the *who, what, where, when, how,* and *why* of collaborative assessment and offers actionable recommendations and tools to support co-assessments in the dual language context. In this chapter, we set out specifically to:

1. Define the essential elements of collaborative authentic assessment in the dual language classroom

2. Make connections to the four pillars of dual language in collaborative authentic assessment practices

3. Distinguish between and among collaborative authentic assessment *as, for,* and *of* learning in the dual language context

4. Explore collaborative reflection as an integral component of the collaborative instructional cycle

Chapter 6: Collaborative Leadership Support for Dual Language Programs

The final chapter of the book focuses on collaborative leadership support. In Chapter 6, we explain how dual language programs get established, grow, and thrive as a result of collaboration with a range of stakeholders' commitment and hard work. We explore ways in which district and school administrators, coaches, and other instructional leaders play a pivotal role in the success of dual language initiatives. The fundamental goals of Chapter 6 are to:

1. Explore three types of collaborative partnerships teachers and administrators form to make transformative decisions in dual language programs

2. Identify and map out teachers' and administrators' essential roles in establishing a collaborative approach to transform dual language programs

3. Establish connections to the four pillars of dual language in collaborative leadership practices

What Is Unique About the Book?

We believe that as you see the artwork and unique sketch notes our illustrator, Claribel González, created for the outside cover of the book and inside each chapter, you will quickly notice a global connection to *space*. Why did we take this approach? Joan has a deep interest in all things related to space, our solar system, the universe, and stars, and Andrea has a brilliant sense of adventure. We recognize that dual language education is best fueled with ongoing motivation and that often we're collaborating with each other, learning from each other, and collectively brainstorming to stay inspired. These are beliefs we hold dear to our hearts, and we tried to translate these sentiments into metaphors that run throughout each chapter and the entire book. We hope they serve as pathways for you to be inspired by multilingual learners, to be aspirational for each other and your communities, to *reach for the stars* with your endeavors, and, most of all, to remember that *the sky is the limit* when it comes to creativity built on informed practices. Feel free to take the whimsical metaphors with a grain of salt (or star dust)! And, notice them in the recurring features that we intentionally infused in each chapter for consistency and continuity as you explore and make discoveries about collaboration in dual language education.

Recurring Chapter Features

Throughout the forthcoming chapters, we employ several recurring features to help you organize your learning and application of the chapter goals and topics. An icon—a unique sketch note designed for this book by Claribel González—will call attention to most of these features. On the following pages, you will find a brief explanation of each of the recurring features as well as an opportunity to apply some of them to the content of this introductory chapter:

Each chapter opens with a brief overview of the content we aim to unpack. We emphasize some key points in each chapter to introduce the main ideas and the connections to research and the fundamental chapter contents.

MISSION CONTROL

In this section of each chapter, we explore established concepts as they relate to the chapter. These explorations serve as research-informed and evidence-based foundations, connecting our prior knowledge, theory, and practice as we bridge to new knowledge and understandings. Each Exploration section also provides you with opportunities and invitations to make critical applications based on the uniqueness of your contexts; your students, families, and communities; your goals; and your own program structures.

EXPLORATION

CAPTAIN'S LOG

Throughout each chapter, we provide you with reflection prompts that are specific to the content of the section. For example, here in Chapter 1, we invite you to reflect and write down your ideas in response to the following two prompts:

1. What stands out for you about this book so far?

   _____
   _____
   _____
   _____

2. What goals do you plan to set for yourself as a result of this book study?

   _____
   _____
   _____
   _____

Through the Students' Eyes

At the beginning of each chapter, we will present a "mini case study" on a student or students and present a short vignette that depicts the topic of the chapter from the student perspective (what students see, do, and experience when the ideas presented in the chapter are enacted).

Through the Educators' Eyes

In this section, we will shift our focus to present the educators' perspectives on what was happening in the vignette and why it matters, and how collaboration impacts the teaching and learning experiences in a dual language context.

NAVIGATION SYSTEMS

In this section, we present field-centered information, research, and theoretically based systems associated with the chapter's key points. We provide viewpoints that guide and steer us from the larger picture (*What the Research Says*) to the program or classroom level (*What Practitioners Say*). The combination of both perspectives offers a systemic look at the chapter topics and some foundational obligations associated with them from practitioners' unique, comprehensive perspectives.

In order to directly address ways to explore collaborative practices in dual language education, each chapter features a brief list of our *Core Beliefs* and *"Let's Agree" Statements*. We take this opportunity to weave in our shared understandings of socially just practices and help readers stay focused on equitable learning opportunities through collaboration in dual language programs.

In Chapter 1, for example, we invite you to consider the following *Core Beliefs* that undergird dynamic multilingualism followed by our *"Let's Agree" Statements*:

STAYING THE COURSE

Core Beliefs

- All students benefit from well-structured and justly implemented dual language programs.
- Equal access to dual language education is a priority for transformed programs.
- The process of authentic language acquisition and intentional learning in the academic context must genuinely stay connected; thus, we believe the most appropriate terminology used to describe this complex process is *language development*.
- Language development is neither static nor linear; it is a fluid and dynamic process.
- Multilingualism via dual language education is a collaborative and collective goal that keeps students, families, and communities at the core.

"Let's Agree" Statements

As we begin our learning journey together, let's make a commitment to the following:

- Let's agree that we must recognize and honor the vast individual differences students bring to the classroom regarding their backgrounds and experiences.
- Let's honor the unique talents and gifts, cultural heritages, and personal powers students share with us.
- Let's agree that language levels cannot define who a student is; instead, each level simply offers a frame of reference to what the student is able to do at a particular moment in a particular domain (Shafer Willner, 2013).
- Let's support multilingualism from socially just and transformative mindsets for all.

In this section of each chapter, we showcase real-world experiences, classroom examples, and/or perspectives that researchers and practitioner scholars shared with us for this book. Some are representative of elementary programs, and others are from the secondary perspective. We also include quotes, photos, and teacher and student work samples to showcase their voices from the field.

LAUNCHED MISSIONS

GEAR UP!

This portion of each chapter provides specific websites, books, links to resources, tools, and other documents to use as samples—all to support your own practices and program development. The *gear* we share is strategically provided for you to, in many cases, adapt so the tools work within the distinctive classrooms, schools, and programs where you're teaching and for the unique students and communities you serve.

TUNE IN!

This section of each chapter was created to provide you with broader opportunities to tune in and listen to other success stories, concepts, and innovative ideas from dual language education programs across contexts. We direct you to selected critical resources that go beyond those in the Gear Up! section and look beyond the contents of the chapter. We sincerely invite you to continue your explorations with some additional print- and web-based resources for your own growth and collaboration.

COUNTDOWN TO LAUNCH

At the end of each chapter, we offer practical application tips in 10 key steps! For Chapter 1, we offer this countdown to guide you to launch your explorations of this book and set your own goals as they relate to your learning:

10. Read the book cover to cover in one night. (Just kidding! But . . . you might not be able to put it down once you begin diving into it.)
9. As you open the pages of the book and broaden your learning, keep an open mind.
8. Question what you read and discuss your noticings and wonderings with your colleagues.
7. Make the reading an interactive process by using the reflection prompts we have included in the book.
6. Remember—nothing is set in stone.
5. Have a sense of adventure to be creative and innovative with your collaboration.
4. Trust the research that defines and supports high-quality dual language education.
3. Experiment with the ideas presented and make them your own.
2. Take your time and celebrate all the steps—even when they feel small.
1. **Aim for the stars!**

Each chapter ends with a final entry into your Captain's Log. As we wrap up Chapter 1 and transition into Chapter 2, we invite you to reflect on your ideas using the following prompts:

CAPTAIN'S LOG: FINAL ENTRY

1. What stands out for you about the *Core Beliefs* and *"Let's Agree" Statements* in Chapter 1? How do they align with your own?

   _____
   _____
   _____
   _____

2. Which three Countdown to Launch steps resonated with you the most, and why?

   _____
   _____
   _____
   _____

Prepare to Take Off

We hope you are as excited as we are about this book. We wrote about collaboration for you via a sincerely collaborative effort. We invite you to enjoy the journey as you embark on new collaborative adventures or enhance your current ones!

Foundations of Dual Language Programs 2

"All instruction is culturally responsive. The question is: to which culture is it currently oriented?"

—Gloria Ladson-Billings

MISSION CONTROL

Chapter 2 is designed to help you gain insight into some foundations of dual language pedagogies as you learn more about the importance of enhancing collaboration within the dual language approach. To begin, let's take a closer look at some history of dual language instruction, what those of us in the field are currently experiencing, where we're heading in the future, and why collaboration is so important for progress. Each part of Chapter 2 will guide you to make direct connections to collaboration in your own programs.

The fundamental goals of Chapter 2 are to:

1. Illustrate essential historical elements of dual language and bilingual education in the United States

2. Describe the role of collaboration across dual language program types and structures

3. Explore the ways in which teacher partnerships contribute to the benefits of dual language education

4. Establish a pathway to building capacity for collaboration in your dual language program

As we monitor the conditions and progress of numerous dual language programs that are well into their journeys, we can probably agree right away that not all "launched" dual language programs are created alike. In fact, your mission's context makes your dual language program unique from any others—even though it's built on a framework of dual language program structures that may be like others. One size does not and should not fit all. Every mission has its own goals—its own flight plan. In Chapter 2, we will explore some collaborative programs to guide you toward creating strategically built-in spaces for collaboration in your dual language program. In addition to sharing these examples with you, we will provide you with ways to develop your own insight as to *where* your programs reside, *whom* they are intended to serve, and *what* you will need to increase collaboration in your context. Even though there is great variation between program types, more than four decades of research have identified four nonnegotiable pillars of effective dual language programs. The first guiding message from Mission Control—whether it's a pre-flight check or an in-flight check—is to invite you to *free-write* some of your ideas about your own program's pillars of:

1. Bilingualism and biliteracy

2. Grade-level academic achievement

3. Sociocultural competence
4. Critical consciousness

In the space provided, note your interpretations of the four pillars of dual language education, whether they relate to a program you're in or one you're about to develop. Bear in mind that you will elaborate on each of these pillars in the latter half of this chapter—so there are no wrong answers here. For now, approach the reflection to freely write your creative ideas and thoughts.

CAPTAIN'S LOG

1. Bilingualism and biliteracy

   _____

   _____

2. Grade-level academic achievement

   _____

   _____

3. Sociocultural competence

   _____

   _____

4. Critical consciousness

   _____

   _____

While we recognize that the majority of the dual language programs in the United States are Spanish–English programs, there is vast diversity across the United States and the world regarding dual language program structures to include 30+ partner languages (Park et al., 2018). We believe you will help us further recognize the splendid cultural, linguistic, socioeconomic, racial, and ethnic diversity of multilingual learners in dual language education by reading this book and continuing your work. We begin the exploration by first aiming our telescopes to gain insight into the importance of collaboration in dual language education from some very specific points of focus. In the next section, we showcase two siblings' experiences in elementary programs. By sharing these composite vignettes that express the benefits of collaboration in elementary dual language programs, we hope to guide you to think vertically, boosting the importance of growing secondary programs. We also invite you to consider these stories through your own lenses and to explore how they might influence your current practices—especially with regard to the role of the English language development (ELD) teacher in the collaboration.

EXPLORATION

Through the Students' Eyes

Milagros and Michael, who are siblings, are both originally from Mexico and living in Chula Vista, California. They moved to the United States when Milagros was in preschool and Michael was in kindergarten, both fully fluent in Spanish. In the school district where they lived, Michael was placed in a transitional bilingual program and received two years of bilingual support in Spanish and was then transitioned to a fully English-speaking environment after completing the second grade. By the time Milagros began kindergarten, the transitional bilingual program had changed to a dual language program, and her mother enthusiastically enrolled her. Here are some things they described about their experiences from what they remembered once they got to secondary school:

Michael: When I started school in California, I spoke Spanish at home. I knew some English from watching TV and seeing movies and listening to some songs. I had some English in school too before we moved to the United States, and I was learning to read and write in Spanish in Mexico. I felt okay going to school because most of the day in the beginning was in Spanish. I learned to read and write some more in Spanish and started to add English. It was a good thing for me in the beginning because I didn't feel so lost at school. School was really different in California than in Mexico, so I felt more comfortable knowing at least I could talk and listen and understand my classmates and teachers. After the second grade I started to be in school with all English all the time. It felt so hard for me—like it was too big of a jump too quickly. I felt forced sometimes to hold back my thinking and writing in Spanish, and I didn't like that. There were many times when I knew the answers to questions and problems but I didn't know how to write them in English, so I just didn't write. I had an ELD teacher who came to work with me a lot, sometimes by myself and sometimes with some other kids. Most of the time she stayed with us in the class, but if we needed extra help, she would pull us out to a smaller room. I still think in Spanish and English and find it more helpful to do that. I wish I could have been in school with some English and some Spanish to keep both languages all the time, so I don't feel like I have to split myself into two parts—Spanish at home and English at school. That doesn't seem to fit the way I think or live.

Milagros: When I started kindergarten, I spoke Spanish most of the time. The teachers were helping me learn to read and write in Spanish and then again in English, which was not the same. When my teachers explained how Spanish works and how English works, it helped me to think about each language and then think about them together, because some things in Spanish are the same as English but other things are different. I remember feeling more comfortable because my teachers encouraged me to speak and write in Spanish in class, just like I did at home. I also had an ELD teacher who came to my class and worked together with my other teachers, and that was good. They would teach us similar things but one more in Spanish and the other more in English, and that helped me think about things a lot more. I wanted to stay in my class, so I liked that she [the ELD teacher] came to us. Some of my friends at school speak English at home, and that was totally fun because they would ask me all the time to help them with their Spanish. I remember we worked together a lot in class. We had lots of activities where we solved math problems together, and we also helped each other write sometimes. I am now in the seventh grade, still at the same school, because we go there until we finish eighth grade. From about the fourth grade on, we had a schedule with a half day in Spanish and a half day in English. I will go to high school next year, and it will all be in English. I really wish I could keep doing half Spanish and half English all the way until I graduate.

Now that you have met Milagros and Michael, let's take a few moments to reflect on what they expressed.

CAPTAIN'S LOG

1. What are some ways you believe Milagros's experience in a dual language program was more beneficial than Michael's experience?

   _____

   _____

   _____

   _____

2. What did you notice about the role of the ELD teacher? What did you notice about what was inferred regarding collaboration between the ELD teacher and the dual language classroom teacher?

   _____

   _____

   _____

   _____

Through the Educators' Eyes

Here is a composite vignette from Milagros's former kindergarten teacher, who represents so many of the dual language teachers in U.S. schools. The dual language teacher who worked with Milagros in her classroom is fully bilingual and biliterate in both program languages of Spanish and English.

My name is Rosa, and I am originally from Puerto Rico. I moved to the States when I was in middle school, and I was an ESL student [that's what they called us at the time—learners of "English as a second language"], in a pullout setting, until I got to high school. I remember all too well that I was in a "sink or swim" situation in all my classes. I knew that I wanted to become a kindergarten teacher in a dual language classroom because I wanted to help students become multilingual rather than giving up Spanish to become "fluent" in English. Even though I am the teacher of record in the class, I want to be sure people know I could not provide the same high-quality instruction without collaborating with the ELD teacher and the bilingual teacher's aide. I remember having Milagros in class several years ago when my colleagues and I were really working out our strategic collaboration schedule. It was a little different then, but not much. We learned over time that we can make things work well when we meet once a week for 90 minutes during a common planning time to co-design lessons and activities. We talk about who will be helping which students during the lessons and what those kids' specific needs are for developing biliteracy—and making connections to the lesson's content topic. We discuss formative assessments and making sure students are given as much access to complex thinking tasks as possible and what student work we can save to show as artifacts for progression in both languages. We look closely at the materials we have and what needs to be tweaked so things line up with our kids' cultural backgrounds. We plan for times when my bilingual aide can help the students as emerging writers in Spanish while the ELD teacher works with a small group as emerging writers in English. We make sure all of us are working with a small group of students on a similar topic with similar language goals, sometimes in Spanish and sometimes in English according to the 90/10 language allocation plan at my school. In other words, 90% of the instructional day is dedicated to one language, and 10% to the other.

Here's a more specific example of something we planned to coordinate an activity for a math lesson. First, we had the students working in small groups to solve math problems together. We gave them realia and structured conversation cards to be sure they all explained their thinking processes to each other. They had to decide on collective answers. They would then explain their thinking and their answers to another small group. We targeted them as emerging writers to "show their work" with numbers in their math journals, and they could write together. They could also draw pictures to help.

Another important thing is that once a month we talk about what these things are doing to help the students build the skills and language they will need in first grade. Once a quarter we meet with the first-grade teachers for a 45-minute working lunch together in our classroom (we're excused from lunch and hall duty that day). We show each other unit plans, and sometimes we discuss certain kids and their needs. We want to be sure our students stay in our school at least through the eighth grade—like Milagros. And we all wish we had a dual language high school for them to go to after that.

The research is clear: Given the opportunity to engage in productive struggle with complex topics while freely drawing from both program languages, multilingual learners stand to benefit in school and in life. The positive impacts of critical thinking for biliteracy development are undeniable. Another common myth about language acquisition has also been debunked: Use of the home language does not impede learning other languages. Furthermore, multilingual learners are too often denied opportunities (Genesee et al., 2006; Walqui et al., 2010) to draw from their home language to advance academic mastery. Let's think about how collaborative processes extend the overall benefits of dual language, including the specifics of students' access to complex thinking for multilingual development.

CAPTAIN'S LOG

1. What stands out to you about the collaborative practices of these three educators—the classroom teacher, ELD teacher, and bilingual teacher's aide?

   _____
   _____
   _____
   _____

2. What did you notice about the things they did regarding students' use of complex thinking skills within their collaboration?

   _____
   _____
   _____
   _____

WHAT PRACTITIONERS SAY

The research is clear that dual language programs benefit all students (Thomas & Collier, 2014). Research also confirms that collaboration and co-teaching improve the instructional cycle to better support all students' academic gains—especially with language learners (Dove & Honigsfeld, 2020b; Greenberg Motamedi et al., 2019). For these reasons, does it make sense to weave collaboration into dual language instruction and program design? We say yes! In Chapter 1, we shared a segment of our interview with Virginia Collier and Wayne Thomas that showcased the importance of dual language education. In this next segment, they share their viewpoints on equity and collaboration in dual language programs.

(Continued)

(Continued)

Dual language education is for everyone—for all students! This also means that teaching in dual language classes is the most challenging assignment of any in education. And yet the teachers can do it! That said, it's challenging to create interactive lessons for the diverse groups of learners coming together for the nonnegotiable of heterogeneous learning. It's also the most exciting environment for learning. Dual language learners as multilingual students are diverse in multiple ways beyond ethnicity—including socioeconomic, academic, language, and cultural backgrounds. We strongly encourage equity and heterogeneity, and that means collaboration among teachers and students. This is a historic issue. Not everyone agrees about diversity in the classroom, and sometimes even teachers struggle with being enthusiastic about teaching in very diverse situations—because it's really hard—but with very rewarding outcomes! That's why collaboration is so critically important, especially in dual language programs.

As you reflect on the benefits and challenges of working in a diverse classroom, what are some of your own personal thoughts and ideas? How would you describe to others why you are an advocate for equity and diversity in dual language education?

WHAT PRACTITIONERS SAY

Parallel to the research on the benefits of collaboration in dual language education, Alma G. Rocha, principal in the Freeport Public Schools in New York, shares her viewpoints on how essential collaboration is for the teachers and the program. She also emphasizes the importance of co-planning (see Chapter 3):

> *In the Freeport school district, the dual language program is not only a way to meet the state criteria to serve students who speak a language other than English, but it serves the community in two important ways. It is a lifeline for Spanish speakers learning English and an enrichment opportunity for English speakers also learning a new language, which is Spanish. It gives all participating students the opportunity to become bilingual and biliterate. Collaboration among teachers is the determinant for the program to succeed. Teachers in the dual language program invest countless hours of planning together in order to maximize their impact. Every minute counts. The time they spend teaching equals the amount of time they spend planning in two languages. Teachers have to make sure dual language students follow the same pacing guides and curriculum maps in addition to participating in the same assessments (in two languages) as any kindergartener in the district.*

Dr. Rocha emphasizes the importance of investing time in planning. How can school leaders ensure the success of collaborative planning in addition to allocating time for it?

Since the benefits of dual language are already extraordinary, we see collaboration as the ideal way for you to add some *booster engines* to your missions—to keep you and your students moving forward. Let's shift our focus to the first of our goals: *illustrate some historical elements of dual language and bilingual education in the United States.* Some readers may question the need for a history lesson in the context of a professional development book. Quite simply, we believe that in order for us to aim forward with equity at the core of our practices, we must explore our past so that we may avoid future injustices and inequities in dual language education. Unfortunately, the turbulent history of bilingual education in the United States includes significant layers of systemic oppression, injustice, and discrimination. Our goal, in the following section, is to portray this history in an authentic manner so that we may learn and transform our futures.

Exploring the Past: A Brief Overview of the History of Dual Language and Bilingual Education in the United States

In truth, while we are a nation of tremendous linguistic and cultural diversity, we have endured deep struggles to provide access to a quality education to our nation's multilingual learners for far too many decades. Oftentimes, the struggles resulted in *English-only* state-level policies that were antithetical to findings in the research on teaching multilingual learners and, ultimately, harmful to children. Those who have worked in the field of education are well aware of the pendulum swings and policy shifts that impact all levels of education systems from boardrooms to classrooms. And, unfortunately, we know too well that educator policies often ignore current developments in research and practice and, instead, are frequently politically driven.

Historically, school districts across the United States established bilingual programs for varying reasons. Transitional bilingual programs were created as a temporary means to transition Spanish-dominant students into English language proficiency. While these efforts were framed as beneficial to multilingual children at the onset, such programs were subtractive (extinguishing the student's home language), rather than additive (sustaining the home language and using it as a leverage point for English language development and academic content mastery) (García, 2014; García & Woodley, 2015). Ofelia García and Heather Homonoff Woodley (2015) explain dynamic bilingualism as follows:

> *[B]ilingual school programs acknowledge that the children hold different degrees of bilingualism because their families speak different languages or because they have lived and worked across national contexts. The bilingualism of these children also cannot be simply added or subtracted whole, since their language practices are already multiple, non-linear, and complex when they come into school.* (p. 135)

The United States is unique in its stubborn adherence to monolingualism. For many generations of students, English-only education was the sole option. English was the language of cultural power, and students were expected to *get up to speed* in their

English language development with minimal supports (García, 2009, 2014). When materials in languages other than English were introduced, they were seen as temporary scaffolds on the pathway to exclusive dominance of English. Similarly, most assessments were conducted in English only (Gottlieb, 2021), which provided teachers with limited insights into student learning, let alone their funds of knowledge (Moll et al., 1992). Rather than valuing the goals of multilingualism or affirming the benefits of culturally and linguistically sustaining practices, the goal of English-only instruction has been to produce monolingual students at the expense of their home languages and cultural identities.

Review Figure 2.1 to get a feel for some of the key enactments and their impacts on the use of languages other than English in our schools. As you do this, think about the possible cultural climates you sense may have influenced some of these enactments. Be sure to note things that surprise you, the enactments that may explain instructional patterns you continue to notice in your own setting, and the potential impacts they have on collaborative practices.

Figure 2.1 A Historical Snapshot of Important Legislation, Enactments, and Policy Trends

ENACTMENTS	SUMMARY	IMPACT ON THE USE OF LANGUAGES OTHER THAN ENGLISH IN U.S. SCHOOLS
Supreme Court Decisions		
Interpretation of the Fourteenth Amendment		
Hernandez v. Texas (1954)	Señor Pete Hernandez was sentenced to life imprisonment after being tried by an all-white jury and convicted of murder. Señor Hernandez claimed that the trial was discriminatory, indicating that Mexican Americans were barred from the jury. "Purposeful exclusion" was unanimously determined, violating the *Equal Protection Clause* of the Fourteenth Amendment. Mexican Americans were viewed as a "special class" entitled to equal protection under the Fourteenth Amendment.	Mexican Americans were protected under the Fourteenth Amendment, aiming to ensure that every legal advancement for one ethnic minority group was a protective win for all.
Interpretations of the Fourteenth Amendment: Civil Rights Act of 1964		
Lau v. Nichols (1974)	The San Francisco school system desegregated in 1971, which resulted in nearly 3,000 Chinese students who needed support in English being integrated back into the schools. Only one-third were provided language development support, which was	The *Lau v. Nichols* case resulted in a unanimous decision in favor of bilingual instruction as a means of helping English learners enhance their proficiency. The case made it easier for students whose home language was not English to access education.

ENACTMENTS	SUMMARY	IMPACT ON THE USE OF LANGUAGES OTHER THAN ENGLISH IN U.S. SCHOOLS
	found to be a violation of the Fourteenth Amendment and the Civil Rights Act.	Some believe, however, that the Supreme Court did not fully resolve the issue given that school districts were left to interpret the ruling for their own means of implementation.
Castañeda v. Pickard (1981)	Mexican American students and their parents stated that the Raymondville (Texas) Independent School District (RISD) discriminated against them because of their ethnicity. They claimed that schools were segregated using racially and ethnically biased grouping methods. According to the *Lau v. Nichols* judgment, school districts were compelled to provide bilingual instruction, but there was no means to assess the school's approach. Initially, the court ruled in favor of the defendant on August 17, 1978, noting that the district had not infringed on any of the plaintiff's constitutional or statutory rights. However, the ruling was appealed in 1981 and eventually decided in favor of the plaintiff.	As a result, districts' plans for English learners must be: 1. Based on "a sound educational theory" 2. "Implemented effectively," with adequate resources and personnel 3. Evaluated as effective in overcoming language barriers
Plyler v. Doe (1982)	Texas education laws were changed in 1975, allowing the state to withhold state funds from local school systems for the education of undocumented children. In *Plyler v. Doe*, the Court ruled that although undocumented immigrants and their children are neither citizens of the United States nor citizens of Texas, they are people and thus entitled to Fourteenth Amendment protections.	*Plyler* maintained that all children, regardless of immigration status, must have equal access to education.
Federal Legislation		
NCLB (2001)	No Child Left Behind (NCLB) was a reauthorization of the Elementary and Secondary Education Act (ESEA). States were mandated to test children in reading and math in Grades 3–8 and in high school. The legislation required that by the year 2014, all children should	States were also required to set English language proficiency (ELP) standards and directly connect them to the state's academic content standards. English learners (at the time referred to as students with limited English proficiency) were included in states' accountability systems. At the time, many states

(Continued)

(Continued)

ENACTMENTS	SUMMARY	IMPACT ON THE USE OF LANGUAGES OTHER THAN ENGLISH IN U.S. SCHOOLS
	have met or exceeded state reading and math benchmarks.	did not have specific English language development (ELD) standards, which resulted in compliance issues. The World-Class Instructional Design and Assessment (now referred to as WIDA) Consortium was developed in 2003, and states began to use the WIDA system of assessments while others developed their own ELD standards.
ESSA (2015)	The Every Student Succeeds Act (ESSA) was signed in 2015, to replace NCLB. The premise of the legislation was to give states more flexibility in how to best assess students' progress with the requirement that state report cards be disclosed.	Under ESSA, schools and districts are required to include students' English proficiency data into Title I structures for accountability purposes. ESSA included several new standards for English learner (EL) education, such as methods for identifying ELs and the use of English competence as a criterion for school quality. ESSA aimed to establish state-level consistency for standardized testing and gave schools an incentive to assess ELs in their first year of enrollment, also with options for exemption, to collect data that may be used to track future improvement.
Select Examples of State Legislation and Regulations		
Massachusetts LOOK Act of 2018	The Language Opportunity for Our Kids (LOOK) Act was unanimously passed by the Massachusetts Senate in 2018 with bipartisan support. This bill established a state Seal of Biliteracy and allowed school districts to offer bilingual programs without the requirement for waivers. It repealed the sheltered English immersion law (2002) that banned bilingual education, which stated "all public school children must be taught English by being taught all subjects in English and being placed in English language classrooms."	The LOOK Act allows school districts more options to better meet students' needs with dual language education as a promoted option to emphasize the value of bilingual students and communities. It also establishes a new Seal of Biliteracy to honor bilingual and biliterate high school graduates.
New Mexico as a bilingual state	New Mexico was the first state in the United States to have a bilingual and multicultural education law, passing the Bilingual Multicultural Education	According to New Mexico's Language and Culture Division, "Developing proficiency in two or more languages for New Mexico students has been the

ENACTMENTS	SUMMARY	IMPACT ON THE USE OF LANGUAGES OTHER THAN ENGLISH IN U.S. SCHOOLS
	Act of 1973. There is no official language of the state, whereas many others note English as the official state language.	commitment of New Mexico educators, legislators, and other government leaders since the state constitution was approved in 1911."
Texas House Bill 3 (2019)	The Texas Legislature passed House Bill 3 (HB3), a widely publicized school finance bill. Under HB3 learners participating in a dual language program receive additional basic education allotment funds.	Overall, this means that schools enrolling students in dual language programs may have additional state funding, which results in added resources to support their schools.
Washington State Transitional Bilingual Instruction Program	Started in 1979 with the most recent update in 2020, the Washington State Transitional Bilingual Instruction Program mandates school districts offer ELs transitional bilingual instruction, through either a bilingual program or an alternative program such as English as a second language.	In the spring of 2021, the Washington State Board of Education adopted the National Dual Language Education Teacher Preparation Standards to oblige their use in all dual language and bilingual teacher preparation programs. We also recognize that Washington State is believed to be one of the first populated regions in the United States with Indigenous groups speaking more than 50 languages. The influence of language and culture remains today with the state's absence of having an official language.
California Proposition 58 (2016)	Proposition 58 repealed California's prior English-only policy of Proposition 227, which had been in effect for nearly two decades.	ELs are now freed up from the requirement to attend English-only classes under Proposition 58. Schools and districts may use a variety of language assistance programs, including bilingual programs taught by teachers who are fluent in both their home language and English, and are required to include community involvement.
Arizona's current English-only stance	In 2000, Arizona passed Proposition 203. The enactment mandated that all public school instruction take place in English. Children who do not speak English fluently are usually placed in a one-year rigorous English immersion program to teach them the language as rapidly as possible while still learning academic subjects. For children who already know English, are 10 years old or	When Proposition 203 was passed in 2000, EL students could no longer receive instruction in their home language while learning English. This led to other regulations that hampered multilingual students, such as one that forced EL students to take English classes in four-hour blocks every day.

(Continued)

(Continued)

ENACTMENTS	SUMMARY	IMPACT ON THE USE OF LANGUAGES OTHER THAN ENGLISH IN U.S. SCHOOLS
	older, or have unique needs that call for a different educational method, parents may request a waiver of these requirements.	While the goal was to help ELs learn English, it has resulted in them missing out on other topics that are important for a well-rounded education, such as art, math, social studies, and science. It has also stopped our EL students from naturally interacting with their English-proficient peers. In 2018, the Arizona House of Representatives passed Senate Bill 1014, which gave districts and schools more flexibility in EL instruction. However, the bill stopped short of entirely repealing the state's ELD requirements.

CAPTAIN'S LOG

After reading about some key historical aspects of bilingual education, we offer you an opportunity to reflect on what resonated with you.

1. What surprises you about any or all of the enactments in Figure 2.1?

   _____
   _____
   _____
   _____

2. How do you think some of bilingual education's history may influence your current setting? What are some potential impacts of the enactments on collaboration in dual language programs?

   _____
   _____
   _____
   _____

Exploring the Present: The Role of Collaboration in High-Quality Dual Language Program Types and Structures

Now here is some good news: We've learned a great deal from research and practice on the programs that afford the most benefit to multilingual learners. In turning our attention to our second goal, we focus on the role of collaboration in programs that are described as additive and dynamic. Dual language learners in additive program structures learn grade-level, rigorous, standards-based content via two program languages. Simultaneously, the students are building multiliteracies in two languages *through* the content, which teachers believe can be extended through their strategic collaboration (Lachance, 2020). The key difference in the additive, dynamic approach is that the learners are never expected to forgo any aspect of their linguistic and cultural backgrounds while adding another via dual language learning. As we describe the benefits of collaboration and co-teaching in dual language education, we will focus on the two dual language program types we briefly mentioned in the introductory chapter:

1. Two-way dual language programs
2. One-way dual language programs

Dual language refers to an educational program design where students learn content and literacy through *two languages*. All dual language programs, regardless of the population and regardless of grade level, use both of the program's partner languages for at least 50% of the instructional day for a minimum of five years (see www.dlenm.org for more). While all programs share the goal of educating students for multilingualism, different programs have somewhat different populations of learners. Of all program types, *two-way* and *one-way* programs have the strongest longitudinal evidence of increases in bilingualism and biliteracy, overall academic gains, and significantly deepened senses of sociocultural competencies (Lindholm-Leary, 2016; Thomas & Collier, 2002).

Two-way dual language programs enroll a balance of speakers from both partner languages. Sometimes, especially in the U.S. context, these groups are referred to as *English dominant* and *partner language dominant*. Of all the program structures we describe, two-way programs demonstrate ideal successes for all students year after year (de Jong & Howard, 2009; Thomas & Collier, 2002).

One-way dual language programs are typically established for students from one language group as they represent the majority of the students (often all) in the program. The programs are considered one-way in structure since there are over 70% of students from the same language group. The students are learning content through a language other than English for at least 50% of the school day while their primary language and literacy skills are also supported. Many international programs mirror this one-way structure as the majority of the participants' home languages are other than English such as Arabic, Mandarin, Portuguese, Dutch, Spanish, and so on.

One-way (world language) immersion programs are commonly established to support speakers of English in learning languages other than English. Some programs are established with a partial one-way immersion structure to introduce aspects such as Advanced Placement language courses in high school, whereas others such as some International Baccalaureate programs may weave language development across other curricular areas such as math, science, cultural studies, and the arts. *World language immersion*, *language immersion*, or *one-way immersion* are some commonly used terms to describe this program structure, so you might be familiar with one or more of the terms based on your setting.

One-way dual language programs may be implemented in a variety of ways based on the local context and the population they serve. Whether or not these legitimate programs are considered developmental bilingual programs or single-language immersion, they are all designed for learners wishing to become fully bilingual and biliterate, and oftentimes multilingual. As we noted in Chapter 1, the linguistic richness and multidimensional home languages the students bring with them to the programs are critical assets, especially with students' development of multilingual identities.

Schools of thought on dual language implementation norms are different in the United States and internationally. In short, context plays a very important role in shaping programs' schools of thought and their implementation norms. One difference we note is regarding language-use ratios and time allocations. Some programs operate with strict language allocations such as 90/10, 80/20, 70/30, 60/40, and 50/50. Some require the ratio of the partner languages to be adjusted annually until a 50/50 ratio is achieved, starting with a 90/10 ratio. A second difference in implementation norms we note is about the use of translanguaging. Some programs embrace more contemporary language practices and encourage the pedagogy of translanguaging and simultaneous language and literacy development in the partner languages, whereas others do not. A third implementation norm where we note difference has to do with districts' departments that house dual language programs. Some programs are housed in their own, stand-alone dual language departments, others in the English as a second language or Title III department, some with the world languages department, and others with magnet programs. In all cases we emphasize the need for deliberate and consistent collaboration.

CAPTAIN'S LOG

The benefits of well-constructed two-way and one-way dual language programs are substantial for academic and sociocultural gains (Howard et al., 2018). Let's stop and reflect on what we've captured so far and make some intentional connections to collaboration.

1. Of the program types we described, which best describes your program (or the program you wish to create)? How do you believe collaboration can enhance the program?

___

2. What are your ideas about the importance of additive/dynamic dual language education? How will you explain this to others in a way that advocates for teacher collaboration for multilingualism?

___

Numerous international schools that are part of the WIDA Consortium also embrace dual language programming (https://wida.wisc.edu/memberships/isc/members).

WHAT PRACTITIONERS SAY

Maha Al Romaihi is the director of Tariq Bin Ziad, a pre-K–5 International Baccalaureate (IB) dual language school in Doha, Qatar, operating under the Qatar Foundation (www.qf.org.qa). She shared the following:

We are an IB school with an international curriculum. We want our students to be fluent English speakers and have more access to universities anywhere in the world when they graduate. But still, we want them to have a strong identity. And one of the most important pillars of their identity is the language of the country. Our plan is to make sure that we provide a balanced dual language program with a set of standards and a framework for Arabic as well. We have an English-speaking homeroom teacher who leads math and science instruction in English. And we have an Arabic-speaking homeroom teacher who does the Arabic language, Qatar history, and the Islamic studies, because it's mandatory in Qatar. Our teachers meet every day to preplan lessons, the curriculum coordinator works with the grade-level teachers once a week, and we regularly work together as a whole

(Continued)

(Continued)

school to look at the curriculum vertically and horizontally. All teachers make authentic connections across the content areas in both languages, and learning is happening in all subjects in an integrated, transdisciplinary way!

What type of vertical and horizontal planning is happening in your own context? Why are these factors important within a dual language program?

Also see how the characteristics of an IB learner profile are displayed bilingually at the Qatar Academy Doha Primary School (Figure 2.2).

Figure 2.2 Arabic/English Banners of the IB Learner Profile

Source: Sana Alavi. Used with permission.

Collaborative Partnerships

Clearly, dual language instruction is far from a "one size fits all" endeavor. Other than the foundational aspects of the *four pillars* of dual language education, there are many combinations of learners, languages, and teachers to explore. A strong rationale for the chapter's third goal—to explore the ways in which teacher partnerships contribute to the benefits of dual language education—is evidence of the effectiveness of collaboration and co-teaching between general education and English language development specialists (Dove & Honigsfeld, 2020b). The current national shortage of highly qualified, bilingual dual language teachers is another reason to support a variety of collaborative models. We simply don't have enough bilingual teachers in the field, nor do we have sufficient numbers of preservice teachers in the pipelines of teacher preparation programs to realistically fill the demand for creating, maintaining, and expanding dual language programs (Guerrero & Lachance, 2018). Dual language administrators are faced with making difficult hiring and scheduling decisions to the extent that even when credentialed bilingual teacher candidates are available to fill positions, they may not have specialized expertise in dual language pedagogy and/or demonstrate skills and knowledge related to how both program languages work with each other. And those teachers who have a functional knowledge of both program languages may require additional support to reach *academic language levels* in one or both languages. The good news is that such barriers aren't insurmountable: Collaboration and co-teaching models draw upon the strengths and competencies of two or more teachers in a manner that enhances the potential for high-quality teaching and learning (Guerrero & Guerrero, 2017).

Keri Ward and Megan Smith, dual language educators in Idaho's Jefferson County School District 251, discuss how their students best work in their classroom as a whole group, in small groups, and individually, and make strategic decisions together about seating patterns that they believe will result in optimal learning. Their informed collaborative decisions intend to promote students' learning of the new content while simultaneously affording their classes leveraged opportunities to use both program languages. This sense of collaboration is quite different from creating a seating chart in isolation and shows us one of many examples of how this teacher partnership contributes to the benefits of dual language education (see Figure 2.3).

In the following section, we provide some clear examples of *collaborative partnerships* that may offer creative and sustainable ways for collaboration and program design. Keep in mind that these examples don't provide the full range of combinations that are possible. We encourage teams (including teachers and paraprofessionals) to collaborate as much as possible, regardless of configuration—starting with co-planning and using assessment data to shape and reshape the instruction being delivered.

Figure 2.3 Partner Teachers Review Students' Academic and Linguistic Progress as Well as In-Class Participation Patterns

Source: Keri Ward and Megan Smith. Used with permission.

In essence, we encourage you to "do what you can!" rather than being hesitant to move forward with a partnership/collaborative approach if partnership teaching or co-teaching in the same classroom isn't feasible. See which of these examples of collaborative partnerships across program models may best align to your context (see more in Chapter 4).

Two bilingual teachers, both using two languages

In some programs, two bilingual teachers with similar proficiency levels in both program languages work in the same classroom at the same time. One teacher delivers instruction through the program language, and the partner teacher teaches through English. The key distinction in this configuration is that both teachers are fully bilingual and biliterate. Multilingual educators can draw from any number of design possibilities with respect to language of instruction and the role of each teacher depending upon the instructional needs of the student, the capacity of individual teachers, and the content being taught. For example, teachers may be taking turns during portions of lessons in different languages such as circle time in English and then again in Arabic without repeating the same information—thus one circle time builds on the next. Another example is interdisciplinary in which a language arts teacher and social studies teacher collaborate to determine crossing over of lesson objectives and topics to teach back-to-back lessons in the same classroom, even if they are using different program languages.

Two bilingual teachers, each using one of the partner languages (side by side)

Teachers may "side by side" teach in one language or the other on a regular basis. Students may alternate their use of program languages throughout the school day, on alternating days, or, in some cases, in slightly longer chunks of time. In this configuration, both teachers are fully bilingual and biliterate. For example, Teacher A delivers Spanish language arts, math, and science through Spanish while Teacher B delivers English language arts, social studies, and technology through English. The students may switch classrooms, or the teachers may change classrooms depending on the numbers of students and the availability of classroom space. In smaller programs, Teachers A and B may always be in the same classroom and move in and out of the leading teaching role as the subjects change. In either case, or in other similar cases, teachers deliver different content-based curricula yet strategically make bridging connections via materials, topics, and lesson activities.

Two monolingual/partially bilingual teachers, each using one of the partner languages (side by side)

In this "side by side" scenario, teachers will teach in one of the program languages daily. A distinction of this configuration is that teachers are fully literate in one of the program languages *but not both*. The teachers may have some conversational proficiency in the other program language but not to the extent to be considered fully bilingual and biliterate. This configuration has some similarities to the prior in that different subject areas are taught through different languages. For example, Teacher A delivers Spanish language arts, math, and science in Spanish while Teacher B delivers English language arts, social studies, and technology in English. Again, the students may change classrooms or the teachers may change classrooms depending on the numbers of students and the availability of classroom space. In smaller programs, Teachers A and B may always be in the same classroom and move in and out of the leading teaching role as the subjects change.

Bilingual paraprofessionals and teacher's assistants

Paraprofessionals frequently play a critical role in meeting students' needs in dual language settings whether they are bilingual or monolingual. Some paraprofessionals may have more of an instructional role, and others may have more of a helper role to assist with things like bathroom breaks, classroom organization, filing, and so on. Without their contributions, many programs would be in danger of insufficient staffing. Far too often they are the unsung heroes who come to our schools on a daily basis, receive little pay, and are committed to the success of dual language programs as much as many other teachers. They deserve our advocacy for expanded career pathways, better compensation, and professional respect.

CAPTAIN'S LOG

After reading a few examples of innovative ways teachers form partnerships, let's reflect on teacher collaboration.

1. What collaborative scenarios does your program have? How are you utilizing the help of bilingual paraprofessionals?

   _____
   _____
   _____
   _____

2. If you are working on a co-teaching approach, what collaborative practices are you able to achieve now?

   _____
   _____
   _____
   _____

The Pillars of Dual Language Education With a Focus on Collaboration

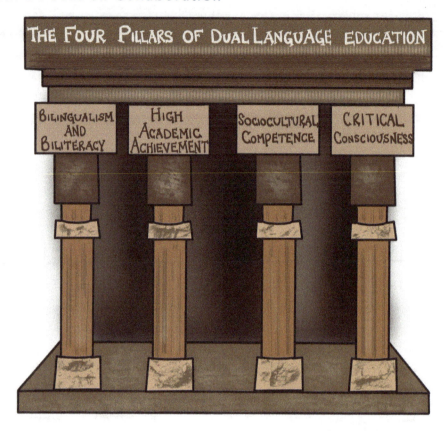

Even with the wide variety of dual language program structures and immense diversity in the dual language learner population, experts in the field agree that high-quality, carefully implemented dual language programs are built on four pillars of foundational support. The first three foundational elements address the development of bilingualism and biliteracy, grade-level academic achievement, and sociocultural competence for *all* students (Howard et al., 2018). More recently, as the field began to recognize and acknowledge the social justice and equity implications of dual language instruction, a fourth pillar was added: *critical consciousness* of educators working within the dual language spheres of impact (Cervantes-Soon et al., 2017; Palmer et al., 2019). The need for the fourth pillar is based on severe inequities within some dual language programs; thus we, too, take the stance that this fourth pillar is both necessary and compatible with the overarching and transformative goals of dual language education. The four pillars of dual language education help us by providing crucial specifications as we collaborate within the planning, teaching, and assessment processes—so let's *commit to collaborating based on the four pillars*!

The First Pillar: Bilingualism and Biliteracy

The bilingualism and biliteracy pillar of dual language affirms that dual language learners develop oracy and literacy in both program languages. To facilitate such development, dual language co-educators design, deliver, and assess instruction in different ways. Some co-creation of lessons and assessments that promote biliteracy may be from the *simultaneous approach* (students are learning or developing in both languages at the same time). Others, depending on the context of the program, may focus on sequentially developing students' languages and literacies. Remembering the diversity in the dual language population as well as learners' stages of development, there are times when dual language collaborators are facilitating lessons that develop literacy in both program languages at a similar pace, whether they occupy the same classroom or are in a side-by-side format with separate classrooms.

In making instructional decisions, teachers take into account the needs of individual dual language learners. Collaborating teachers should closely examine and discuss which curricular transformations are necessary to give breadth and depth for literacy and content development in both languages. These collaborative conversations are different from simply agreeing to teach literacy for each language separately (Howard et al., 2018). When dual language teachers collaborate about curricular transformations throughout the instructional cycle, the activities they plan, the materials they use, and the assessments they administer with transformations in mind expand students' opportunities to interact with one another (Honigsfeld & Dove, 2019). Some nonnegotiables for success include students' collective problem solving, participating in deep discussions, co-thinking, and writing about rigorous, thematically connected, and critically conscious topics in both program languages.

The Second Pillar: Grade-Level Academic Achievement in Both Program Languages

The next pillar is that of grade-level academic achievement in both program languages. For many years, the guiding assumption in the United States held that multilingual learners needed to reach a certain level of English language proficiency before being taught content. Fortunately, this myth has, for the most part, been debunked. Students in dual language programs gain proficiency *in both languages* while learning content. Every state has content standards for academic subjects studied in school. Likewise, states have language development standards. In combination with the use of multiple sets of standards, dual language teachers are uniquely positioned to facilitate lessons filled with rich and rigorous opportunities for students to take risks with using new language in new ways. Many educators would agree that dual language teachers are the only educators who simultaneously use multiple sets of language development standards in both program languages as well as content standards, synchronizing language development in two languages concurrently with content development. In Figures 2.4 and 2.5, we see some examples of bilingual anchor charts from Collinswood Language Academy, part of Charlotte-Mecklenburg Schools in North Carolina, where dual language educator Elia Alarcon reinforces language and content via a math lesson. The anchor charts support students' simultaneous growth in grade-level math skills, the use of the language of math, and Spanish language development.

Figures 2.4 and 2.5 Bilingual Math Anchor Charts

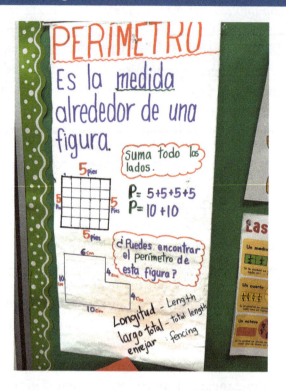

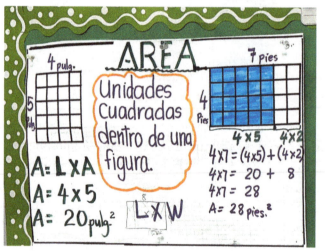

Source: Elia Alarcon. Used with permission.

The Third Pillar: Sociocultural Competence

The third pillar of dual language education substantiates the need to consider students' languages and backgrounds as a vital part of their educational experiences and growth. We call upon our dual language educators to see this pillar as a much deeper goal than cross-cultural understanding. Surface-level recognition of concepts and traditions that seem to represent students' cultural groups and social norms—for example, international dress day or international foods day—will do little to honor and affirm students' cultural identities. Instead, we advocate for planning, delivering, and assessing dual language classroom experiences that positively shape and reshape multilingual learners' individual identities, including self-perception within a local community and society as a whole (de Jong & Howard, 2009; Feinauer & Howard, 2014). Dual language teachers and multilingual students develop positive attitudes through consistent and deliberate opportunities for examining, reflecting upon, and interacting with each other in a manner that sincerely honors others' identities and language use. Both teachers and students participate in a process of multidimensional identity development, appreciating different ethnicities, languages, cultural assets, and community contributions in ways that disrupt society's inequitable norms.

The Fourth Pillar: Critical Consciousness

Students' positive academic and sociocultural growth as a result of dual language education has been documented for decades (Lindholm-Leary, 2012; Thomas & Collier, 2017). A newer development has been the call for a conscious acknowledgment of the continued inequities in dual language education programs (Palmer et al., 2019). In particular, some programs privilege the English-speaking students at the hindrance of the minoritized bilingual learners (Cervantes-Soon et al., 2017; Roda & Menken, under review). Dual language educators are obliged to skillfully collaborate in order to better advocate for the systematically oppressed linguistic status of the emergent bilinguals so they are no longer viewed as subpar. We embrace Carla España and Luz Yadira Herrera's (2020) call for six essential practices to center the voices and experiences of Latinx students, which may also be directly transferred to all multilingual emergent bilinguals' identities. We adapted these six recommendations to further support building students' critical consciousness in dual language classrooms:

1. Become familiar with your students' unique journeys that contributed to the formation of their complex identities.

2. Understand and leverage your students' language choices and practices.

3. Understand and leverage your students' and their families' literacy choices and practices.

4. Thoughtfully learn about your own privileges and be in solidarity with your students' experiences and opportunities.

5. Closely examine the local, state, and national policies, practices, and narratives that impact your students' personal, familial, and academic lives.

6. Understand the intersectional and multidimensional nature of your students' identity development and how they have experienced marginalization.

Let's recognize this is no simple task, especially in our current, turbulent political environment. Disrupting inequities takes courage, time, savvy, and well-crafted communication skills. Advocates must be able to articulate the proven benefits of dual language programs, based on long-term research and successful program results. Let's take great caution in examining our own beliefs and practices that may inadvertently feed deficit thinking with respect to multilingual learners and the languages and regional dialects they bring to the classroom.

CAPTAIN'S LOG

1. How do you see yourself as a collaborator in light of the four pillars of dual language education?

   _____
   _____
   _____
   _____

2. What recommendations would you offer other educators regarding effective, collaborative ways to build equity within a dual language program?

   _____
   _____
   _____
   _____

LAUNCHED MISSIONS

Let's meet two dual language kindergarten teachers, Alejandra Aguilera and Liliana Grajeda, from John F. Kennedy Elementary School in Port Chester, New York. The two collaborating kindergarten teachers are from a 90/10 two-way dual language program, both delivering instruction in Spanish for 90% of the instructional day. These two teachers consistently reflect on what's working well and where they need to make some shifts in their journey's plans, an essential element of effective collaboration.

In the beginning of their paired experiences, they met regularly to work out some overall logistics of lessons but also took time to have very focused conversations about biliteracy instruction, to ensure their practices took biliteracy instruction into account rather than teaching each program language individually (Howard et al., 2018). Despite their varying levels of teaching experience, Señorita Grajeda works diligently to have exchanges of ideas with Señorita Aguilera to be sure she feels like a valued and equal colleague. In fact, Señorita Grajeda looks to Señorita Aguilera as a mentor regarding technology and digital tools. At the same time, Señorita Aguilera still considers Señorita Grajeda as her mentor teacher and professional colleague with valuable insight. They also shared the importance of collaborating with their monolingual colleagues in other subject areas and the overall benefits of working together.

Señorita Grajeda shares:

This year we tried to meet once a week and tried to really look at our plans. First, we talked about all our experiences during the week. Let's say how they [the students] are doing. For example, they are learning the vowels in Spanish. Then we made the projections for the following week. Let's continue with the next steps in vowels, and let's say what we are going to do with that in [Spanish] reading. Sometimes, we exchange ideas about materials and resources. For instance, we often plan to try this new thing with the kids, a new strategy, or a new activity. I love technology, so I always want us to try working in Google Slides and to try different activities in technology. Let's say we are teaching the vowels; we use technology for activities. We are transferring from the traditional way of teaching into a more technological way. The benefits are that we see the progression and the growth of the students. That's the most important role for us. We talk about our students and our situations and our experiences and exchange ideas. This is something that worked for me, and maybe she [my partner teacher] will also say something about an activity that worked for her and suggest that we try and see if it is going to work for my students in my classroom. The advantage is that we really discuss what we see in the growth and the progress of the students. In terms of planning, it allows us to save more time. We can decorate the wheel instead of reinventing it.

Señorita Aguilera shares:

How did it go? What worked for you? What didn't work for you? What can we do next? Those are the questions we ask each other regularly to see how we can collaborate and plan. I see her [my partner teacher] as a mentor because she keeps teaching me about lessons and assessments. I learn from her, and she learns from me. We also talk to the monolingual teachers regularly. We are always doing curricular planning with teams, discussing things that we have been working on, and we share ideas. That way, all the teachers can benefit from our collaboration. We talk a lot about [Spanish] language and reading, and that helps the other teachers understand what we are doing with our students and what they will do with the students.

CAPTAIN'S LOG

1. How do you see Alejandra's and Liliana's collaboration as beneficial, therefore extending the successes of dual language in a 90/10 two-way kindergarten program?

   _____
   _____
   _____
   _____

2. Why are the regular meetings with the grade-level teachers so important for extending collaboration efforts?

   _____
   _____
   _____
   _____

NAVIGATION SYSTEMS

The way we conceptualize the navigation system toward successful capacity building through collaboration is multifaceted. We already know that dual language is highly beneficial academically, linguistically, and socioculturally across all student learning groups. Keeping the key benefits of dual language education in mind will help you navigate the way you collaboratively plan, implement, and assess instruction for your students in this context:

1. Multilingual learners display higher levels of cognition and critical thinking in both program languages.

2. Multilingual learners exhibit higher outcomes on high-stakes assessments across language, socioeconomic, racial, and special education groups.

3. Multilingual learners demonstrate wider ranges of cultural competence and are able to problem-solve in collaborative ways that are more multidimensional than monolingual students (Feinauer & Howard, 2014).

4. Dual language programs, when constructed as enriching and accelerated for *all* students rather than being viewed as a necessary means of remediation for English learners who need to catch up to their monolingual peers, facilitate language-rich environments that cannot easily be re-created in monolingual schools (Escamilla et al., 2014).

What we need to focus on is how to extend these benefits by strategically enhancing collaboration in all program structures. Our field-based research shows us that when you build capacity for collaboration informed by four dynamic components (see Figure 2.6), you're moving forward to ensuring what all multilingual learners deserve—a bright future. The components are:

1. Research Findings: To inform your collaborative practices with research on the benefits of collaboration and dual language, emphasizing the need to combine both approaches

2. Leadership Commitment: To create and foster leadership commitment to collaboration

3. Practitioner Learning: To enhance your collaborative practices by making them ongoing and reflective, to continuously shape and reshape your work

4. Dynamic Lived Experiences: To position the rich, authentic life events, encounters, and everyday practices both you and your dual language learners bring to your classrooms as a focal point

Figure 2.6 The Four Dynamic Components of Informed Collaboration

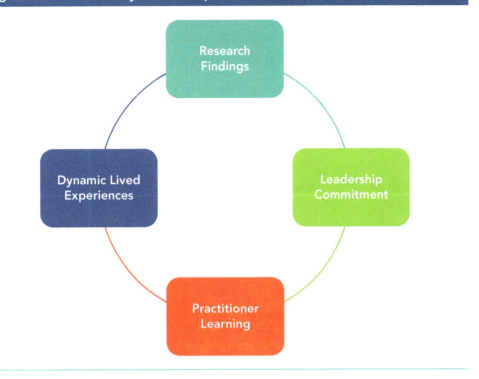

1. How do these four dynamic components inform your collaboration?

   _____
   _____
   _____
   _____

2. What other sources of information or experience enhance your collaborative practices?

   _____
   _____
   _____
   _____

CAPTAIN'S LOG

STAYING THE COURSE

We have found that oftentimes educators are able to identify aspects of inequities but then may struggle with addressing them in ways that promote action and change (Nordmeyer et al., 2021). In this section, let's focus on some core beliefs and agreements that undergird equitable dual language instruction.

Difficult conversations about our beliefs, biases, and values call for safety measures. As we think about the following *Core Beliefs* and articulate some *"Let's Agree" Statements*, remember to commit to an overarching belief that helps us stay on the course of empowerment, equity, and strength for all dual language programs, even when there is turbulence on the journey—especially when we collaborate with each other. Many educators have dedicated themselves for years or decades or perhaps their entire careers as advocates, trailblazers, and activists in settings ranging from schools and communities to Capitol Hill in Washington, DC. Let's amplify their stories with our co-creations as we move forward.

Core Beliefs

We share the belief that dual language education for multilingualism is *the* tool for social transformation (Wayne Thomas and Virginia Collier, personal communication, December 21, 2021). We embrace that collaborative, well-structured dual language programs employ culturally relevant pedagogies. The facilitation of collaborative instruction, based on the four pillars of dual language, does more than teach a mainstream curriculum in two languages. Rather, dual language teachers who collaborate work together with their students to design and deliver multilingual lessons that confront issues of race, class, language and power dynamics, gender, and other inequities (Cervantes-Soon et al., 2017; Palmer et al., 2019).

1. Longitudinal research shows the academic success of every group and subgroup participating in high-quality dual language programs. These research findings help us to stay the course.

2. Critical consciousness regarding aspects of the dual language education program structure is an extraordinarily complex system of interwoven tethers, some of which have very distinct meanings for people. Programmatic context, systems of linguistic power, and interpretation of equitable access to high-quality dual language education shape our core beliefs (Cervantes-Soon et al., 2017; Palmer et al., 2019).

3. Only when we are transparent and well prepared to take an informed approach regarding inequities can we move toward dismantling them (Kibler et al., 2021).

"Let's Agree" Statements

Based on the core beliefs, let's make a commitment to sharing and upholding the following:

1. Dual language education is for all students!

2. All multilingual learners should be viewed as gifted assets in school and in our communities.

3. The characteristics of high-quality programs include collaboration between and among educators.

4. Developing capacity for collaboration within the context of dual language programs is a complex process that requires a shared understanding of research-informed, evidence-based practices.

CAPTAIN'S LOG: FINAL ENTRY

1. What are some additional core beliefs you might add to the list we provided?

   _____
   _____
   _____
   _____

2. How might you expand the *"Let's Agree" Statements* to make them unique to your context?

   _____
   _____
   _____
   _____

GEAR UP!

Before we move forward with our chapters that dive into co-planning, co-delivering, and co-assessing dual language instruction, we invite you to explore some foundational resources that will help strengthen your work to enhance collaboration in your dual language program at any and every level. The "Questions to Begin the Conversation" inventory helps promote reflection and action toward ensuring that you are building capacity for collaboration into your dual language program (see Figure 2.7)—whether you are starting from the very beginning of creating a new program, polishing one that is already in place, or aiming to grow a program to include additional grade levels (keep going to secondary levels!).

Figure 2.7 Questions to Begin the Conversations

REFLECTION QUESTIONS	STAKEHOLDERS WITH WHOM TO COLLABORATE	HOW TO PREPARE FOR A COLLABORATIVE CONVERSATION (WHAT INFORMATION, EVIDENCE, OR RESOURCES WILL YOU NEED?)
Why create, enhance, or expand our dual language program? How do we describe that equity for multilingual learners is at the center of our initiatives?		
How will the beneficial outcomes for our community and for our students be extended with teacher collaboration?		
Who are the intended participants in the program (*remember equity*), and how will they benefit by having educators who collaborate?		
Which program type is best for our students, and how will we build in collaboration?		
What are the time allotments within the program, and how do they work for collaboration?		
Which subjects will be taught through which program languages?		

REFLECTION QUESTIONS	STAKEHOLDERS WITH WHOM TO COLLABORATE	HOW TO PREPARE FOR A COLLABORATIVE CONVERSATION (WHAT INFORMATION, EVIDENCE, OR RESOURCES WILL YOU NEED?)
Who will teach both grade-level content across two or more languages and language skills, and how will these teachers collaborate?		
Which teachers do we already have, and which will we need to recruit?		
How will we build in our program culture of collaboration as we recruit teachers?		
How will we describe to others the benefits of collaboration from a critically conscious perspective?		
What culturally relevant curricular materials and multidimensional supports are already available in grade-level content that facilitate multilingualism? What additional materials do we need?		
How will our teacher partners collaborate to use the available resources and materials? What additional key resources do we need?		

TUNE IN!

The momentum of growth in dual language education is being propelled by more and more educators' awareness of the elements of high-quality programming. Research and policy also support dual language programs. In addition to the tools and reflections you've used so far in Chapter 2, here are a few books and guides, links to organizations, and links to Web resources to support your work:

Books and Guides

Beeman, K., & Urow, C. (2013). *Teaching for biliteracy: Strengthening bridges between languages.* Caslon.

Collier, V. P., & Thomas, W. P. (2009). *Educating English learners for a transformed world.* Fuente Press.

Collier, V. P., & Thomas, W. P. (2018). *Transforming secondary education: Middle and high school dual language programs.* Fuente Press.

Escamilla, K., Hopewell, S., Butvilofsky, S., Sparrow, W., Soltero-González, L., Ruiz-Figueroa, O., & Escamilla, M. (2014). *Biliteracy from the start: Literacy squared in action.* Caslon.

García, O. (2020). Translanguaging and Latinx bilingual readers. *The Reading Teacher, 73*(5), 557–562. https://doi.org/10.1002/trtr.1883

García, O., Ibarra-Johnson, S., & Seltzer, K. (2017). *The translanguaging classroom: Leveraging student bilingualism for learning.* Caslon.

Gottlieb, M. (2021). *Classroom assessment in multiple languages: A handbook for teachers.* Corwin.

Gottlieb, M. (2022). *Assessment in multiple languages: A handbook for school and district Leaders.* Corwin.

Hamayan, E., Genesee, F., & Cloud, N. (2013). *Dual language instruction from A to Z: Practical guidance for teachers and administrators.* Heinemann.

Howard, E., Lindholm-Leary, K., Rogers, D., Olague, N., Medina, J., Kennedy, F., Sugarman, J., & Christian, D. (2018). *Guiding principles for dual language education* (3rd ed.). Center for Applied Linguistics.

Thomas, W. P., & Collier, V. P. (2014). *Creating dual language schools for a transformed world: Administrators speak.* Fuente Press.

Thomas, W. P., & Collier, V. P. (2017). *Why dual language schooling.* Fuente Press.

Professional Organizations and Web Resources

- ACTFL (formerly the American Council on the Teaching of Foreign Languages): www.actfl.org

- Association of Two-Way & Dual Language Education (ATDLE): https://atdle.org

- Center for Advanced Research on Language Acquisition (CARLA): https://carla.umn.edu/immersion/resources.html

- Center for Applied Linguistics: www.cal.org
- Dual Language Education of New Mexico: www.dlenm.org
- Massachusetts Department of Education: www.doe.mass.edu/ele/look-act.html
- Migration Policy Institute: www.migrationpolicy.org/programs/nciip-english-learners-and-every-student-succeeds-act-essa
- Multistate Association for Bilingual Education, Northeast: https://mabene.org
- TESOL International: www.tesol.org/search?query=dual%20language

As we finish up Chapter 2 and get ready to focus on collaborative planning in Chapter 3, think about how you want to get started on using the content of the chapter to launch your own mission. As you count down to launch, remember to think openly regarding equity and access to your program and consider the following ideas:

COUNTDOWN TO LAUNCH

10. Reflect upon the ways in which collaboration is already built into your program.

9. Identify areas where collaboration can be expanded.

8. Feel confident to be creative and innovative for leveraging collaborative practices for multilingualism.

7. Keep learning about dual language education and share your expertise with others.

6. Ask and collectively answer the hard questions about equity and access to high-quality dual language education. How will you collaborate to involve parents and community stakeholders in this process?

5. Be committed to collaborate using the four pillars of dual language instruction as the cornerstones of your program structure and goals.

4. Commit to actions that promote collaboration—remembering that your colleagues have important insights even if they are still on the path to developing familiarity with dual language education.

3. Collectively identify the types of student data your school or district already collects and how you can collaborate regarding the use of the data.

2. Collaborate to share a wide range of creative ways to assess and report students' and programmatic successes, including those from students themselves.

1. Put students first and involve them as leaders and co-creators of the dual language program.

CAPTAIN'S LOG: FINAL ENTRY

Based on Chapter 2 and its learning goals, take a moment to identify your key takeaways. Here are some questions to consider: What is directly applicable to your context? What is something you learned that is completely different from your context? What do you feel is your biggest challenge at the moment? How might you address that challenge in small steps? What are some future goals or steps you wish to take? What might be challenging for you to discuss with your collaborative partner(s)?

_____
_____
_____
_____
_____
_____

Collaborative Planning in Dual Language Programs 3

"When you change the way you look at things, the things you look at change."

—Dr. Wayne Dyer

MISSION CONTROL

Collaborative planning is an essential component of dual language programs regardless of the model of instruction. Partnering teachers and other members of the school community collaborate for the sake of their multilingual learners. This chapter defines the *who, what, where, when, how,* and *why* of collaborative planning and offers actionable recommendations and tools to support co-planning in the dual language context. More specifically, the goals of Chapter 3 are to:

1. Define the essential elements of collaborative planning in the dual language classroom

2. Identify the purpose and key practices of co-planning using the four pillars of dual language instruction

3. Review and evaluate collaborative planning protocols and tools

EXPLORATION

Before we launch our exploration into collaborative planning, let's look at this topic from the perspectives of one student and her teachers in a Vietnamese–English fourth-grade dual language classroom. We wish to elevate these voices here by briefly sharing their experiences and invite you to consider them through your own lens as well as through some key research findings.

Through a Student's Eyes

My name is Minh, and I am in the fourth grade. I love going to school. I am excited to see my friends, even if sometimes I am a bit nervous in class. I know I must do well in school. My teachers and my parents both expect me to learn as much as I can, both in Vietnamese and in English. I started in a Vietnamese dual language program in kindergarten where half of the students spoke Vietnamese and the others spoke English [a two-way program]. I was born in the United States, but both my parents came here from Vietnam when they were much younger. My grandma only speaks Vietnamese, and our culture and language are very important to the family. My name Minh means "clever, intelligent person" in Vietnamese, and I know my family wants to make smart choices for me and wants me to have a better life in America.

And here is what her teachers think about Minh:

Minh enjoys that she gets to use both her languages at school. She can read and write in Vietnamese with just as much confidence as she does in English; she has friends whose home languages are English, Spanish, and Vietnamese and enjoys learning with them and from them. She prefers writing poetry in Vietnamese, though, whereas science reports and social studies document-based analyses come with more ease in English. Recently she began to be more conscious of—and occasionally even puzzled by—the significant differences between her two languages. For example, the adjectives must follow nouns in Vietnamese, while adjectives come first in English. Words like easy-peasy, super-duper, *and* goody-goody *are rare and playful in English, but such repetitive or rhyming reduplicative use of words is quite common in Vietnamese, offering a refinement or a new shade of meaning of the original word.*

She has long noticed how the dialect her family uses slightly differs from that of her teachers and the teaching assistant: Originally from Can Tho in southern Vietnam, her family uses five tones; her teachers and the teaching assistant (both from northern regions) apply six tones, but she can easily comprehend and communicate with everyone. She looks forward to making some of these comparisons in class, with her family, or on her own and lights up each time she can make some new discoveries for herself about what languages can do and how her two languages and dialects work.

Minh is developing metalinguistic awareness about her languages and dialects both intuitively and through her participation in a dual language program. As Ofelia García (2014) also notes, "language is an inseparable part of all human action, intimately connected to all other forms of action, physical, social and symbolic. Language is a set of practices that express agency, embodied and embedded in the environment" (p. 149). Knowing this, what might be the unique role teacher collaboration can play in supporting Minh's dual language development?

CAPTAIN'S LOG

_____

_____

_____

_____

Through the Educators' Eyes

We are Minh's fourth-grade partner teachers. We also work with a part-time bilingual teaching assistant, and all three of us meet regularly during our assigned weekly collaborative planning time. We have been looping with the class since third grade, so this is the second year we are working together as a team in support of the same two-way dual language class. Our official planning time is limited to two periods per week combined with our lunch period, so we often do "lunch and plan," too. We like to look back at the previous week and compare notes about how students make progress in the core content areas across the two languages, as well as in their cross-cultural understandings and critical thinking. In our collaborative conversations, we discuss ways to infuse our students' cultural heritage in the curriculum and are attentive to their emerging bicultural identities. We frequently survey our students to get input from them and guide them to set goals for themselves.

To make our planning time more efficient, we look at available formative student data and review the appropriate curriculum and scope and sequence guides prior to our common meeting time. When we sit down to plan, we like to start with some brief celebrations (or noticings) before we take a deeper dive into the upcoming lessons. Early on, we have established several classroom protocols for instructional consistency that we periodically revisit such as beginning- and end-of-day routines, processes for transitioning from large-group to small-group instruction, and clear expectations for self- and peer assessment and goal setting that students regularly engage in. We also made an agreement that we will not stress if we cannot finish planning everything on the spot: Instead, we will work on making some deliberate overarching decisions regarding goals and objectives, as well as key instructional practices that support the development of content, language, literacy, cultural and critical consciousness, and ways our students can demonstrate their new learning through key activities, tasks, and projects. We make sure our teaching assistant has meaningful tasks in each lesson. Then we hash out roles and responsibilities during our planning period and finish planning using a shared Google Drive on our own.

WHAT THE RESEARCH SAYS

Intentional planning and collaborative conversations about students' simultaneous development of academic, linguistic, cross-cultural, and critical consciousness are key to success. We chose two key points from current research to connect to this scenario. One invites explicit focus on planning for metalinguistic awareness, and the other reminds us of the importance of collaborating to ensure that students engage in self- and peer assessment and goal setting with clear expectations (see Chapter 5 for more on this):

According to WIDA (2020), *"The explicit teaching of how language works can help multilingual learners expand what they can do with language, thereby growing their language toolbox. We want our students to become increasingly aware and strategic in their use of language to negotiate meaning and achieve their purposes in various contexts"* (p. 20).

Margo Gottlieb (2021) emphasizes the importance of collaborating to engage multilingual learners: *"From the first day to the close of the school year, students should be participants in classroom instruction and assessment"* (p. 14).

How are these ideas from current research reflected in the collaborative planning vignette from Minh's partner teachers? How could they be further strengthened during co-planning time?

Ready to Launch the Exploration

Common sense, evidence-based practice, and empirical research all support the notion that dual language programs cannot thrive without sustained teacher collaboration. In this section, we will explore the key questions that arise related to collaborative planning—*who, what, when, where, why,* and *how*—to ensure impactful program implementation and consistent and rigorous yet highly supportive learning experiences for all students.

Who Collaborates With Whom?

While partner teachers are expected to closely work together, collaboration may involve several educators in a dual language context. Some collaborations may be regularly scheduled and sustained; others may only occur occasionally or on an as-needed basis. Consider the following list and reflect on what collaboration may look like in each of the scenarios when partner teachers collaborate with:

- Each other and other dual language partnerships
- Teaching assistants or paraprofessionals assigned to their class
- Other grade-level teachers (on the elementary level)
- Other content-area teachers (on the secondary level)
- Other bilingual and dual language educators
- English language development (ELD) specialists
- Special education teachers
- Instructional coaches
- Instructional leaders and administrators
- Parents or guardians
- Community liaisons or other members of the larger linguistic community

Collaboration may greatly vary in each case: Collaborating with teaching assistants may focus on the effective and efficient day-to-day management of resources, connecting with parents invites a two-way dialogue about their children's progress, and collaborating with instructional coaches allows for self-assessment, goal setting, and ongoing, job-embedded professional learning opportunities for the team. We fully embrace what Margarita Calderón and her colleagues (2019) also claim: "The success of dual language programs depends on collaboration between teachers, administrators, and students. In a dual language school, teachers are well-prepared to co-teach and students to co-learn" (p. 163). So, collaboration may even be perceived to be the norm; do you agree?

What Is Collaborative Planning?

For our purposes, this is how we are going to define *collaborative planning*. Also referred to as *co-planning*, it is a process that supports the consistent, high-quality implementation of standards-aligned language and core content curricula alongside developing cultural and critical consciousness while allowing dual language educators and other collaborating educators (such as special education teachers, teaching assistants, paraprofessionals, instructional specialists, and others) the opportunity to coordinate and refine their plans for instruction and assessment (Honigsfeld & Dove, 2022).

CAPTAIN'S LOG

Did you have the same definition of *co-planning* in mind before you began reading this book? Reflect on the following list of ideas we gleaned from working with or interviewing collaborating dual language educators. Do you embrace any of the same notions?

Co-planning is:

- An agreement to welcome the use of both languages for co-planning purposes and to create an equitable, inclusive work environment for the partnership
- A joint commitment to excellence in both languages
- Critically listening to each other and building a trusting professional relationship
- An establishment of shared goals, learning intentions, and measurable outcomes for all students
- A concerted effort to make sure all students are developing academic, linguistic, and cultural competence in two languages
- An endeavor among educators to ensure that grade-level standards are met while equity of languages and cultural understandings are addressed
- An opportunity to leverage multilingualism

What else may be an important aspect of co-planning? How do *you* define collaborative planning for your team?

_____
_____
_____
_____

Consistent, intentional collaboration—especially co-planning—cannot happen in a vacuum. Administrators and collaborating educators must work together to create the logistical support for collaborative planning. When teachers have the opportunity to work together for sustained amounts of time, on a regular basis, with clear goals and agendas in place, their collaborative efforts, creativity, and professional commitment to the goals of dual language education must be recognized and appreciated. For effective teacher collaboration, ample time is needed, so as collaborating educators, you could share:

- Personal and professional beliefs and evidence-based best practices

- Commitment to the practice of collaboration and support for your partnership

- Expertise in content, knowledge of literacy and language development, cultural understanding, and pedagogical skills

- Instructional resources and bilingual supplementary materials that are scaffolded and differentiated

- Appropriate technology tools and creative ways to meaningfully integrate them into the curriculum

- Instructional strategies that represent research-informed practices for critical engagement

- Approaches to collaboratively teaching your classes (if applicable)

- Ways to group your students and optimize the learning space(s) available for instructional delivery

When and Where Does Collaborative Planning Take Place?

While teachers and administrators alike recognize the importance and value of collaborative planning, their most frequently cited concerns seem to be related to its logistics. Time often proves to be the greatest barrier. Yet, when we fully commit to allow for common planning time during the regular school day by building co-planning sessions into our master schedules, we alleviate the pressure on teachers and their assistants to figure out when and how they can find time to co-plan. When collaboration time is secured prior to or at the beginning of the academic year, teachers can work on mapping out the curriculum for the year. Revisiting and revising these curriculum maps periodically (such as at the beginning of each quarter) ensures a closer alignment between the planned or intended and the actual, taught curriculum.

WHAT PRACTITIONER RESEARCHERS SAY

Shera Simpson and Elizabeth Howard (2021) suggest starting the year with a co-planning map that helps streamline the collaborative planning and aid in the complex decision-making process:

> *The co-planning map asks tandem teachers to consider both the "what" and the "when" of co-planning for the year. First, you and your partner teacher brainstorm all of the recurring activities that you will need to work on together in the technical domains of co-teaching (curriculum, instruction, assessment, family communication, and classroom management), as well as the interpersonal aspects of your co-teaching relationship . . . You then take those activities and determine the "when" of co-planning, by distinguishing co-planning topics that need to be addressed weekly (such as lesson pacing) from those that require less frequent—but perhaps more intensive—discussion (such as curriculum mapping), as well as those that require ongoing attention through asynchronous tasks that partner teachers take care of on their own time. (para. 4)*

What tools have you used to map out your collaboration or co-planning?

Collaboration may take place in person or virtually, synchronously and asynchronously. Prior to 2020, most educators opted for face-to-face meetings for collaboration. The global crisis that the COVID-19 pandemic brought about resulted in some significant shifts in the way we use technology for teaching and collaboration. One silver lining of virtual or hybrid teaching and learning turned out to be that teacher collaboration and co-planning also went online: Most teachers we work with agree that examining standards and other resources, reviewing and aligning curriculum maps, co-planning units and lessons, sharing ideas and best practices, and co-developing instructional materials can be accomplished virtually with a lot more ease.

WHAT PRACTITIONERS SAY

Vanessa Aspiazu and Sean Kennedy are fifth-grade dual language educators in Port Chester Public Schools in New York. This is what they shared about the dynamic relationship and communication patterns they have established as well as finding time over the years:

> *We just communicate whenever we need to. It is very fluid, and we obviously—yes, we do have our boundaries and whatnot—but because we've been together for so long, it's just very easy to shoot each other a text. We communicate routinely every Friday, when we send each other a really long email to just update one another on the classes that we've been with for the week so that we can start preparing for*

the incoming class, so it is very fluid. We call, text, Zoom, email. In person, we just stop by each other's rooms. It's awesome! We just walk into each other's rooms, a lot, because things pop up all the time and sometimes it's not that easy to communicate. Well, it's just kind of an open-door policy and reminding each other, "We have to do this!"

How does Vanessa and Sean's communication resemble yours with your partner teachers?

Why Is Collaborative Planning Necessary in Dual Language Programs?

Collaborative curriculum development and collaborative planning (also referred to as co-planning) have been well established across grade levels, content areas, and instructional programs (e.g., Sleeter & Carmona, 2017). For example, special education inclusion as a program design and inclusive instructional choices for students with disabilities have decades of research and implementation grounded on the practice of collaboration among general and special education teachers (Beninghof, 2020; Friend & Cook, 2012; Murawski & Lochner, 2017; Peery, 2019; Villa et al., 2013). Collaborative service delivery models for English learners have been recognized as a way to ensure equity (Yoon, 2022) and to offer similar benefits by integrating content and language development (Honigsfeld & Dove, 2010, 2012a, 2015, 2019). Intentional planning has been at the core of all these initiatives (Honigsfeld & Dove, 2022).

Professional learning communities (PLCs) call on teams of teachers to engage in sustained collaboration and co-planning (DuFour & DuFour, 2012; DuFour et al., 2016; Marzano et al., 2018; Mattos et al., 2016). Establishing shared goals and committing to ongoing joint professional explorations are among the hallmarks of the PLC movement supporting both teacher agency and shared ownership of evolving pedagogies.

By design, many dual language programs are based on a partnership between two or more educators who come to the practice with language, literacy, and cultural knowledge and skills in their respective languages and combine their expertise through regular collaboration and co-planning. At other times, dual language teachers forge additional partnerships and collaborate with ELD teachers, who may provide additional language instruction, or special education teachers (such as occupational and physical therapy providers, speech–language pathologists, and other support personnel), who may offer in-class support to ensure that students' complex academic, linguistic, sociocultural, and social-emotional needs are met.

Collaboration in dual language programs demands both commitment and healthy risk-taking in the interest of promoting biliteracy development. Collaborating dual language teachers will be more effective when they each have a basic understanding of the partner languages' oracy and literacy patterns. In dual language settings, collaborative planning obliges conversations regarding each language's communication patterns for various language functions, both spoken and in writing. For example, in English, students are often expected to "get straight to the point" in their productive domains of communication. Ideas are expressed in a linear fashion. In other languages such as Diné, Mandarin, and Spanish, the communication patterns are much less linear. Students would perhaps be expected to express ideas and knowledge in a culturally decorated and/or circular pattern (Collier & Thomas, 2009).

CAPTAIN'S LOG

From the critically conscious view, collaborative planning must include some "prickly" yet very necessary conversations on the topics of curricular materials, representation, access, and equitable participation. Choose one of the following questions for your reflection:

How will students be able to see themselves in literature and anchor text selections, in both languages? How will students who speak the minority language have equal access to leading discussions?

_____

_____

_____

_____

WHAT PRACTITIONERS SAY

Teacher collaboration to support dynamic bilingual, bicultural, and biliteracy development could cause a cosmic shift in school culture, which we learned about when we interviewed Mats Haaland, director of English as an additional language (EAL), and Chelsea Wilson, director of teaching and learning, at Nansha College Preparatory Academy, a secondary immersion school in China. This is what Mats had to share:

> A few years ago, we pivoted toward having far more structure and support for our collaborative co-teaching teams by ensuring that our master schedule provided teachers with ample co-planning time and aligning their schedules for intentional co-teaching. Our EAL specialists have really flourished with this added support by becoming fully recognized members of their teaching teams. They have been able to consistently integrate their language acquisition expertise with our curriculum so that our students' needs as multilingual learners can be met consistently in the classroom.

Chelsea added:

One thing that I've been really, really happy to see on our campus is that we have seven learning teams that are being led by seven different members of faculty this semester. We have visitations happening as part of those learning teams where we have lots of people going into each other's classrooms to just take a look and see what's happening—what they can pull into their own instructional practice. I have people send me messages all the time saying, "Hey, I'd really like to get into someone's classroom to see X. Who is doing something like this that I can see?" So, we've moved toward this place where people recognize that their most valuable learning opportunities are their colleagues. And that is, I think, really powerful to have as a staff culture.

What challenges do you think Mats and Chelsea had to overcome to ensure everyone is on board with this new initiative?

How Do Dual Language Educators Co-Plan?

Based on the four pillars of dual language education, we present a four-dimensional collaborative planning framework (see Figure 3.1).

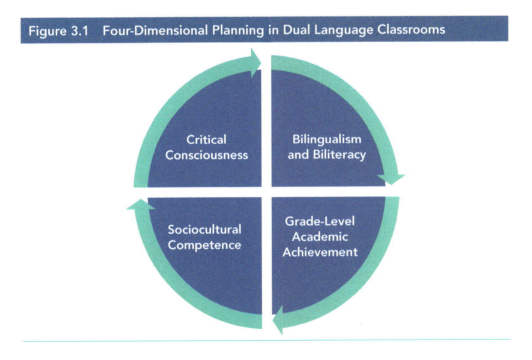

Figure 3.1 Four-Dimensional Planning in Dual Language Classrooms

When all four dimensions are considered together, collaborative planning maximizes teacher effectiveness and meaningfully impacts students' language acquisition and literacy learning in both languages. In addition, students' grade-appropriate core content knowledge and skills develop along with sociocultural understanding and critical consciousness. Co-planning is vitally important whether your team includes dual language partnering teachers or additional service providers such as special education teachers with or without the opportunity to co-deliver instruction. Collaborative planning upholds all other work that is done in the dual language classroom.

How do your students benefit from collaborative planning? In a purposefully planned lesson, they will:

- Receive rich, multidimensional, culturally and linguistically responsive, and sustaining curricula across the content areas

- Participate in instruction based on multilevel, differentiated unit and lesson plans

- Engage in learning tasks that integrate content, language and literacy development, sociocultural competence, and social-emotional growth

- Build cross-cultural understanding and positive identity development

- Develop critical understanding of and engagement with complex concepts (especially related to social justice and equity)

To establish a shared understanding of the four pillars, we invite partnering dual language teachers and other collaborating educators to discuss their beliefs and overarching goals for their students. You can use the *Co-Planning Pillars and Priorities Crosswalk Grid* in Figure 3.2 to develop a shared understanding of the four pillars and establish shared priorities for the upcoming school year regarding the curriculum, instruction, assessment, and community building.

Figure 3.2 Co-Planning Pillars and Priorities Crosswalk Grid

PRIORITIES → PILLARS ↓	CURRICULUM	INSTRUCTION	ASSESSMENT	COMMUNITY BUILDING
Bilingualism and Biliteracy				
Grade-Level Academic Achievement				
Sociocultural Competence				
Critical Consciousness				

If you design your own co-agreement, you and your colleagues can jointly decide what to prioritize; most partner teachers tend to focus on building partnerships, determining routines and structures, establishing collaboration norms and commitments, and mutually agreeing on some other critical points (see Figure 3.3 for an excerpt from the *Partnering for Literacy Success* document that includes essential mindsets, as well as teacher and leadership agreements, from Matt Hajdun and his team at the Columbus School in Envigado, Colombia).

Figure 3.3 Biliteracy Agreement for Partnering for Literacy Success at the Columbus School in Envigado, Colombia

Essential Mindsets:

- As bilingual learners, our students have double the assets, not half.
  - Asset-based vs. deficit-based
- All students are capable of learning additional languages.
  - Growth mindset vs. fixed mindset
- We are all literacy teachers.
  - Team teachers vs. language teachers
- Students must make frequent connections between partner languages with equity and balance.
  - Integration vs. two monolingual approaches
- Collective efficacy has the greatest impact on student learning.
  - Team teaching vs. individual islands

Source: Matt Hajdun. Used with permission.

NAVIGATION SYSTEMS

Collaborative planning cannot be accomplished on the fly! Due to the complex nature of co-planning and the significant impact it has on instruction and assessment, it may be best approached through two lenses: First, let's zoom out and establish some co-planning essentials and anchor strategies that support long-term planning; next, let's zoom in and refine our co-planning practices to ensure successful day-to-day collaborations!

Co-Planning Essentials

María Santos and colleagues (2012) offer a useful basic navigation system that starts out by taking a content-embedded linguistic angle of collaborative planning and suggests that when you collaborate with your colleagues, you begin by determining how to respond to students' developing needs by addressing the following:

1. Language progressions—What levels of proficiency are represented in your class? How do your students learn language, in terms of both general language acquisition and discipline-specific academic language and literacy development?

2. Language demands—What kinds of linguistic expectations and opportunities are embedded within specific texts and tasks with which your students engage across the core content classes?

3. Language scaffolds—How can specific representations and instructional strategies be used to help students gain access to the core concepts as well as to the language they need to learn?

4. Language supports—How can your classrooms and schools be organized to support students in continually building a deep understanding of language and content?

In the dual language context, this framework needs to be expanded to also ensure (a) equitable language and literacy development in both languages, (b) grade-level core content attainment, (c) cultural competence, and (d) critical consciousness. In order to apply these important considerations for dual language classes, we have created a planning template incorporating this critical framework that can be used when jointly planning instruction (see Figure 3.4).

Figure 3.4 Integrated Focus on Planning for Dual Language Teaching

FOCUS	KEY QUESTIONS	PLANNING NOTES
Language Progressions	*What levels of language proficiency do our plans address?*	
	What language learning standards do we target and assess?	
Language Expectations and Opportunities	*What content standards do we target and assess?*	
	What academic languages—general and subject-specific—are embedded in the target content?	
	What opportunities do our students have to practice the four key language uses (narrate, inform, argue, explain)?	
Language Scaffolds	*What scaffolds are needed to support comprehension of language and content through interpretive modes of communication (listening, reading, viewing)?*	
	What scaffolds are needed to support application of language and content through expressive modes of communication (speaking, writing, visually representing)?	

FOCUS	KEY QUESTIONS	PLANNING NOTES
Community and School Language Supports	What school-based supports can we tap into for this unit of study?	
	What out-of-school, community-based supports can we tap into for this unit of study?	
Cultural Competence	What materials can help students develop cross-cultural competence?	
	What learning tasks and activities can students engage in to demonstrate cross-cultural competence?	
Critical Consciousness	How have we ensured that both program languages are given equitable attention?	
	What aspect(s) of critical consciousness have we woven into the lesson content and/or materials?	
	What opportunities have we planned for our minoritized dual language learners to serve in linguistic leadership roles?	

Co-Planning Anchors

When you regularly engage in joint planning with your partner teachers and other collaborating educators, you can accomplish a lot. These professional conversations will range from the immediate, unique, and varied needs of your students to the academic complexities and linguistic expectations of the learning standards in core content areas—from ways your students develop multilingual and multicultural identities to the opportunities for critical engagements with larger concepts such as societal injustices, from simple translations of monolingual materials to the use of multidimensional, thought-provoking resources and learning activities. No small feat! So, anchoring your co-planning can help with this task. We have learned one such approach from Susan Pryor, who, in her former role as biliteracy coach for Cicero School District 99 in Illinois, frequently facilitated collaboration between dual language and general education teachers, the goal of which was to develop integrated curriculum units that can be applied in both dual language and general education classrooms in the same school. She invited collaborating teachers to accomplish some overarching tasks first (Pryor, 2018) before they focus on the nuances of instructional strategies and supplementary resources. We adapted her work to suggest the following co-planning anchor activities:

1. Unpack the target standards:
    - ⇒ Connect the standards to objectives and authentic assessment tasks.
    - ⇒ Establish key learning activities (support all four pillars of dual language education).

2. Review trends and patterns of student data:
    - ⇒ Establish what prior knowledge is needed for the unit.
    - ⇒ Consider what concepts and skills need to be retaught or spiraled into the new unit.

3. Develop new content or enhance existing content of the unit:
    - ⇒ Focus on essential questions.
    - ⇒ Identify the big ideas and enduring understandings.

4. Select key language and literacy targets:
    - ⇒ Examine the content and establish the language and literacy expectations of the unit.

Co-Planning Refinements

During co-planning, rely on each other's expertise and resources to complete additional dimensions of unit or lesson planning:

- Map out instructional procedures for reaching the objectives you determined for your students. For example, consider a dynamic version of the gradual release of responsibility (GRR) model, in which you and your students fluidly move among the phases of GRR—modeling, teacher-directed and student-led guided practice, and independent work.

- Align instructional practices to bridge instruction in the two languages. For example, pinpoint opportunities for intentionally transferring academic concepts and skills students have learned in one language to the other language.

- Co-create or curate instructional resources with cultural authenticity and cross-cultural competence. For example, have students create cultural stories with their own illustrations to be shared with other groups of students across the school community.

- Co-develop learning activities, tasks, and projects for critical engagement. For example, invite students to examine the same historical events from multiple perspectives based on a choice board and create a project.

- Consider the range of language proficiency levels present in the classroom and target the academic language and literacy development of all learners. For example, establish crosscutting strategies such as the use of graphic organizers for all students, but differentiate the tool by providing a partially completed or visually enriched version of the same tool for some students.

- Integrate individualized education program (IEP) goals into their lesson plans. For example, if you have students with 504 plans or IEPs, review the types of appropriate modifications and accommodations these individual learners need.

- Agree on formative assessment tools to be used to inform your instruction. For example, plan on creating goal-setting and self-assessment tools with your students and determine how you can effectively monitor students' progress.

CAPTAIN'S LOG

What other professional priorities do you have for collaborative planning? How do you jointly determine these professional goals?

_____

_____

_____

_____

How will you plan to discuss moments when you view something as inequitable in a lesson, especially when you disagree with your collaborative partner(s)?

_____

_____

_____

_____

STAYING THE COURSE

Collaborative planning means opening your door to your colleagues, opening your plan book to a new page, or turning on your laptop or computer—and opening your mind to new ideas! It often means going outside your comfort zone, where unfamiliar experiences and unforeseen challenges or conflicts may await. At the same time, collaborative planning is an opportunity for dual language educators to maximize ways to leverage their cultural and linguistic assets, profoundly empowering students. Collaboration may also offer tremendous comfort and support—knowing that you are not alone as you work together for your students' academic, cognitive, sociocultural, and linguistic benefits.

Core Beliefs

We share the belief that dual language programs must go beyond *curricularizing* the two languages involved: We cannot merely plan for language and literacy development in two languages. Instead, as discussed in Chapter 2, we must offer literacy and content through two languages, build on the four pillars of dual language instruction, and promote:

- Bilingualism and biliteracy
- Grade-level academic achievement
- Sociocultural competence
- Critical consciousness

"Let's Agree" Statements

If we want to ensure successful dual language program implementation, both curriculum design and ongoing collaborative planning must include the following four dimensions:

1. Let's intentionally draw on all educators' and students' strengths as we focus on planning for bilingualism and biliteracy across the content areas.
2. Let's offer multiple pathways and student-centered authentic explorations to our students as they work toward grade-level academic achievement in both languages.
3. Let's strategically support students' multidimensional identity development and sociocultural competence.
4. Let's challenge ourselves and our students to critically examine multiple perspectives and develop criticality across cultural experiences and content areas.

Co-Planning for Key Instructional Practices

Some aspects of co-planning related to content and language development standards may be familiar to you due to planning and implementing literacy instruction across content areas. However, other elements for consideration are quite unique to the dual language classroom. First, there is a need for collaborating teachers to have a basic understanding of literacy patterns in both program languages. For example, if you are in a side-by-side program configuration and you and a colleague teach different content subjects through a different partner language, you each must focus on literacy building in both languages. You can be intentional to use teaching and learning strategies for the languages to build on one another rather than the use of activities that were designed for a monolingual lesson and then simply translated.

Co-Planning for Multilingual, Multimodal, and Multilevel Practices and Resources

Dual language learners need both access to and opportunities to comprehend and produce oral and written discourse that is multilingual, multimodal, and available at multiple reading levels. Using these various dimensions for introducing and creating text will allow your students to have multiple entry points into the content they are learning as well as provide supports to build competency in language use, cross-cultural competence, and critical understanding. Furthermore, dual language learners need activities that facilitate leadership opportunities with each other for deep and meaningful, co-created language learning.

Multilingual discourse practices and multilingual texts allow dual language learners to draw on their multiple linguistic resources and help develop multiliteracies. Relying on students' home languages and rich dialects, and tapping into their cultural histories, affirms their personal identities and further supports learning additional languages.

Multimodal approaches to serving dual language learners are getting increasing attention, whether they are recognized as scaffolding tools or more. We agree with Scott Grapin (2019), who advocates for a strong vision of multimodality, according to which language serves as a meaning-making tool across all content areas and all modalities. It is important to keep in mind that multimodal discourse includes a wide range of possibilities, such as listening to a podcast, watching a video recording or screencast, or presenting information through a combination of visual and textual resources. Multimodal expression honors students' communicative practices across all grade levels, all proficiency levels, and all content areas.

WHAT THE RESEARCH SAYS

According to WIDA (2020),

Multimodality, the use of multiple means of communication, is an essential way for all students to access and engage in the content areas. In addition to the use of spoken and written language, students also communicate through gestures, facial expressions, images, equations, maps, symbols, diagrams, charts, videos, graphs, computer-mediated content, and other means. (p. 12)

(Continued)

(Continued)

Previously, Moje (2015) argued, *"Multimodal representations are de rigueur in laboratories, archives, and field work. Opportunities to read and write (or compose) multimodal forms are critical for fostering disciplinary literacy skills because they are part and parcel of actual disciplinary practices"* (p. 264).

Why is multimodality so important? What is your strongest argument for planning for multimodality?

Multilevel discourse recognizes that students may progress through their language and literacy development in stages over time. When students have access to content—more specifically, to text on multiple reading levels—they may be able to access key concepts and information and engage in learning activities with their peers. When text is provided on two or more levels, students may work on the independent level alone, on a higher-level text with peers, and on the grade-level (instructional-level) text with their teachers.

Co-Planning for Bridging

The Bridge is gaining widespread acceptance across dual language classrooms. It is an instructional opportunity within the dual language context that occurs when you bring the two languages together intentionally and engage in linguistic comparisons of the two languages. Through this practice, students transfer academic concepts and skills they have learned in one language to the other and, in the process, develop or deepen their metalinguistic awareness and cross-linguistic strategies.

When you plan for The Bridge, you can begin by determining topics, thematic connections, content standards, and textual materials. Karen Beeman and Cheryl Urow (2013) emphasize that these instructional details are mapped out prior to planning specifically for The Bridge:

> *The instructional elements that come before The Bridge—developing oracy and background knowledge, reading comprehension, writing, word study, and summative assessment—are planned and conducted in one program language, the language of heavy lifting. During The Bridge, when students and teacher[s] engage in contrastive analysis activities of their languages, the two languages come together. After The Bridge, extension activities are conducted in the other program language.* (p. 49)

While planning for The Bridge, make sure you and your partner teacher discuss your own language use within the context of the unit or the lesson. In the classroom, model specific language use and make direct connections between the languages for the students (see Figure 3.5 for a snapshot of a student learning to read both in Arabic and in English). For further examples, consider:

- The sound system (phonology and syllables): Phonemic awareness and letter–sound correspondence are needed to learn to read in English. In Chinese, unlike in alphabetic languages like English, most words consist of two or more characters or syllables (rather than letters). Learning to read in these two languages will be a fundamentally different experience.

- Word formation (morphology): Some languages such as French and Arabic have complex verb and noun conjugations, and others such as English do not. Some languages use prefixes and suffixes extensively, whereas others apply prepositions and postpositions (e.g., Japanese and Korean).

- Sentence structure (syntax and grammar): There are two common word orders—SVO (English) and SOV (Japanese)—as well as some other less common orders among the world's languages, in which the subject (S), the verb (V), and the object (O) may occupy their positions in a sentence.

- Semantics: Many languages share cognates as well as false cognates, so it is important to establish the difference for your students; for example, *encontrar* (Spanish) and *encounter* (English) are cognates, but *embarazada* (Spanish) and *embarrassed* (English) are not.

- Language use (pragmatics): Many languages (French, Spanish, German, Russian, etc.) distinguish between using a formal and informal or familiar *you*.

Figure 3.5 Anchor Chart Support for Retelling a Story and Learning to Read in Two Languages

Source: Sabina Rahman. Used with permission.

We agree with Kathy Escamilla and her colleagues (2014) who suggest that dual language teaching must provide as many opportunities as possible for the students to develop and use metalinguistics for biliteracy and engage in meaningful explorations of how the partner languages work.

Co-Planning for Translanguaging

García and Wei (2014) define translanguaging as a process in which "bilingual speakers select meaning-making features [from multiple languages] and freely combine them to potentialize meaning-making, cognitive engagement, creativity, and criticality" (p. 42). When you support your students' full linguistic repertoires, many researchers and practitioners believe that learners' academic, linguistic, sociocultural, social-emotional, and critical cognitive development may be optimized. However, in *Guiding Principles for Dual Language Education*, Elizabeth Howard and colleagues (2018) remind us to consider "that if the two [program] languages are used concurrently, the use of both languages should be strategic" (p. 52).

Collaborative planning for strategic use of translanguaging in lessons ensures the creation of a classroom that is a safe and supportive space where students' multilingual talents are used authentically, regularly, and with purpose. With these practices we can also ensure equitable use of both program languages rather than any greater emphasis given to the majority language with English-dominant learners. Some educators might perceive translanguaging pedagogy as the sole responsibility of the bilingual educator, especially in classrooms that are serving emergent bilingual students with different abilities.

Ofelia García and colleagues (2017) provide examples of how collaborative planning can leverage the development of bilingualism and biliteracy in the classroom. Recognizing it as a promising practice, you can work together to plan for a "*coriente/* current" of translanguaging via heterogeneous grouping, the creation of activities that allow students to ask and answer culturally thought-provoking questions and that facilitate frequent opportunities to solve real-world problems to promote critical consciousness. All of this can be done with the recognition that authentic, dynamic language use and metalinguistic discoveries are essential for multilingual learners. When you intentionally co-plan for students' authentic use of language, they can communicate with each other in one language or the other, or even in a combination of program languages, when appropriate. Based on Cristian Solorza and colleagues' (2019) work, some intentionally planned activities may include:

1. Conducting frequent and deliberate pre-assessments

2. Creating flexible language spaces for inquiry-based or play-based learning

3. Using instructional materials that invite flexible, dynamic language use and access to content in both languages

4. Building peer support that helps facilitate bridging between languages

5. Using translanguaging as an ongoing support

Many educators agree that students benefit from the opportunity to make meaning and to express themselves freely in their language choices. These practices help students feel confident to articulate their learning in complex ways.

Co-Planning for Academic Language and Disciplinary Literacy

Language and literacy development in dual language contexts is multifaceted and complex. Students' progress through the levels of language proficiency (from entering to bridging levels) and levels of literacy in both program languages. Learners of all ages and language groups engage themselves as readers to make meaning of text as robust, whole people. Simply put, students' lives and experiences shape the ways in which they navigate reading. Biliteracy development is a highly dynamic process, so you will want to collaborate in very strategic ways. It is crucial that you and your collaborating partners shift away from ideas regarding static reading levels combined with retrofitting monolingual literacy development approaches in both partner languages. Instead, plan to work closely with your partner teacher(s) to understand what is necessary for the students to interact with the texts *as readers* in both partner languages. Zhihui Fang and Dana Robertson (2020) have recently recognized that "an emerging shift is taking place from teaching basic language skills (e.g., fluency, vocabulary) and generic cognitive strategies (e.g., inferencing, summarizing) to teaching discipline-specific language and literacy practices" (p. 240). In the dual language classroom these processes are even more dynamic in nature since they happen in two languages.

Basic dynamic biliteracy refers to literacy skills that are crucial for understanding texts from the home and community such as family-told stories, songs sung at home, and other kinds of culturally rich, literacy-based resources. A more in-depth way of looking at teaching letters and sounds is to teach reading and writing for biliteracy from a more dynamic view. In order for emergent bilingual students to gain reading comprehension, they must immediately connect their own experiences to the text. Therefore, when co-planning for basic biliteracy, it's crucial to determine when approaches like sound correspondence, decoding in English, and accessing high-frequency words are appropriate or when other biliteracy strategies are needed.

Intermediate literacy indicates skills that are common to many reading tasks and include developing dynamic fluency when reading, understanding generic academic words and phrases, and applying general comprehension strategies to everyday and academic readings. This is where most of the interactions with literacy take place: Students develop essential comprehension skills and experience cross-disciplinary practices of reading and writing in both languages.

Disciplinary literacy specifies biliteracy skills that are essential to understanding and producing text that is unique to the various content areas, such as literature, history, science, mathematics, music, or any other subject matter (Shanahan & Shanahan, 2020). According to one of the most frequently cited definitions, disciplinary literacy is "grounded in the beliefs that reading and writing are integral to disciplinary practices and that disciplines differ not only in content but also in the ways this content is produced, communicated, and critiqued" (Fang, 2012, pp. 19–20). Students in dual language programs engage in disciplinary practices in both languages.

Let's recognize that students in dual language programs may have intermediate literacy skills in one language or one content area such as geometry, while showing emerging skills somewhere else such as computer science. Based on students' ongoing language development levels and the objectives of the lesson, consider one or more levels within the context of the same lesson or unit. The most important recommendation is to not wait for students to develop what is labeled as fluency in one language before planning for all three levels of literacy.

When you plan for dual language and literacy support, use Figure 3.6 to cross-reference student language and literacy development levels.

Figure 3.6 Co-Planning Template for Language and Literacy Levels

LEVELS OF LANGUAGE PROFICIENCY*	LEVELS OF LITERACY		
	BASIC	INTERMEDIATE	DISCIPLINARY
Entering–Emerging	• Recognize common words and phrases • Make connections to experiences in the text • Demonstrate themselves as active readers	• Understand common academic words in simple text • Find information in simple text	• Develop vocabulary for essential content concepts • Write simple phrases or sentences to express content concepts
Developing	• Understand most common words in both program languages • Read and comprehend two- to three-paragraph text with predictable content	• Comprehend main idea and details in short, factual academic texts • Convey ideas and opinions in simple paragraphs in both program languages	• Develop strategies to understand authentic texts that are increasingly complex or contain unfamiliar topics • Develop ability to write organized and cohesive texts in both program languages
Expanding–Bridging	• Express deeper connections to home and community in texts • Find main idea and details consistently and understand key words in full-length academic readings • Work alone or in pairs to comprehend texts that are increasingly complex	• Make inferences and understand authors' purpose and point of view • Write about a variety of topics and display clear organization and topic development in both program languages	• Read and comprehend grade-level texts that are conceptually and/or linguistically complex • Write about various topics, using a variety of sentence structures for stylistic purposes

*This chart uses three combined levels of proficiency, and the labels are based on the WIDA standards. The three levels approximately correspond to Levels 1 & 2, Level 3, and Levels 4 & 5 on a five-point scale.

Source: Adapted from Honigsfeld and Dove (2022)

Disciplinary literacy is also grounded on the fairly well-established practice of content and language integration. Adding sociocultural and critical consciousness to planning takes you beyond the dichotomy of content and language goals or objectives and ensures students make connections to cultural identities as invaluable resources across all content areas. As collaborative teachers in dual language programs, you are committed to designing lesson activities that promote student communication in multidimensional ways and draw on students' cultural capital to simultaneously support their development of strong multilingual identities. At the core of this approach to planning is ensuring rigor as well as student voice, active participation, and critical engagement with the content, with academic language and (bi)literacy practices, and with students' and their peers' cultural experiences and authentic selves. See Figures 3.7 and 3.8 for a sample third-grade curriculum map in English and Arabic from dual language school Tariq Bin Ziad in Qatar.

As suggested by Amanda Kibler and her colleagues (2021), "critical and dialogic educational practices provide a space for students to learn through multiple voices and perspectives" (p. xiii). In the dual language classroom where their literacy is squared (Escamilla et al., 2014), students also engage in disciplinary literacy practices across their languages. In their content classes, students actively participate in academic conversations with peer and teacher guidance and support. Here are some examples of how to do that across the four core content areas and beyond (please note that these tips can be transferred to other contexts and content areas):

- In the program language of math, engage students in math talk and draw special attention to (a) the way students explain their thinking and (b) the precision of language needed to fully engage in disciplinary practices.

- In the program language of social studies, have students pose their own questions, establish their own line of inquiry, participate in respectful debates, and have critical conversations around issues students sincerely care about.

- In the program language of science, engage students in task-based discussions that build on hands-on explorations and multiple representations such as diagrams, outlines, sketches, and digitally recorded responses as well as in inquiry that provides additional opportunities for multilingual oracy.

- In language arts classes that are typically offered in both program languages, select nonfiction and fiction pieces to discuss those that are relevant to students' cultural experiences and invite students to share their own examples; use "pairing" strategies that simultaneously introduce the informational/nonfiction and fiction versions of a topic across the two languages; embrace multiliteracies as you explore multimedia resources, video clips, and films in addition to print-based materials.

- In music, invite students to share personal and cultural experiences with music and songs related to the lesson in either or both program languages.

Figures 3.7 and 3.8 Excerpts From the Tariq Bin Ziad Program of Inquiry in English and Arabic

Tariq Bin Ziad Program of Inquiry 2021-2022

Theme	Who We Are	Where We Are In Place and Time	How We Express Ourselves	How the World Works	How We Organize Ourselves	Sharing the Planet
	An inquiry into the nature of the self; beliefs and values; personal, physical, mental, social and spiritual health; human relationships including families, friends, communities, and cultures; rights and responsibilities; what it means to be human	An inquiry into orientation in place and time; personal histories; homes and journeys; the discoveries, explorations, and migrations of humankind; the relationships between and the interconnectedness of individuals and civilizations, from local and global perspectives	An inquiry into the ways in which we discover and express ideas, feelings, nature, culture, beliefs, and values; the ways in which we reflect on, extend and enjoy our creativity; our appreciation of the aesthetic	An inquiry into the natural world and its laws; the interaction between the natural world (physical and biological) and human societies; how humans use their understanding of scientific principles; the impact of scientific and technological advances on society and the environment	An inquiry into the interconnectedness of human made systems and communities; the structure and function of organizations; societal decision making; economic activities and their impact on society and the environment	An inquiry into rights and responsibilities in the struggle to share finite resources with other people, with other living things; communities and the relationships within and between them; access to equal opportunities; peace and conflict resolution

PS 3

	Who We Are	Where We Are In Place and Time	How We Express Ourselves	How the World Works	How We Organize Ourselves	Sharing the Planet
Central Idea	Different characteristics and abilities shape people's identities and make them unique.		Ideas and feelings can be communicated in a variety of modes.	Water is a shared resource for living things that can be investigated.	Routines help people adapt to a new environment and organize themselves.	
Lines of Inquiry	-Characteristics of self -Recognizing differences -What shapes our identities and makes us unique? -How I am changing overtime		-Identifying and describing feelings and ideas -Ways to communicate with others -Responding to others	-How water behaves -Our responsibility for water -Using skills as scientists to investigate	-Routines in our life -Roles and responsibilities within a group -Importance of routines in our lives.	
Key Concepts	Form, Function change		Form, Connection	Function, Form, Responsibility	Form, Function, Perspective	
Related Concepts	Self – Similarity, difference-abilities, growth		Feelings, Communication modes	Conservation, Water	Routines, Organization, Adaptation	
Learner Profile	Thinker - Open-minded		Communicators, Thinker	Principled, Inquirer	Balanced, Reflective	
Approaches to Learning	Self-management, Thinking		Social skills, Communication	Self-management, Research skills, Social skills	Social skills, Self-management	
Subject Integration	Science - PSPE		PSPE-Language-Arts	Science, Maths, Arts, Islamic	PSPE, Science	

برنامج الوحدات البحثية لمدرسة طارق بن زياد

Theme	من نحن	أين نحن في الزمان والمكان	كيف نعبر عن أنفسنا	كيف يعمل العالم	كيف ننظم أنفسنا	مشاركة الكوكب
Central Idea	البحث عن طبيعتنا الذاتية فيما يخص معتقداتنا صحتنا الذاتية البدنية والعقلية الروحية والاجتماعية البحث عن علاقتنا الإنسانية بما في ذلك أصدقائنا مجتمعاتنا وثقافاتنا إضافة إلى حقوقنا ومسؤولياتنا والبحث عن معنى كلمة كائن بشري	البحث عن وجهتنا في الزمان والمكان تاريخنا الخاص موطننا ورحلاتنا الاكتشافات والهجرة البشرية البحث عن العلاقات بين الحضارات الشخصية والمحلية والعالمية من وجهة النظر هذا البحث يتم	البحث عن الوسائل التي نكتشف ونعبر عن أفكارنا مشاعرنا طبيعتنا ثقافتنا معتقداتنا وقيمنا البحث عن الوسائل التي نستعين بها على إظهار إبداعنا وتطوير وتقدير ما يجعلنا نتذوق الجمال	البحث عن العالم المادي وقوانينه التفاعل بين العالم الطبيعي (المادي والبيولوجي) وبين المجتمعات الإنسانية وكيفية استخدام الإنسان فهمه للمبادئ العلمية والتفكير وتأثيره في مجتمعنا ومحيطنا	البحث عن الترابط بين الأنظمة والمجتمعات الإنسانية البحث عن هيكلية المنظمات ووظيفتها البحث عن اتخاذ القرارات والنشاطات الاقتصادية وتأثيرها على الإنسانية والمحيط	البحث عن حقوقنا ومسؤولياتنا حيث نكافح للمشاركة في الموارد المحدودة مع الآخرين والكائنات الحية الأخرى البحث عن مجتمعاتنا والعلاقات فيما بينها وكيفية الوصول إلى المساواة والسلام وحل النزاعات
Lines of Inquiry	ما الذي يشكل هويتنا - كيف تتغير هويتنا عبر الزمن - خصائص الذات		تحديد ووصف المشاعر والأفكار	كيف تتشكل الأمطار - كيف يمكن استخدام الماء - أهمية الماء للاكتشافات	الوظيفة التي يمكن أن يلعبها الروتين في حياتنا - أهمية الروتين والمسؤوليات في حياتنا	
Key Concepts	الشكل - الوظيفة - التغيير		طرق التواصل مع الآخرين	الوظيفة - الشكل - المسؤولية	الوظيفة - المسؤولية - التنظيم	
Related Concepts	النمو - التشابه والاختلاف - التغيرات		الرد على الآخرين - الشكل - الارتباط	الترشيد - الماء	الروتين - الأنظمة - التأقلم	
Learner Profile	مفكرون - ذوو مبادئ		مفكرون - متأملون - الحاجات النفسية - التواصل - المتأمل - المشاعر	ذوو مبادئ - متأملون - مشاركون	ذوو مبادئ - متأملون - مشاركون	
Approaches to Learning	مهارات إدارة الذات - مهارات التفكير		مفكرون	المهارات الاجتماعية - المهارات الفكرية	المهارات الاجتماعية - مهارات إدارة الذات	
Subject Integration	العلوم - التربية الشخصية والبدنية		التقوى - الدراسات	العلوم - الرياضيات - التربية الشخصية - المهارات الفكرية	العلوم - التربية الشخصية والاجتماعية والبدنية	التربية الشخصية والاجتماعية والبدنية - العلوم

Source: Dalal Ali Ahmed. Used with permission.

- In visual arts, have students describe their plans for their work, explain the processes they engaged in, and share their final products in either or both program languages.

Student-to-student interactions in both program languages support the development of academic discourse and communicative competence across topics and content areas. "By providing multiple opportunities for students to negotiate meaning in disciplinary conversation together, we can engage multilingual learners in the interactions that, over time and with appropriate modeling, enable them to become increasingly effective in expressing and exploring ideas" (Nordmeyer et al., 2021, p. 65). Sustained, authentic, and well-supported academic conversations coupled with similarly sustained, authentic, and well-supported literacy opportunities pave the way to equitable classroom experiences for all students. See the checklist in Figure 3.9 to guide your reflection and self-assessment of your collaborative planning and instruction.

Figure 3.9 Self-Assessment and Reflection Checklist

- ☐ Is the content challenging and rigorous yet accessible cognitively and well supported linguistically equally in both languages?
- ☐ Are bridging and translanguaging intentionally planned for?
- ☐ Is the new learning culturally and linguistically relevant and meaningful to all students?
- ☐ Are the lesson materials and lesson tasks instructionally and linguistically scaffolded in both program languages rather than reduced or simplified?
- ☐ Are the students able to engage in grade- and age-appropriate academic language and biliteracy practices?
- ☐ Is the new knowledge connected to prior knowledge or background knowledge authentically representative of the students' lived experiences and cultural understandings?
- ☐ Have you checked your resources and materials for bias and accuracy?
- ☐ Can students equally engage in discussions as critical thinkers and speak, write, read, and listen critically and authentically about the target content?

Co-Planning for Scaffolding

We typically refer to scaffolding as practices that support learning until students can participate in or complete a task independently. Lev Vygotsky (1978) first described the zone of proximal development (ZPD) within his sociocultural theory, characterizing it as "the distance between the actual developmental level as determined by independent problem solving and the level of potential development as determined through problem solving under adult guidance or in collaboration with more capable peers" (p. 86). Bridging the distance between what learners can do by themselves and what the next level of learning is that they can achieve with the help of a more knowledgeable other heavily depends on social interaction for learning to take place.

Pauline Gibbons (2015) highlights the three major characteristics of instructional scaffolding as follows:

> It is *temporary* help that assists a learner to move toward new concepts, levels of understanding, and new language.
>
> It enables a learner to know *how to do something* (not just what to do), so that they will be better able to complete similar tasks alone.
>
> It is *future oriented:* in Vygotsky's words, what a learner can do with support today, he or she will be able to do alone tomorrow. (p. 16)

Gibbons (2015) also points out Vygotsky's argument that supports are gradually internalized. The students' socially created dialogues shift from the temporary, externally provided scaffolds to the use of their own inner speech as a vital resource to guide their learning and problem-solving skills. When co-planning for scaffolding in the dual language classroom, collaborating educators may focus on the following three levels of support (Bunch et al., 2015):

1. Macro-scaffolding is planned for longer-term implementation across a unit or multiple lessons and gives students the opportunity to gradually build understanding, skills, and competence in their academic practices that include language, biliteracy, and content development as well as cultural and critical consciousness. "At the macro level, the overall design of the unit supports students by linking lesson to lesson in articulated ways, deepening and enriching understandings of central ideas, processes, and the language required to express those ideas" (Bunch et al., 2015, p. 12).

2. Meso-scaffolding refers to lesson design features that offer structures to support students through the flow of each lesson. Think of it as the arc of teaching—every lesson has a beginning (or launch), middle (exploration), and end (closure) where students make specific metalinguistic connections between both program languages.

3. Micro-scaffolding is the small-group or individual "in-the-moment" support teachers offer as needed. This approach allows teachers to focus on specific academic, language, and literacy skills that are embedded in the lesson. Bunch and his colleagues (2015) captured the essence of this practice as follows:

> While the teacher carefully plans tasks which will develop her students' potential over time, the most important part of scaffolding occurs in the moment, as the teacher observes how students work, what skills are maturing, which ones need further support to ripen, and what may be misunderstood. Then, teachers contingently offer the appropriate support to redirect, deepen, or accelerate specific students' development. (p. 16)

What does scaffolding actually look like? What choices are available to collaborating teachers? At what point do students internalize scaffolds, and how do we teach them how to do that? Recently, Andrea Honigsfeld and Maria Dove (2022) identified nine scaffolding approaches from practice-based (Gibbons, 2015; Levine et al., 2013), research-based (August, 2018), and standards-based (WIDA, 2020) publications, as well as from their own field-based research and observations. Here we added three more dimensions to support and scaffold for cultural competence and critical consciousness (see Figure 3.10). Rather than being overwhelmed by the sheer number, consider this as a choice menu—not every scaffolding technique will fit every lesson; not every scaffolding approach will result in the desired outcomes for all students; and not all 12 types of scaffolds will have strategic purpose in every class period, so you will need to choose which scaffolds align with the learning goals. You can also chunk and focus on a cluster of scaffolding strategies. Finally, some of these scaffolding approaches may overlap, and the utility and applicability of each must be determined by the context of each lesson or unit. We also advocate for using these scaffolds across partner languages.

Figure 3.10 Summary of Multidimensional Scaffolding Approaches

SCAFFOLDING APPROACH	BRIEF DESCRIPTION
Critical	Supporting students with both (a) deep, analytical thinking and (b) working toward social change and equity
Cultural	Supporting students in developing cultural competence across languages
Digital	Technology-based tools and techniques
Environmental	Physical and virtual learning context
Graphic	Schematic or visual representations
Instructional	Supporting students through the entire learning experience by strategic lesson delivery
Interactive/Collaborative	Participatory supports to enable communication and role definition and task completion
Linguistic	Supporting language and literacy development at the word, sentence, and discourse dimensions
Multilingual	Using two or more languages for self-expression, meaning making, and communicating with others
Multimodal	Expressive (speaking writing, visually representing) and interpretive modes of language (listening, reading, viewing)
Multisensory	Auditory, visual, tactile, and kinesthetic experiences
Social-emotional	Affective supports and relationship building

Source: Adapted from Honigsfeld and Dove (2022).

Consider the following questions when you and your collaborating teachers make a choice about scaffolding:

- What are the most urgent needs of your students?
- What is the purpose of each type of support, and who will benefit most from each?
- What subgroups of students will need differentiation, and how will scaffolds support those needs?
- What types of scaffolds does the upcoming unit or lesson require for equitable access to the core curriculum and language and literacy development?
- What types of scaffolds does the upcoming unit or lesson require for meaningful student engagement in academic practice?
- When is it appropriate to remove scaffolds and make way for student independence?
- How are you ensuring student ownership of the scaffolds so students know when and how to mentally access them on their own?

In the following vignette, Amy Mosquera from the Adelante Educational Specialists Group shares an example and the rationale for co-creating a biliteracy curricular framework that is designed both to enhance teacher collaboration and to develop students' proficiency and literacy in both languages, have access to high levels of engagement with the core content, and develop both critical thinking and cross-cultural understanding. As you review this example, consider the way the pillars of dual language education are intentionally addressed.

In dual language programming, the goals are very clear: bilingualism and biliteracy, grade-level academic achievement in two languages, and sociocultural competence (Howard et al., 2018). An integrated curricular framework sets a strong foundation to meet these goals and also enhances collaboration between teachers. Best practice in a dual language program is to develop content-integrated units that are aligned to state standards while maintaining equal status of both languages. A paired curriculum map that is content integrated and aligned to all state standards is one important piece in supporting a successful "marriage" where teachers are able to collaborate and make connections for students across languages.

In a dual language partnership, it is important to have a strong "marriage" between the two language partners. Three pivotal Cs to remember when developing a strong dual language "marriage" are commitment, communication, and collaboration. When the three Cs are present, teachers are then equipped to use these paired units to collaborate and plan and capitalize on making strong cross-linguistic connections for their students.

LAUNCHED MISSIONS

(Continued)

(Continued)

The first step in developing this curricular framework is to develop a standards-based scope and sequence for language and literacy development in both languages. This scope and sequence provides the road map for what standards the teachers will teach and in what language. This scope and sequence, separated into themes and big ideas, should include not only literacy standards but also content standards as well as language proficiency standards. It outlines what themes and units are taught in the target language and what is taught in English. Without this road map, teachers do not have a clear understanding of what should be taught in each language. It becomes more difficult to make connections between the two languages and collaborate with teammates when the language environments are not thoughtfully paired and connected.

The demographics in our school districts are changing. Many of our students now enter school as simultaneous bilinguals and should be instructed as such. It's important to provide instruction that connects the languages and allows for students to use their entire linguistic repertoire. Paired literacy has been researched as an effective way to enhance biliteracy instruction with emerging bilingual students. This approach is an essential component of the Literacy Squared biliteracy model (Escamilla et al., 2014). In this approach, students are taught reading and writing in two languages, simultaneously, beginning in kindergarten. Literacy instruction in one language is not delayed until the student has literacy skills in the other language. Integrated biliteracy units foster the connection for students in literacy, exposing them to a variety of genres and content. When dual language programs develop content-integrated biliteracy units without paying special attention to the literacy standards, they run the risk of these units being so content driven that literacy is not explicitly taught.

When working with teams, it's important to develop curriculum maps that designate one language to do the heavy cognitive lifting by integrating content and literacy while the other language supports and connects to the other language without duplicating or translating. There is also the issue of lack of time. Traditionally, in dual language, each language is trying to fit in not only literacy but also a content-integrated unit according to the content allocation. This approach relies heavily on content teaching in a short amount of time, which causes teachers to teach at the surface level without having time to dig deeper into the learning and stretch students. When teachers feel rushed for time and feel the need to "cover" everything, they run the risk of leaving student learning behind.

There are many ways to make connections across language environments. One way is to pair informational text with literature text. For example, if the heavy lifting is being taught in English and is focusing on the content area of social studies, with the theme of community, one can connect and support that theme in Spanish by focusing on identity—focusing on how we fit into our community. Then teams can *select informational texts paired with literature texts in English but also do the same in Spanish with texts that really highlight a student's identity. One fourth-grade team was so creative when they taught a science unit on dangerous weather. The heavy lifting was done in English with the science content. The teacher used mainly informational, content-focused texts while her counterpart focused on myths and legends. You might wonder what the connection between those two topics is. The team found beautiful authentic myths and legends from a variety of Latin American countries written in Spanish. They chose myths and legends that focused on weather. Their performance task was for students to create an informational slide show in English on how to stay safe during dangerous weather, and then in Spanish, students collaboratively wrote a myth incorporating weather phenomena. The teacher did not have to re-teach the content information in Spanish; students were automatically able to transfer what they learned in English into their myths in Spanish. This type of connection could not have been possible without the strong paired curriculum map coupled with collaboration and planning with the teachers. Additionally, this team planned together every week to ensure they were pairing standards and concepts. Students were able to see the connection between what they were learning in one language to what they were learning in the other. Developing these maps and biliteracy units takes time and commitment from the administrators as well as the teachers. Time and resources must be dedicated to planning this curricular framework to ensure that there are connections being made across languages and there is also an equitable amount of quality resources dedicated to each language. In Figure 3.11, you will find some examples of paired biliteracy units.*

Figure 3.11 Examples of Paired Literacy Units

COGNITIVE HEAVY LIFTING	PARTNER LANGUAGE
Science Unit: Plants and Animals	Alma Flor Ada Author Study
Science Unit: Earth's Changes	How I've Changed Over Time
Social Studies: Roles and Responsibilities in Our Community	My Home Community
Social Studies: Economy and Financial Literacy	Personal Experience: Saving Money and Working Toward a Goal

Source: Amy Mosquera. Used with permission.

Providing a strong paired curriculum map or scope and sequence elevates collaboration between teachers and provides a road map that teams are able to follow to foster connections for students. Ensuring teachers have this road map, but also collaboration time built into their schedule, is key. It's all about connections!

CAPTAIN'S LOG

After you have read Amy's vignette demonstrating the importance of co-developing paired curriculum, consider the following two issues: (a) How are the pillars of dual language education intentionally planned for? (b) How do or would you engage in similar collaborative efforts with your colleagues?

_____

_____

_____

_____

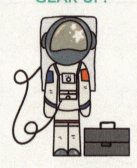

GEAR UP!

Your collaborative planning needs to be well supported with tools and protocols that guide the planning process as well as help you reflect on the effectiveness and impact of that process. Here we recommend you begin by equipping yourself with a Basic Tool Kit.

Get Started With a Basic Tool Kit

Each time you collaboratively plan, you want to use some essential tools and resources to support success—and you want to capture your own co-created notes to keep up with your great ideas for progress! Your Basic Tool Kit should include (a) Figure 3.12, the Co-Planning Focus Form for Dual Language Instruction: A Week-at-a-Glance Tool, and (b) Figure 3.13, the Checklist for Collaboratively Planning Based on the 12 Dimensions of Scaffolding. Here are some other resources to add to your starter kit, all of which can be used together or strategically selected for your lessons and units:

- Grade-level core content standards
- Language development standards
- Curriculum maps; scope and sequence charts
- Content-area texts and teachers' guides; bilingual instructional resources
- Collaborative planning framework or action plan to accomplish co-planning tasks
- Technology tools for co-planning
- Your co-created notes related to current topics and scaffolds you believe will support students' development of their multilingual identity, cross-cultural competence, and critical consciousness

A lot of teachers like to use a planning tool that offers key information at a glance. Try (or adapt) the co-planning tool in Figure 3.12 that connects content, language, culture, and critical consciousness. Earlier in the chapter we also discussed the importance of scaffolding. The checklist in Figure 3.13 expands on the summary chart and helps you with your joint planning and reflection. Use a simple yet effective log or journal to jointly keep track of your notes for supporting students' multilingual identity development.

Figure 3.12 Co-Planning Focus Form for Dual Language Instruction: A Week-at-a-Glance Tool

Classroom Teachers: _____ Other Collaborators: _____ Grade: _____

For the Week of: _____

Overarching Focus for the Week:

	FOCUS ON CONTENT AND CRITICALITY	FOCUS ON LANGUAGE AND CULTURE	NOTES ABOUT STUDENTS
Monday			
Tuesday			
Wednesday			
Thursday			
Friday			

Formative and Summative Assessment Plan:

Source: Adapted from Honigsfeld and Dove (2019)

Figure 3.13 Checklist for Collaboratively Planning Based on the 12 Dimensions of Scaffolding

SCAFFOLDING DIMENSIONS	WAYS TO ADDRESS THE 12 DIMENSIONS IN THE DUAL LANGUAGE CONTEXT
Critical	☐ Connecting teaching to social context ☐ Addressing social justice and equity ☐ Interpreting and engaging with material from the perspectives of marginalized groups ☐ Modeling authentic discourse (written and oral) for balanced program language use ☐ Practicing how to assess and respond to the language and power dynamics inside and outside of the school
Cultural	☐ Connecting text selection to social context ☐ Facilitating academic oracy with cultural relevance ☐ Learning topics that enrich students' multilingual identities ☐ Structured debate techniques with multilingual connections ☐ Exploration of home, community, and school cultures
Digital	☐ Multilingual multimedia presentations ☐ Digital recordings in both program languages ☐ Digital storytelling in both program languages ☐ Multilingual e-books, blogs, web-based books ☐ Digital whiteboards ☐ Instructional apps
Environmental	☐ Maintaining high expectations for all students ☐ Multilingual, print-rich classroom ☐ Class displays reflect students' cultural and linguistic diversity from an assets-based stance ☐ Instructional resources meet students' learning preferences ☐ Areas for learning meet with students' preferences for feeling safe and comfortable
Graphic	☐ Outlines ☐ Charts ☐ Maps ☐ Tables ☐ Timelines ☐ Thinking Maps™ ☐ Graphic organizers
Instructional	☐ Questioning techniques: Surface to deep (Bloom's taxonomy) ☐ Modeling in the partner languages according to your program design ☐ Demonstrating ☐ Guided practice ☐ Chunking information ☐ Mentor texts that are authentic to the program language ☐ Teacher clarity

SCAFFOLDING DIMENSIONS	WAYS TO ADDRESS THE 12 DIMENSIONS IN THE DUAL LANGUAGE CONTEXT
Interactive/Collaborative	☐ Whole-group learning ☐ Small-group learning ☐ Paired learning ☐ Reciprocal teaching ☐ Peer tutoring ☐ Jigsaw reading ☐ Project-based learning
Linguistic	☐ Contextualizing key terms/phrases ☐ Sentence frames and starters ☐ Building fluency through collaborative participation
Multilingual	☐ Translanguaging ☐ Multilingual resources made available ☐ Multilingual modes of expression embraced
Multimodal	☐ Richly illustrated print-based texts in both program languages ☐ Digital resources—films, video clips, interactive web pages ☐ Incorporating speaking, writing, interacting, reading, and listening (SWIRL) ☐ Multilingual graphic representations of concepts ☐ Student choice
Multisensory	☐ Realia (real objects) ☐ Manipulatives ☐ Illustrations ☐ Audio representations ☐ Video representations ☐ Songs, dance, and movement
Social-emotional	☐ Community building ☐ Micro-teaching (supporting individual students as needed) ☐ Offering frequent and targeted feedback ☐ Using multiple group configurations to encourage interaction ☐ Daily emotional check-ins ☐ Individual goal setting ☐ Collaboratively establishing norms and expectations ☐ Equitable approach to both program languages

Source: Adapted from Honigsfeld and Dove (2022)

Paired literacy is a puzzle with many unique and multidimensional pieces. It takes place when students, simply stated, are developing literacy in two languages at the same time. Literacy instruction in either language isn't postponed or omitted, and there isn't a transition to English-only literacy. That way, students co-develop literacy and, with increased student-to-student interaction, co-create biliteracy. We spotlight the importance of your collaboration to facilitate students' consistent use of one language to help them develop the other, and we're rallying for you to create, foster, and grow environments rich in holistic biliteracy. We invite you to use the paired literacy tool in Figure 3.14, which we created based on Kathy Escamilla and colleagues' work in *Biliteracy From the Start* (2014). As you consider each piece of the paired literacy puzzle, we hope these spaces for you to record your ideas will help you with your collaborative work.

Figure 3.14 Paired Literacy Tool

	AUTHENTIC CROSS-LANGUAGE CONNECTIONS	CROSS-LANGUAGE/ METALANGUAGE STRATEGIES	TEACHER COLLABORATION OPPORTUNITIES
Content Goals (connected to standards)			
Literacy Goals			
Oracy Goals			
Students' Spaces to Write in Both Partner Languages			
Language Structure Elements			
Authentic Assessments			

The goal of this chapter was to offer a solid framework; a current, critical perspective; and essential tools that support collaborative planning regardless of the dual language program model you are using. We invite you to look beyond the content of the chapter and continue your exploration with some additional print- and web-based resources.

Books and Articles

Escamilla, K., Hopewell, S., Butvilofsky, S., Sparrow, W., Soltero-González, L., Ruiz-Figueroa, O., & Escamilla, M. (2014). *Biliteracy from the start: Literacy Squared in action*. Caslon.

Espinoza, C., & Ascenzi-Moreno, L. (2021). *Rooted in strength: Using translanguaging to grow multilingual readers and writers*. Scholastic.

Honigsfeld, A., & Dove, M. G. (2019). *Collaborating for English learners: A foundational guide to integrated practices*. Corwin.

Honigsfeld, A., & Dove, M. G. (2022). *Co-planning: 5 essential practices to integrate curriculum and instruction for English learners*. Corwin.

Howard, E. R., Lindholm-Leary, K. J., Rogers, D., Olague, N., Medina, J., Kennedy, B., Sugarman, J., & Christian, D. (2018). *Guiding principles for dual language education* (3rd ed.). Center for Applied Linguistics.

Web-Based Resources

Jeff Zwiers offers a range of tools that support planning for academic language development at https://jeffzwiers.org/tools.

The Massachusetts Department of Elementary and Secondary Education invites teachers to use the following Collaboration Tool that may be adapted for the dual language context as well: www.doe.mass.edu/ele/instruction/collaboration-tool.docx.

TUNE IN!

We had a lot to say about collaborative planning! Our goal was not to overwhelm but to offer choices and inspiration for making some critical decisions on how to best prepare for instruction in the dual language classroom. To get started, consider the following practical tips for implementing collaborative planning:

10. Establish and nurture your professional partnerships.
9. Advocate for and/or secure sustained collaboration time.
8. Create a shared collaborative framework.
7. Establish a structure or routine for collaborative planning.
6. Establish a structure or routine for consistent instructional practices.
5. Use the four pillars of dual language instruction as the cornerstones of your collaborative planning.
4. Bring an open mind and readiness to learn from your colleagues.
3. Put students first: Plan for your students rather than plan to deliver a lesson.
2. Share your ideas, talent, and spirit as well as your critical questions and reflections.
1. Celebrate often!

COUNTDOWN TO LAUNCH

CAPTAIN'S LOG: FINAL ENTRY

Based on Chapter 3, identify your key takeaways. What is directly applicable to your context? What could be a stretch for you at the moment? What are some future goals or steps you wish to take? What might be challenging for you to discuss with your collaborative partner(s)?

_____

_____

_____

_____

Collaborative Teaching in Dual Language Programs 4

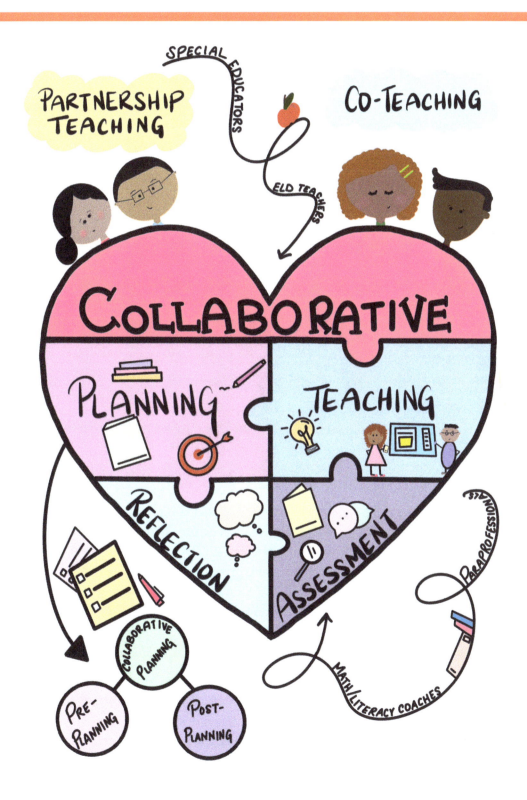

"In a dual language school, teachers are well-prepared to co-teach and students to co-learn."

—Margarita Calderón et al. (2019, p. 163)

MISSION CONTROL

Chapter 4 introduces collaborative teaching approaches as pathways to offering equitable and rigorous yet well-supported instructional delivery within the dual language context. More specifically, the goals of this chapter are to:

1. Differentiate between partnership teaching and co-teaching and define each practice in varied dual language contexts
2. Identify the place partnership teaching and co-teaching occupy within the collaborative instructional cycle
3. Explore several approaches to partnership teaching
4. Describe and evaluate seven co-teaching models

EXPLORATION

Before we launch our exploration of collaborative teaching, let's look at this topic from the perspective of a student and his teachers. When teacher collaboration becomes more visible to students and makes its way into the dual language classroom through co-delivery of instruction, students and teachers both experience a unique way of building community.

Through a Student's Eyes

Jose-Luis is in sixth grade and has been participating in a dual language program since kindergarten. His elementary school ended in fifth grade, when he moved on to a much larger middle school slightly outside his immediate neighborhood. He takes the bus with his cousin every day and is getting used to the new routines in the middle school, where he has several core content teachers. In fifth grade, his classroom teacher taught the class both in Spanish and in English but on alternate days. His parents wanted him to continue developing his Spanish language and literacy skills, and Jose-Luis was looking forward to seeing what it would look like in middle school.

Middle school is very different. I have a lot of teachers, we move around from class to class, there are before-school and after-school activities, and I have my own locker. My schedule looks very different too. My main content classes are either in block or have a lab component every other day. First it was all very confusing, but now I get it. Also, this year I don't have English language arts and social studies separately. Here they call it Humanities 1, and I have two teachers teaching it together. I never had that in elementary school, so it is interesting to get used to: Ms. Rodriguez speaks mainly in Spanish and teaches a bit more about the history behind events. She likes to explain how everything is connected in the world. Mr. Van Antwerp speaks in English to us in class, but in the hallway or sometimes during small groups, he speaks Spanish, too! We have topic exploration stations three to four times a week, so we work in small groups with our classmates. We have to research and design "summatives" for each unit and create them once in Spanish and then for the next unit in English. The class presentations have to alternate between the two languages, which can be tricky but is also a lot of fun! The teachers mix us up for each unit, which is okay because I am friendly with everyone. We know this is a new program because the teachers survey us once a month and ask a lot of reflection questions not just about the material but also about how the class is going. I think most kids like it. Creative arts, math, and humanities are my favorite subjects.

What challenges has Jose-Luis faced adjusting both to middle school and to a co-taught, integrated course? What might have contributed to his successful transition?

_____

_____

_____

_____

CAPTAIN'S LOG

Through the Educators' Eyes

We are Jose-Luis's co-teachers and would like to start by offering a little bit of background: Originally, the dual language program was established as a K–5 initiative in the district. Based on student and parental input, the leadership team agreed that there is a clear need for it to be sustained, and several unique pathways were created for continuation into the middle and high schools. One of them is a co-taught humanities class, which is designed to be a three-year course bridging sixth, seventh, and eighth grades. The humanities class meets every day for an 80-minute block period. We are both co-delivering instruction using the partner languages strategically. Each unit has a "language lead," whereas small-group activities use bridging and translanguaging practices to engage students in the topic in both languages. We want our students to develop conceptual understanding while also using their full linguistic repertoires. Others include a Spanish language and literacy class and a PBL [project-based learning]–based science course taught in English "tag teaming" with a lab class conducted in Spanish. We volunteered for the pilot program to create the dual language interdisciplinary humanities course. We not only co-teach the class and integrate the language arts and social studies curriculum, but also implement the dual language instructional approach for the benefit of the students who wish to continue it in middle school.

As co-teachers, we feel we are well suited for this initiative due to our unique preparation and professional experiences. Here is a bit of our own background: One of us (Ms. Rodriguez) was born, raised, and educated in Peru and has been a dually certified social studies and Spanish teacher for close to a decade. This is her first opportunity to combine her areas of certification and expertise and to formally collaborate with a colleague. The other of us (Mr. Van Antwerp) has just started his fourth year as a sixth- and seventh-grade English language arts (ELA) teacher, and from the beginning of his career in the school, he has regularly co-taught with either a special education teacher or an English language development (ELD) teacher. When the opportunity came to develop and pilot a new curriculum and try a collaborative approach to teaching it, he was the first to volunteer. As an avid traveler, he has visited several Central and South American countries and enjoys speaking Spanish conversationally, so he was excited to use his love of languages in the context of his classroom as well.

The top three collaborative tasks we committed to when we set up our partnership include:

1. Curriculum mapping and alignment (to ensure that the essential questions and the enduring understandings align to the other grade-level courses in ELA and social studies as well as to support disciplinary literacy development across languages)

2. Collaborative planning that considers curriculum maps, core content standards, and the students' academic and linguistic progress in both their languages

3. Establishing a co-teaching routine that allows for both of us to co-deliver instruction but, more important, supports a student-centered learning environment that has a lot of station teaching and PBL opportunities

Our pilot program is still a work in progress. We as co-teachers are a work in progress! As we continue to develop this initiative, we hope to explicitly bridge our students' academic and linguistic competencies in a shared, safe, and affirming learning environment.

WHAT THE RESEARCH SAYS

Based on Harvard psychologist Richard Hackman's work on team effectiveness, Amy C. Edmondson (2012) notes that "well-designed teams are those with clear goals, well-thought-out tasks that are conducive to teamwork, team members with the right skills and experiences for the task, adequate resources, and access to coaching and support" (pp. 12–13). When dual language educators form strong teams or partnerships, they, too, must have clear goals, complex skills and experiences, appropriate resources, and access to ongoing coaching and other types of support, as evidenced in the chapter opening vignette.

How do you perceive partnership teaching and co-teaching could uniquely position teachers to enhance their effectiveness? What skills do teachers need to be successful with collaborative instructional delivery?

Ready to Launch the Exploration

Depending on the program model implemented in schools, we differentiate between two major approaches to collaborative instructional delivery in the dual language context: *partnership teaching* and *co-teaching*. There are many unique similarities and differences between these two main approaches to co-instruction, but let's start with some straightforward, simple definitions:

1. **Partnership teaching** happens when two teachers systematically align their instruction and work with the same group of students but *do not (or rarely) co-deliver instruction in the same physical setting.*

2. **Co-teaching** takes place when two teachers physically *share the classroom space and take responsibility for all students through integrated instructional practices.*

Notice that we did not specify that the two teachers are dual language partner teachers. They may or may not be! Partnership teaching and co-teaching partnerships may also include ELD teachers, special education teachers, literacy or math intervention providers, and other educators, such as paraprofessionals or instructional aides (also referred to as teaching assistants).

WHAT THE RESEARCH SAYS

Laura Hamman-Ortiz and Deborah Palmer (2020) highlight two-way bilingual education (TWBE) classrooms as they

> *provide rich and complex spaces for exploring identity negotiation, as these environments deliberately integrate students from diverse backgrounds and experiences, whose daily languaging and learning experiences are intimately tied to their emerging sense of self and other within the larger context of language ideologies, institutional labels, and sociopolitical systems.*

Martin Scanlan and Lauri Johnson (2021) remind us to take on the roles of "boundary spanners, border crossers, and advocates" (p. 227) to achieve equity on behalf of multilingual learners. Partnership teaching and co-teaching present themselves as an opportunity for deliberate *boundary spanning and border crossing* by virtue of creating a shared, translanguaging bilingual, bicultural space that successfully facilitates student agency through dynamic meaning making in two languages. We believe that educators in dual language classes that embrace partnership teaching or co-teaching are well positioned to create or further enhance equitable bilingual learning spaces that consider diversity among students regarding cultural, academic, linguistic, and social-emotional development (Nordmeyer et al., 2021).

Why does equity matter? What are the challenges and actionable steps that may be taken to achieve equity in dual language spaces? How can partnership teaching or co-teaching support these goals?

For successful implementation, both partnership teaching and co-teaching require a commitment to the entire collaborative instructional cycle consisting of co-planning, co-teaching (or partnership teaching), co-assessment, and co-reflection. While our focus in this chapter is on collaborative instructional practices, we recognize that they never happen in a vacuum; thus we feel compelled to revisit the components of the collaborative instructional cycle and highlight some key tools and protocols that support successful implementation (see Figure 4.1).

Figure 4.1 Key Tools and Protocols Supporting the Collaborative Instructional Cycle

Collaborative Planning
- Planning protocols with clear norms and expectations
- Standards
- Curriculum maps
- Scope and sequence guides
- Unit and lesson planning templates

Collaborative Teaching
- Partnership agreements for collaborative teaching
- Partnership teaching routines and structures
- Co-teaching models

Collaborative Reflection
- Collaborative conversation protocols
- Appreciative inquiry protocols
- Goal setting for continuous improvement

Collaborative Assessment
- Formative and summative assessment measures
- Student self-assessment
- Progress-monitoring tools
- Data analysis protocols

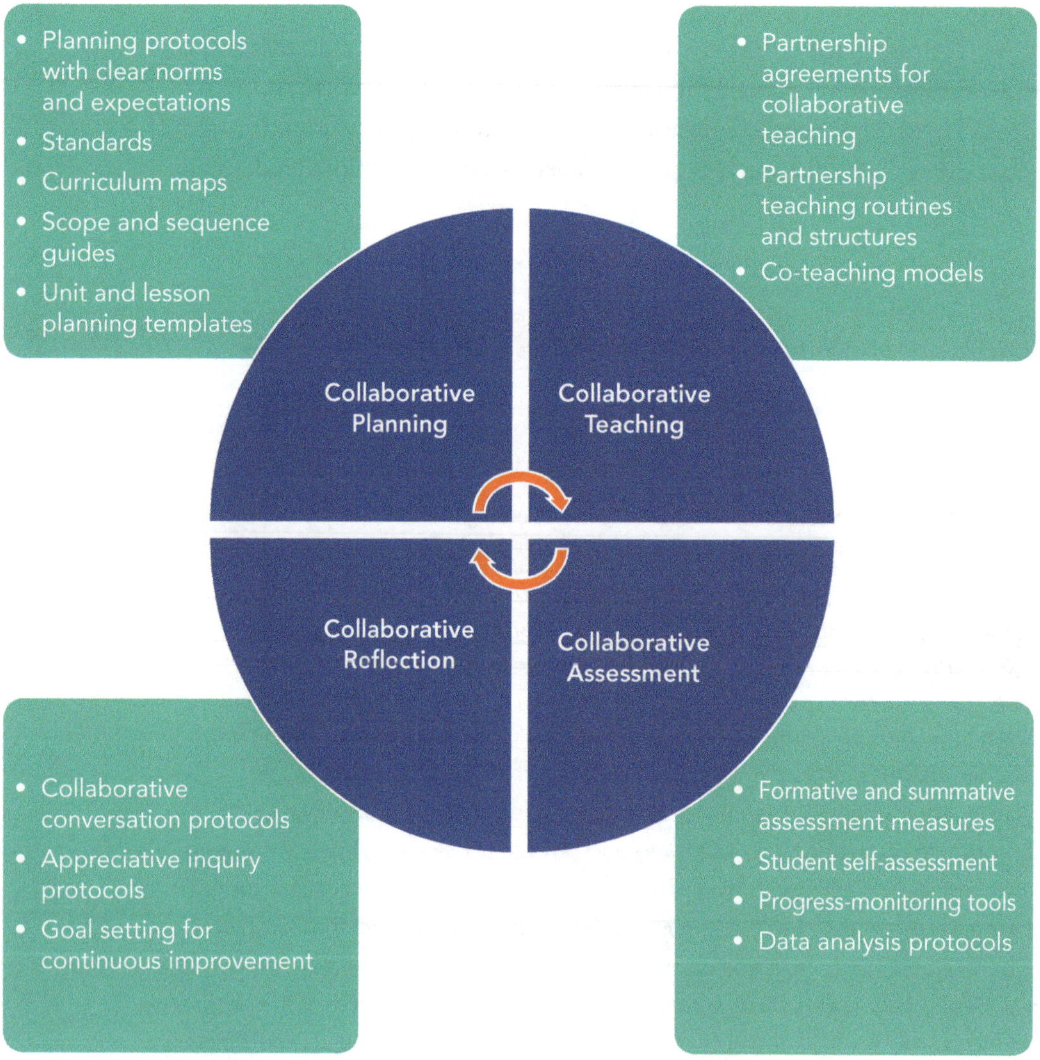

WHAT PRACTITIONERS SAY

Caitlyn (Kate) McNally, a second-grade dual language teacher at Henking School in Glenview, Illinois, shared with us how she engages in collaborative practices including co-teaching:

I attend weekly team meetings (eight classroom teachers and two EL [English learner] teachers) to discuss the second-grade scope and sequence of the core curriculum. After meeting with the team, I adapt the scope and sequence to meet the needs of my dual language class. I also meet in a "mini team" (four classroom teachers and one EL teacher) to be more specific about unit details, receive feedback, and so on. I attend monthly dual language meetings with the kindergarten dual [language teacher], first-grade dual [language teacher], multilingual coaches, administrators, and our executive director of multilingual services, where we discuss data and curriculum topics. I also collaborate with a monolingual general education classroom, so my dual language students have integrated social and academic time with general education students. Five of my students receive special education services, so I also work closely with my special education co-teacher. She and I plan on a weekly basis to discuss lesson content and language support for math. I teach both in English and in Spanish, but my colleague is English speaking only, so we review bridging supports together (such as pre-teaching, visuals, [and] manipulatives). We implement multiple co-teaching models (such as station teaching, parallel teaching, and teaming) so students have the opportunity to learn through explicit teaching in both languages. As co-teachers, we work together to recognize the importance of content, communication, and support for dual language students since the goal is to analyze and solve math problems and apply math concepts in both languages. We believe that every subject can have language objectives, so we focus on language expectations with students through teaching math content. We use strategic grouping of students based on language usage and levels, math ability, and some other academic and linguistic factors. Before we begin each unit, we pre-assess students, and then group them to best meet their needs.

How are Kate's experiences similar to or different from yours? What is unique about this collaborative partnership when compared to your own situation?

Co-planning and co-assessment as well as regular collaborative reflection on the teaching and learning experiences in the dual language classroom are critical dimensions of successful collaborative instruction. In Chapter 3, we made a strong case for collaborative planning and offered strategies and tools to support successful implementation. In Chapter 5, we will do the same regarding co-assessment and co-reflection. Here, we will continue to focus on what co-instruction may look like.

CAPTAIN'S LOG

What experiences have you had with partnership teaching or co-teaching? What worked, and what needed adjustments? If you are just starting out with teacher collaboration, what are you most interested in or excited about regarding partnership teaching and co-teaching? What questions or concerns might you have, and how are you going to share them with others?

_____

_____

_____

_____

Partnership Teaching in Two-Way Programs

Two-way programs are frequently designed to rely on two teachers collaborating and coordinating instruction for two groups of students. Partnership formation and sustained, intentional collaboration are often a hallmark of these programs. Do you recognize any of these basic configurations? How do they compare to your context?

Scenario 1:

Group 1/Class 1 begins the day with Teacher 1 in Language 1.

Group 2/Class 2 begins the day with Teacher 2 in Language 2.

Halfway through the day, the two groups are swapped:

Group 1/Class 1 finishes the day with Teacher 2 in Language 2.

Group 2/Class 2 finishes the day with Teacher 1 in Language 1.

Scenario 2:

Group 1/Class 1 spends an entire day with Teacher 1 in Language 1.

Group 2/Class 2 spends an entire day with Teacher 2 in Language 2.

The groups and teachers switch every day.

Scenario 3:

Group 1/Class 1 spends an entire week with Teacher 1 in Language 1.

Group 2/Class 2 spends an entire week with Teacher 2 in Language 2.

The groups and teachers switch every week.

If none of the above scenarios fit your context, how about some further possibilities?

- Through partnership teaching, some units of study are taught in Language 1, and others are in Language 2. Alternatively, some larger, interdisciplinary units of study are started in Language 1 and then finished in Language 2 with strategic bridging of topics and materials.

- Each teacher of the dual language partnership focuses on designated core classes (year-round, for example, Teacher 1 teaches language arts and social studies in Language 1, and Teacher 2 teaches science and mathematics in Language 2).

- In some secondary programs, the language partnerships may be more at the grade level rather than the classroom level. Each teacher delivers instruction in one of the two partner languages in one specific content area, and the school's schedule is created based on which teachers deliver which content subjects in the partner languages. For example, language arts, music, and social studies are delivered in one program language while a second language arts class, math, science, and physical education are delivered in the other program language.

As you make connections to your own classrooms and schools with the scenarios, you may also be thinking about teacher availability based on areas of teaching certification, languages needed, and state-level hiring parameters. Ultimately, we recognize that there are many variations for successful partnership teaching.

WHAT PRACTITIONERS SAY

Blake Ramsey, French dual language educator and program coordinator at Fort Greene Preparatory Academy in Brooklyn, New York, shared with us how his department ensures that partnership teaching is successful.

Partnering in our dual language immersion (DLI) program is essential to solid instruction in two languages. Regardless of the model, it is vital to have a partner who can cross-reference objectives for horizontal and vertical alignment of language objectives, content objectives, and skills objectives. The students in the French dual language program at Fort Greene Preparatory Academy in Brooklyn, New York, receive instruction in the target language for 50% of core classes in addition to weekly language labs and advisory classes. Science and social studies are taught exclusively in French, whereas English language arts and math are taught exclusively in English.

My partner teacher Sarah Brooks and I have specialized into two departments as well as forming our own Dual Language Department. My partner meets several times a week with the Social Studies Department whereas I meet with the Science Department two to three times per week. My colleague and I then meet two to three times a week to hone in specifically on the skills and language objectives after solidifying units with our respective content teams. See Figure 4.2 as an example of our collaboration: Generally, my partner teacher and I team up in each other's lessons to sift through entry tickets, which give us data to inform our small groupings. In this particular case, I pulled a small group of language learners to review key vocabulary on the theme of voluntary movements. My partner teacher supported native language students and the language learners whose entry tickets demonstrated readiness for the collaborative inquiry portion of the lesson.

Similar to other practitioners in previous chapters, Blake talks about alignment. He focuses on aligning three types of objectives. How do you work across content and language goals and expectations with your dual language students?

Figure 4.2 Dual Language Co-Teachers in a Science Class

Source: Blake Ramsey and Sarah Brooks. Used with permission.

Dual language classes that have two teachers collaborating naturally allow for partnership teaching with the following benefits:

- Content and language objectives may be co-constructed by the partner teachers.

- Objectives as well as instructional and assessment practices may be aligned across the partner languages.

- Curricular continuity may be established and reinforced through intentional curriculum mapping and alignment work (horizontal and vertical).

- Interdisciplinary thematic units may be co-developed and delivered in tandem.

- Consistent routines and structures may be utilized across content areas and languages.

- Attention to bridging may be co-created to support dynamic multilingual development.

- Consideration for cultural nuances and critical consciousness may be emphasized.

- Partnership teaching at the secondary level may significantly differ from the elementary dual language context. Let's see some examples of how partnership teaching is implemented across the grade levels.

What does it look like in the *elementary classroom* when dual language teachers or other educators engage in partnership teaching?

- In a kindergarten class, while one dual language teacher teaches a unit about farm animals and how they help people survive, the other dual language teacher teaches songs, chants, and counting games with farm animals, thus thematically connecting learning in two languages.

- Addressing the same essential question in second grade while exploring why friendships are important, students read *My Diary From Here to There* by Amanda Irma Pérez (2009) with Spanish- and English-integrated text included throughout the book, bridging portions of the story in both languages.

- Studying the genre of autobiographies in fourth grade, students read several mentor texts in their home language arts class connected to the social studies curriculum. They create a timeline of their own lives, storyboard their major life events, and write their own autobiography with the help of an ELD teacher during the designated ELD period.

- Exploring the topic of refugee relocation in the two languages of Hmong and English, the two teachers coordinate how to build students' backgrounds; activate culturally relevant, critically conscious prior knowledge; and create extension and enrichment activities based on shared objectives.

What does it look like in the *secondary classroom* when dual language teachers or other educators engage in partnership teaching?

- Sixth-grade students conduct science experiments to compare the physical properties of substances to then co-create scientific reports in Language 2 on density, boiling points, and melting points. Then, sixth-grade social studies teachers in Language 1 facilitate activities for students to collaboratively write a parallel type of report describing physical properties of limestone and granite found in the pyramids of Giza.

- In seventh grade, students expand their argument-writing skills in Language 1 by citing text-based evidence and offering explanations for their reasoning—teachers across languages and content areas enhance students' thinking skills and use of expressive language skills by having them prepare speeches related to the topic of exploration.

- In a ninth-grade math class, students examine finding the diameter and circumference of circles, with an emphasis on describing the steps in the process. They engage in task-based discussions that use hands-on explorations and multiple representations such as diagrams, conversation prompts to support the language of describing steps in a process, sketches, and video-recorded responses, as well as inquiry that provides additional opportunities for oracy in Language 1. Then, in a Language 2 language arts class, the students discuss a different topic yet utilize the language of describing the steps in a process, solidifying the language development across both languages and content areas.

- In eleventh grade, when students are preparing for standardized assessments, teachers across the languages and content areas intentionally teach similar study skills and test-taking strategies for consistency and reinforcement.

WHAT PRACTITIONERS SAY

Partnership teaching may be implemented based on frequent and consistent collaborative planning or based on joint, collaborative projects. The coordinated efforts are well reflected in what Nidia Vaz-Correia and Vanessa Kittilsen, middle school dual language teachers from Patchogue-Medford Union Free School District in New York, shared with us:

We are teammates, meaning we teach different content areas but share the same students. We refer to the two of us and our students as the Dual Language Team. Being sixth-grade teachers, we collaborate before the year begins to establish similar classroom routines, discipline procedures, and student/parent communication. Throughout the year, we meet frequently to reflect on lessons and to share with one another what seems to be working, and sometimes not working, well. Both of us have backgrounds working with English learners (Vanessa was an English as a new language [ENL] teacher prior to this role, and Nidia a bilingual teacher), so we both place a strong emphasis on language development in English and Spanish. Sharing a similar teaching philosophy—of putting language at the core of everything we teach—is essential to maintaining the integrity of the program.

Nidia and Vanessa emphasize the importance of a shared teaching philosophy. How can you relate to this in your own context?

Co-Teaching

Co-teaching by definition requires that lessons are jointly delivered—with two educators sharing responsibility for all students as they co-deliver instruction. Co-teaching frameworks have emerged in the special education inclusion context. Most experts on co-teaching to support students with special needs talk about four to six possible co-teaching arrangements. The models of co-teaching vary based on (a) roles and responsibilities each teacher takes on and (b) grouping configurations including the number of groups and group size as well as goals for groups. Richard Villa and his colleagues (2013) have four distinct models of instruction:

Supportive: One teacher takes the lead while the other teacher facilitates learning by rotating among the students.

Parallel: Two teachers work with approximately even sized groups in different parts of the classroom.

Complementary: One teacher works on enhancing the instruction previously provided by the other co-teacher.

Team teaching: Both teachers share the instruction for the entire class as well as collaboratively planning, teaching, and assessing all of the students in the classroom.

But these four models may not be the co-teaching configuration you have heard of. Wendy Murawski (2009), in *Collaborative Teaching in Secondary Schools: Making the Co-Teaching Marriage Work!*, outlines five common approaches for co-instruction: one teach, one support; parallel teaching; station teaching; alternative teaching; and team teaching. Susan Fizell (2018), Marilyn Friend and Lynn Cook (2016), and most others present six co-teaching models in their work, typically labeled as follows: one teach, one observe; one teach, one drift—or circulate; parallel teaching; station teaching; alternate teaching; and team teaching.

When six models are considered, the supporting roles one teacher may take on are more distinguished. Yet others further expand these commonly identified models to capture some variations, such as Katherine Perez (2012), who builds on Friend and Cook's basic set of six models by supplementing them with five additional variations, or Anne Beninghof (2020), who identifies nine approaches to co-teaching—adding more nuances to the choices collaborating teachers have when sharing instruction within the same classroom.

In an extensive body of work by one of the authors of this book, Andrea Honigsfeld, along with Maria G. Dove, a special emphasis is placed not only on the collaborative instructional cycle that consists of co-planning, co-teaching, co-assessment, and co-reflection for the sake of English learners, but on seven distinct co-teaching models as well (Dove & Honigsfeld, 2018). In this chapter, we will apply their seven models to dual language classrooms.

CAPTAIN'S LOG

Reflect on any opportunity you have had to share (a) a bilingual classroom space, (b) responsibility for the same group of students, or (c) a teaching–learning cycle with another teacher in your current dual language context or during prior assignments. What decisions and discussions did you and your colleague have to engage in?

_____

_____

_____

NAVIGATION SYSTEMS

If collaborative planning means symbolically opening your door to your colleagues, collaborative teaching requires that those classroom doors swing wide open and welcome one or more colleagues for a shared instructional experience! As collaborating teachers, you must establish shared beliefs about learning and teaching all children in your care and, more specifically, translate your understanding of how students acquire a new language and develop academic, literacy, critical thinking, and social-emotional competence into collaborative routines and structures. The navigation system we offer here can help strengthen partnership teaching and/or co-teaching in dual language programs.

A Systemic Look at Co-Teaching

We will start by taking a closer look at the seven co-teaching arrangements. You will notice that in the first three cases, the two teachers work with one large group of students taking on different roles and responsibilities. In the next three models, there are two groups of students split between the two cooperating teachers. In the final model, multiple groups of students are engaged in a learning activity that is facilitated and monitored by both teachers. As you explore these seven arrangements, we invite you to make immediate connections to your program's type, structure, and language allocations. We recognize again that there are different dual language program configurations and that your context will shape these co-teaching models. For example, think about how each arrangement may have logistical differences in a 90/10 setting with language allocations assigned to content areas versus a 50/50 setting where language use is determined by subject area, units of instruction, or a morning/afternoon schedule. The bottom line is that all seven co-teaching arrangements can work with any program's language allocation as long as you consider its logistics. Based on Andrea Honigsfeld and Maria Dove's work, we named the models using the group configurations and teacher roles:

1. One Group: One Leads, One "Teaches on Purpose"
2. One Group: Two Teach Same Content
3. One Group: One Teaches, One Assesses
4. Two Groups: Two Teach Same Content
5. Two Groups: One Pre-Teaches, One Teaches Alternative Information
6. Two Groups: One Re-Teaches, One Teaches Alternative Information
7. Multiple Groups: Two Monitor/Teach

Each of these configurations may have a place in any co-taught classroom, regardless of the grade level, the content area, language of content delivery, or the designated teacher assignment. In the following section, we encourage you to consider both the rationale for using each of the co-teaching models and ways to make the most out of them. We invite you to pilot various co-teaching models in your classes to see which ones allow you to respond best to the students' needs, the program's time and language use allocations, the specific content being taught, the type of learning activities designed, and the participating teachers' teaching styles and preferences.

Model 1. One Group: One Leads, One "Teaches on Purpose"

In this model, presented in Figure 4.3, one teacher assumes the lead role, and the other teacher serves in the role of "teaching on purpose," which refers to giving short, focused mini lessons to individual students, pairs of students, or a small group of students. Teaching on purpose might involve a follow-up to a previous lesson or a check and extension of what is presently being taught based on a teachable moment. Teachers who implement teaching on purpose may also keep a written log of information for each student who needs follow-up. You will also consider the strategic use of partner language(s) based on your program's structure.

REASONS TO USE THIS MODEL:	HOW TO MAKE THE MOST OF IT:
• The curriculum is accessible to everyone. • All students receive equal benchmark instruction. • Formative data may be produced via logs (for follow-up). • Constant monitoring of student understanding is possible. • Personal, individualized attention may be given to students in need.	• Plan for purposeful one-on-one or small-group interactions with specific language use in mind. • Come prepared with tools, strategies, and ideas for bridging and translanguaging. • Alternate teacher roles of leading and teaching on purpose. • Avoid one teacher taking all the responsibility for teaching.

Figure 4.3 What Does Model 1 Look Like?

Image credit: New America

Model 2. One Group: Two Teach Same Content

As shown in Figure 4.4, Model 2 involves two teachers directing a whole class of students. Both teachers are working cooperatively and teaching the same lesson at the same time. For example, one teacher presents a lesson, and the other teacher interjects with examples, explanations, and extensions of the key ideas. Either teacher can provide strategies to assist the students in better remembering and organizing the information presented. In the context of dual language, depending on the grade level and program structure, the teachers may teach the content in the same program language or utilize both with bridging (*avoiding repetition*) when appropriate.

REASONS TO USE THIS MODEL:	HOW TO MAKE THE MOST OF IT:
• It allows for collegial observation. • It provides immediate reinforcement/remediation. • It allows for the ability to take notes and offers authentic modeling. • It adds clarity to the lesson. • It is very effective when done well.	• Commit to a good amount of planning for this model. • Practice a smooth back-and-forth between teachers, with specific use of the partner languages based on the program's allocations. • Define roles and responsibilities. • Become thoroughly familiar with the lesson content and the bridges to other lessons.

Figure 4.4 What Does Model 2 Look Like?

Image credit: **New America**

Model 3. One Group: One Teaches, One Assesses

In Model 3, shown in Figure 4.5, two teachers are engaged in conducting the same lesson with consideration of partner language use; however, one teacher takes the lead, and the other teacher circulates the room and assesses targeted students through observations, checklists, and anecdotal records. The observing teacher may also take notes on which activities successfully engaged students, caused confusion, and so on.

REASONS TO USE THIS MODEL:	HOW TO MAKE THE MOST OF IT:
• There is opportunity to carefully observe students in action. • There is opportunity to collect authentic data across both program languages. • The observing teacher can focus on specific subskills and language practices. • The observing teacher may offer peer feedback on what worked and what did not work for individual students to the colleague who teaches.	• Design a data collection tool. • Share student data across and inclusive of both program languages. • Use evidence about student learning to inform other models (such as Model 5, 6, or 7). • Make sure you take turns assessing/observing and leading instruction, with specific connections to bridging content. • Move into other models of co-teaching as needed (such as Model 1) with specific consideration of if, when, and how the partner language use may change.

Figure 4.5 What Does Model 3 Look Like?

Image credit: New America

Model 4. Two Groups: Two Teach Same Content

The students in a Model 4 class form two heterogeneous or homogeneous groups, and each teacher works with one of the groups (see Figure 4.6). The purpose of using two smaller groups is to provide additional opportunities for the students in each group to interact with the language, the materials, the teacher, and each other; to critically think and provide answers with a connection to partner language use; and to have their responses monitored by the teacher. As we noted for Model 2, Model 4 may also include teaching the content in the same program language or utilizing both with bridging (*avoiding repetition*) depending on the grade level and program structure.

REASONS TO USE THIS MODEL:	HOW TO MAKE THE MOST OF IT:
• It decreases class size (small groups). • It provides individualized instruction. • It leads to more interaction due to a lower student–teacher ratio. • It provides a safe environment for students to take more risks with both languages. • You can swap groups to allow for fresh perspectives or new ways of learning with each teacher. • It offers an alternative way to learn same content. • It leads to intentional differentiation. • It can be used with homogeneous or heterogeneous groups.	• Consider using two different instructional approaches for the two groups (SMART Board vs. manipulatives). • Make sure all students experience working with both teachers with bridged topics. • Use a jigsaw approach. • Share goals/objectives, embrace teacher creativity and autonomy when delivering small-group instruction and consider partner language use in both small groups. • Avoid teaching *two* unconnected, separate mini lessons. • Avoid *repeating* the same lesson in both languages. • Be mindful of the noise level. • Utilize classroom space creatively.

Figure 4.6 What Does Model 4 Look Like?

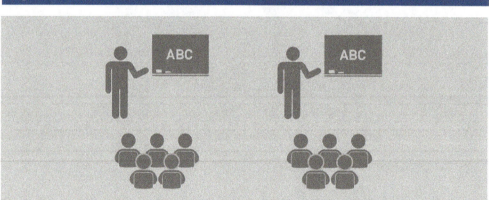

Image credit: **New America**

Model 5. Two Groups: One Pre-Teaches, One Teaches Alternative Information

As demonstrated in Figure 4.7, teachers using Model 5 assign students to one of two groups, based on their readiness levels related to a designated topic or skill. Students who have limited prior knowledge of the target content or skill will be grouped together to receive instruction with a connection to partner language use. The teacher working with that group will have the opportunity to prepare students to bridge the gap in their background knowledge.

REASONS TO USE THIS MODEL:	HOW TO MAKE THE MOST OF IT:
• Focused attention may be given to subgroups' unique needs. • It is ideal for tiered lessons and tasks or other forms of differentiated instruction. • It allows for building vocabulary (or other language features) for one group of students and expanding the same of another. • It allows for building background knowledge across languages.	• Monitor the time allowed for pre-teaching information to one group. • Offer enrichment, extension, bridging, and translanguaging opportunities for the other group. • Be mindful of the environment and find ways to reduce distractions or control the noise level.

Figure 4.7 What Does Model 5 Look Like?

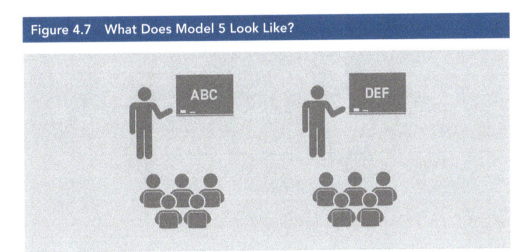

Image credit: New America

Model 6. Two Groups: One Re-Teaches, One Teaches Alternative Information

In Model 6, shown in Figure 4.8, teachers assign students to one of two groups, based on their readiness or mastery levels regarding the designated learning objective. One teacher will focus on previously presented material and offer the group an opportunity for reinforcement, practice, or application with consideration to partner language use. The other teacher may challenge the students to extend their learning through enrichment activities. In this flexible grouping arrangement, the group to which students are assigned is temporary and relates solely to their knowledge and skills regarding the designated topic. As the topic and skills that are addressed change, so does the group composition.

REASONS TO USE THIS MODEL:	HOW TO MAKE THE MOST OF IT:
• It is ideal for differentiating. • It is flexible—only students who need re-teaching or reinforcement will get it. • It provides enrichment for students who have demonstrated mastery.	• Plan the re-teaching task to be completed at the same pace with the enrichment task and consider partner language use. • Offer enrichment, extension, bridging, and translanguaging opportunities to all students.

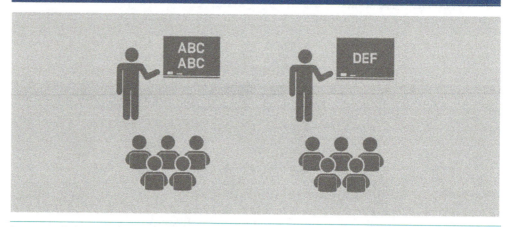

Figure 4.8 What Does Model 6 Look Like?

Image credit: **New America**

Model 7. Multiple Groups: Two Monitor/Teach

The multiple-group format of Model 7 allows all or most students to work in either heterogeneous or homogeneous groups, with selected students grouped for specific, skills-based instruction (see Figure 4.9). This model can be particularly effective in language arts at the elementary level when students require specific and intensive small-group instruction or at the middle school level when students participate in literature circles or inquiry circles. Science or computer labs may also easily lend themselves to such instruction. Model 7 is also conducive to learning centers or learning stations, where students rotate from center to center (in the elementary classroom) or from station to station (in the secondary classroom) while two teachers monitor the learning.

REASONS TO USE THIS MODEL:	HOW TO MAKE THE MOST OF IT:
• There is total engagement due to movement. • More individualized attention is offered. • There is increased student participation and engagement.	Mix up group membership to avoid a stagnant group formation. Vary teacher roles: • Each teacher takes a group, and there are one or more independent groups.

REASONS TO USE THIS MODEL:	HOW TO MAKE THE MOST OF IT:
• Co-teachers can cover more of the curriculum if the jigsaw technique is used. • It lends itself to multicultural, multilingual interaction. • There is extensive opportunity for peer learning.	• One teacher stays with a group; the other teacher facilitates the remainder of the groups. • Both teachers facilitate and monitor learning in all the groups with specific partner language use.

Figure 4.9 What Does Model 7 Look Like?

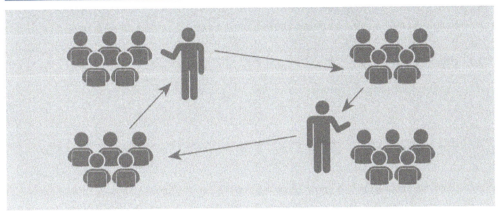

Image credit: New America

What Is Unique About Co-Teaching in the Dual Language Context?

During any of the co-teaching configurations, co-teachers will share the responsibility for planning instruction, implementing the lessons, and assessing student performance and outcome. Depending on your local context, who those partnering teachers are, your program's structure and time allocations, the amount of time you have to co-teach, and how you define the goals of co-teaching will vary significantly. As we also noted in each of the seven co-teaching models, there may be variations with teachers' strategic program language use. Given the diversity within dual language programs, we recognize that teaching the content in the same program language or utilizing both languages with bridging (*avoiding repetition*) depends on the students' needs, the grade-level scheduling, and the program structure. Special education teachers, bilingual paraprofessionals, and/or academic intervention service providers may indeed focus on different aspects of biliteracy development.

What *is* constant is that in a co-taught classroom, the teachers not only work alongside each other in a range of configurations but share a deep-rooted commitment to learning for all students. In dual language programs, these commitments and goals also include the four pillars of dual language education. In all seven co-teaching configurations, both teachers give significant attention to students' development of bilingualism and biliteracy, grade-level academic achievement, sociocultural competence, and cultural consciousness. We invite you to take another look at the *How to Make the Most of It* columns from the seven models section and reflect on how you may draw connections to the four pillars based on your students and the community your program serves.

STAYING THE COURSE

We share the belief that the success of collaborative instructional delivery (be it partnership teaching or co-teaching) depends on a variety of complex factors.

Core Beliefs

Reflect on the following list and decide what resonates with your belief system:

- *Collaborative practice:* You willingly and voluntarily engage in all three phases of collaborative practice: planning, implementing, and assessing instruction.
- *Cross-cultural and interpersonal skills:* To effectively co-teach, you pay special attention to and further develop your cross-cultural understanding, communication, critical consciousness, and interpersonal skills.
- *Bridging and building content knowledge and linguistic competence:* You recognize that students bring a wealth of life experiences and complex linguistic repertoires to the classroom. The challenge is to activate such prior knowledge and successfully connect it to new learning or, when needed, effectively build background knowledge so your students can understand the new content and develop language and literacy in two places.
- *Consistent and supportive teacher behaviors:* You embrace that they are role models to their students and are constantly being observed by them. So, building a cohesive, dual language learning community sends a clear message to all students: Two teachers are in charge who share equal responsibilities.

"Let's Agree" Statements

For collaborative teaching to result in impactful instructional practices and enhanced student learning, we invite you to agree to the following five premises (and develop further agreements for your own partnership):

1. Let's establish open communication from the onset and co-create structures and routines that benefit our collaboration.
2. Let's outline our personal goals for the partnership, our philosophy about educating language learners, and our expectations for student performance and success, as well as our strengths in working within the dual language context.

3. Let's commit to engaging in the entire collaborative instructional cycle of collaborative planning, teaching, assessment, and reflection.
4. Let's identify the roles and individual responsibilities for each collaborative member of the partnership.
5. Let's use, adapt, or create co-planning structures, co-teaching models, and collaborative tools and techniques and select those that are mutually agreed upon.

WHAT THE RESEARCH SAYS

Jason Greenberg Motamedi and colleagues (2019) conducted a longitudinal study comparing the impact various program models have on student learning:

> [They] found that elementary ELL [English language learner] students in dual language and co-teaching programs started kindergarten with lower levels of English language proficiency than their peers in pull-out programs and those whose parents waived ELD services. However, ELL students in dual language and co-teaching programs made greater grade-to-grade English language proficiency growth compared to students in pull-out programs and students whose parents waived ELD services. This faster growth allowed ELL students in the dual language and co-teaching programs to catch up with their peers by the end of elementary school. (p. 1)

Fred Genesee and Kathryn Lindholm-Leary (2013) also suggest that when content and language instruction are integrated, there is "authentic communication in the classroom about matters of academic importance that provides critical context for learning the communicative functions of the new language" (p. 6).

What are the implications of these research findings for your own context?

Bridget Costa and Jessica Manriquez, first-grade dual language partner teachers, have been collaborating for two years at Woodland Academy in the Worcester Public Schools in Massachusetts (see Figure 4.10). They shared with us several artifacts documenting their co-teaching practice and reflections on how they developed their collaboration. They work in the context of a one-way dual language classroom where all students are Spanish speakers, and they are simultaneously developing Spanish and English language and literacy skills.

LAUNCHED MISSIONS

(Continued)

(Continued)

Figure 4.10 Bridget Costa and Jessica Manriquez: First-Grade Dual Language Partner Teachers

Source: Bridget Costa and Jessica Manriquez. Used with permission.

We developed a co-planning agreement that helps define our roles and responsibilities and how we commit to a cycle of pre-, co-, and post-planning (see Figure 4.11).

Figure 4.11 Co-Planning Agreement

PLAN FOR COLLABORATIVE PLANNING	CORE CONTENT TEACHER	EL TEACHER
Pre-Planning	• Review lessons • Plan interactive read-aloud (IRA) and centers • Preview topic/theme and vocabulary	• Preview lessons • Preview data • Concept development • Preview topic/theme and vocabulary
Collaborative Planning	• Plan centers: Spanish • Roles and responsibilities • Make a list of cognates	• Plan centers: English • Roles and responsibilities • Make a list of cognates
Post-Planning	• Reflect • Review data/progress	• Reflect • Review data/progress

Source: Bridget Costa and Jessica Manriquez. Used with permission.

We have also created a brief agreement regarding our communication and reflection.

> **Communication**
>
> We agree to:
>
> - Meet in person
> - Exchange emails
> - Send texts
>
> **Reflection**
>
> We agree to:
>
> - Share student information
> - Evaluate structures and co-teaching models
> - Be open and honest
>
> *To ensure consistency, we developed a routine we tend to follow most days during our co-taught class time (see Figure 4.12).*

Keep in mind that Bridget, the ELD specialist, spends two class periods a day in the classroom, while Jessica is the classroom teacher delivering instruction in Spanish. In addition, music, physical education, technology, and art are taught by English-speaking educators. The combination of the time Bridget and the specials teachers are dedicating to delivering instruction via English ensures the 70/30 language allocation.

Figure 4.12 Daily Lesson/Routine

INSTRUCTIONAL CONTEXT	CO-TEACHING APPROACH	CORE CONTENT TEACHER FOCUS	EL TEACHER FOCUS	SPECIAL CONSIDERATIONS
Morning message	EL teacher facilitates (T, Th) Core teacher leads (W, F)	Phonemic awareness and wordplay in Spanish	Phonemic awareness and wordplay in English	Biliteracy language development
Translanguaging lesson	Two teachers teach at the same time	Metalinguistic awareness, biliteracy development	Metalinguistic awareness, biliteracy development	Biliteracy language development
Small groups/ guided reading	Rotation model	Guided reading: Spanish	Supports skill and language oracy	Every day for 15 minutes: Biliteracy language development
Read-aloud (F only)	One teacher teaches, the other assesses	School pace assessments	Leads read-aloud	Biliteracy language development

Source: Bridget Costa and Jessica Manriquez. Used with permission.

(Continued)

(Continued)

We frequently utilize translanguaging approaches when both teachers teach at the same time. Here is an example of a lesson plan we recently developed.

> **Objective:** Students will be able to identify similarities and differences in cognates using visuals and written language in order to develop metalinguistics within English and Spanish.
>
> **Vocabulary:** *mammal, reptile, amphibian, camouflage, adaptation, hibernation*
>
> **Activity:**
>
> - Present an anchor chart with vocabulary written in both languages (Spanish = red, English = blue).
>
> - Introduce the topic.
>
> - Both teachers switch off displaying a photo and asking what the word is in the teacher's native language.
>
> - Students discuss similarities and differences as well as definitions via turn and talk or as a whole group.
>
> - Sing the "We are bridging, because we're bilingual" song. Note: A bridge is made with arms to show the bridging of both languages.

Bridget's Small Group

Language Standard and Key Use (WIDA, 2020)	ELD-LA.1.Inform.Interpretive ELD-LA.1.Inform.Expressive
Language Expectation	Describing attributes and characteristics with facts, definitions, and relevant details
Language Function	Orally using noun groups to add description and precision that answer questions about an animal's physical characteristics
Language Feature	Using compound sentences to add details Creating labeled drawings to support information

Jessica's Small Group

Language Standard and Key Use (WIDA, 2020)	ELD-LA.1.Inform.Interpretive ELD-SC.1.Inform.Expressive
Language Expectation	Students will be able to identify and restate the main topic and key details in order to show comprehension of texts read. Students will be able to describe and write about a topic presented from informational text in order to demonstrate understanding of facts and details.
Language Function	Students will use sequence words (*first, and, then, next, last*) to clarify facts learned within an informational text.
Language Feature	Students are expected to use simple and complex sentences, with proper punctuation. When demonstrating what they have learned through a visual representation, students will add labels to show details in their drawings.

And finally, we would like to share some of our reflections on how we approach collaboration, co-planning, and co-teaching.

Bridget: *Jessica and I both have the best interest of our students at heart. We want them to feel successful and confident in their skills. Because we share the same philosophy, we are always communicating about our students and lessons whether it be in passing, via text message or email, or meeting after school at least once a week. It doesn't feel like added work or loss of time since we view collaboration as part of our everyday routine.*

When it comes to co-planning, we start by checking to see what the topic or theme of our curriculum unit is. Then we decide who will teach what during our small groups. If the particular unit is rich in new vocabulary, such as an informational unit on animal research, I might decide to go a week ahead of Jessica so I can pre-teach certain terminology and build background knowledge about the subject by using realia, songs, and movement to create experiences that help the learning to stick. We then pull out cognates within the vocabulary that we use for our translanguaging lessons.

(Continued)

(Continued)

Jessica: *I teach more standards-based lessons because those skills will grow with the students through the units, topics, and subjects. Since we are a 70/30 Spanish/English program and we are implementing a one-way dual language model, Bridget teaches more of the rich language that can be transferred during our translanguaging lessons, always keeping in mind how we can provide rich language experiences to our students. We know that our students only learn to sequence events once; it's not different when sequencing in Spanish or English—it would be the same skill.*

Bridget: *At the beginning of the year, I was hesitant with co-teaching. I was always worried about "stepping on toes" and self-conscious about my lack of Spanish. Now, since beginning our translanguaging lessons, I feel very comfortable stepping in, and I feel as though our teaching time together has a good flow. I realize too that it is good for our students to see me as a language learner just like them, and they feel as though they are my teachers. My students and I are together in the language acquisition process.*

Jessica: *I love co-teaching with Bridget. I have always had to be my own EL teacher within my classroom or had a different model of co-teaching. I never had someone in my classroom at the same time I did teaching the same overarching unit/theme in a different language. I have taught self-contained dual language or had a co-teacher where I was the Spanish component and she was the English component, but we each had our own classroom and would switch kids. I would teach Spanish language arts, science, and social studies, and she would teach English language arts and math.*

Bridget: *All students benefit from co-teaching, but there is one student in particular who comes to mind. The way he thinks and approaches learning is a lot different from his peers. He has a very creative mind, and is always wanting to build, draw, and create. He also requires a lot of structure. I feel as though my co-teacher's strengths lie within her structure and routines, and I view myself as being strong in creativity. With me, he is able to make connections through movement and song, and is given "outside of the box" methods to show what he knows. With Jessica, he is able to have the security of knowing what will come next, and her calm demeanor makes him feel safe and nurtured. From both of us, our student gets exactly what he needs for him to be successful.*

Jessica: *I also believe that all students benefit from co-teaching, especially in our situation (dual language). They get such different approaches to language and content because Bridget's and my teaching styles are different. I would like to consider my teaching style as structured and routine based, with a calm- and focus-driven goal in mind. I see how our students have gained so much from both Bridget and me. I see how they make those connections from what they do with her in her table and whole-group instructional lessons in Spanish.*

Bridget: *Co-teaching in dual language classrooms is all about working together toward one common goal in order to gain a new perspective on who your students are and all of the amazing things they are capable of. Children contain so many puzzle pieces inside of their brains. These pieces are their learning styles, personality traits, language, culture, strengths, and insecurities. These puzzle pieces must come together in the learning process to enable the students' growth, and each child's puzzle is different. Concurrently, it is the teachers who are figuring out how to put these pieces together, and every teacher has a different strategy. When two teachers with two different skill sets are working on these puzzles toward one common goal, they are gaining new insights to who these students are. In turn, the students are accessing learning from two different perspectives through different instructional approaches and languages. It's amazing to see our students grow throughout the year going from being dominant in one language to effortlessly switching languages. They know when they are with Jessica they speak Spanish and with me they speak English, but simultaneously, in social and academic conversation, if they are unsure of a word, they are able to code switch, and both languages are seen as one.*

Jessica: *Collaborating with a co-teacher in a dual language classroom has been the best thing I have done in my educational practice as a teacher. Being able to learn so much from Bridget and her approaches to language-rich instruction as an EL teacher has opened my eyes on how I could add those approaches when teaching students' in their home languages. At first, we both struggled with what we each had to teach and oftentimes were teaching the same standards in both languages, but as we continue to collaborate and reflect, we see each lesson with a different perspective with an overarching goal/unit/theme. We can now easily see what she can teach while I support or vice versa. I am lucky to have such a strong EL teacher who easily lends herself to be so flexible and supportive.*

Bridget and Jessica continue to work on their co-teaching practice and focus on planning effective cross-language connections during the preview–view–review lesson sequence during English-targeted instruction.

CAPTAIN'S LOG

After you read this vignette illustrating collaborative teaching in a dual language classroom, consider the following two questions: (a) What evidence of partnership building and intentional dual language pedagogy can you identify? (b) If you could meet Bridget and Jessica, what questions would you have for them?

_____

_____

_____

_____

GEAR UP!

In a collaborative teaching situation, key details can be carefully planned ahead of time and further negotiated as the collaborative practice unfolds. A good place to start is to have a conversation with your collaborative teaching partner or team in order to answer the following general and specific questions:

1. What will our partnership teaching or co-teaching arrangement look like?
2. What are our hopes and fears (or concerns) about our collaborative teaching?
3. What are our expectations for sharing the responsibility for the curriculum and the students through a collaborative approach to teaching?
4. What are our "nonnegotiables"—anything necessary for each of us to function as a fully productive member of the team?

If a classroom space and instructional time are also shared, consider discussing the following:

1. If we use multiple models for instruction during one teaching session, how will the classroom's overall design accommodate their use?
2. Which areas of the classroom will be designated as shared spaces?
3. Where will teaching resources be kept for easy access for all co-teaching partners?
4. How will one classroom accommodate each teacher's need for personal space?

Rethinking Teaching Spaces for Optimized Learning

A classroom designed for one instructor might not be adequate for co-teaching situations. Therefore, co-teachers must plan and manage the teaching space in a way that enhances lesson instruction and corresponds with the selected co-teaching model. (See Figure 4.13 for a summary of the seven co-teaching models we introduced earlier in this chapter aligned to specific space requirements and recommended suggestions.)

Figure 4.13 Co-Teaching Models and Organizing Classroom Space for Equity and Maximizing Instructional Intensity and Student Engagement

CO-TEACHING MODELS	SPACE REQUIREMENTS	SUGGESTIONS TO CONSIDER
One Group: One Leads, One "Teaches on Purpose"	Space for students to work in small groups	• Desks or tables arranged in clusters • A carry-all bag for resources and supplies for "on purpose" teaching
One Group: Two Teach Same Content	Room sufficient to divide students into two groups	• Separate teaching spaces • Chart easel, whiteboard, etc. • Place to house resources and materials • Seating arranged in horseshoe or circle • May be situated in different rooms
One Group: One Teaches, One Assesses	Area for the whole class to gather together	• Carpeted area • Chart easel, whiteboard, etc. • Place to house resources and materials
Two Groups: Two Teach Same Content	Whole-group seating area	• Carpeted area • Chart easel, whiteboard, etc. • Interactive whiteboard • Computer with projector • Seating arranged in horseshoe or circle
Two Groups: One Pre-Teaches, One Teaches Alternative Information	Small- and large-group seating arrangements	• Separate teaching spaces • Hands-on materials • Computers/interactive whiteboards • May be situated in different rooms
Two Groups: One Re-Teaches, One Teaches Alternative Information	Small- and large-group seating arrangements	• Separate teaching spaces • Hands-on materials • Computers/interactive whiteboards • May be situated in different rooms
Multiple Groups: Two Monitor/Teach	Areas designated for small groups and center or station learning	• Areas of the room for each learning station • Baskets for needed materials • Portable boxes or folder-type centers that can be easily adapted to different classroom spaces

TUNE IN!

The goal of this chapter was to offer a solid framework; a current, critical perspective; and essential tools that support collaborative planning regardless of the dual language program model you are using. We invite you to look beyond the content of the chapter and continue your exploration with some additional print- and web-based resources.

Books and Articles

Beninghof, A. M. (2020). *Co-teaching that works: Structures and strategies for maximizing student learning* (2nd ed.). Jossey-Bass.

Cohan, A., Honigsfeld, A., & Dove, M. G. (2020). *Team up, speak up, fire up! Educators and the community working together to support English learners.* ASCD.

Dove, M. G., & Honigsfeld, A. (2018). *Co-teaching for English learners: A guide to collaborative planning, instruction, assessment, and reflection.* Corwin.

Dove, M. G., & Honigsfeld, A. (2020). Is there magic in co-teaching? In M. G. Dove & A. Honigsfeld (Eds.), *Co-teaching for English learners: Evidence-based practices and research-informed outcomes.* Information Age.

Honigsfeld, A., & Dove, M. G. (Eds.). (2022). *Portraits of collaboration: Educators working together to support multilingual learners.* Seidlitz.

Web-Based Resources

Review this blog post discussing an integrated co-teaching (ICT) dual language program designed to meet the needs of children who are acquiring a second language and who have also been identified as having a disability: Rodriguez, D. (2016). *Teaching bilingual learners with disabilities in an integrated co-teaching dual language program.* Colorín Colorado! https://www.colorincolorado.org/article/teaching-bilingual-learners-disabilities-integrated-co-teaching-dual-language-program

Watch this video introducing team teaching in dual language classes: Los Angeles Unified School District. (n.d.). *Team teaching and self-contained classrooms in dual language education* [Video]. Multilingual and Multicultural Education Department, Dual Language/Bilingual Programs Office. https://lausd.wistia.com/medias/q981na7my7

COUNTDOWN TO LAUNCH

Consider the following practical tips for implementing collaborative teaching:

10. Make sure your partnership teaching or co-teaching is strongly rooted in ongoing professional relationship building and respect for each other.

9. Collaboratively plan, assess, and reflect to maximize collaborative teaching, paying close attention to partner language use according to your time allocations.

8. Start from an asset-based perspective: What are your strengths as educators, and how can you build on them?

7. Focus on curriculum alignments, language use allocations, and bridging.

6. Define roles and responsibilities according to your program's structure and partner languages.

5. Establish collaborative teaching routines and structures that offer safety and familiarity as well as cut down the amount of planning needed.

4. Maximize instructional intensity, especially during co-teaching when there are two teachers in the room working with all the students.

3. Create an affirming multilingual space where collaboration among students can thrive.

2. Work from clearly established goals while avoiding scripted collaborative lessons.

1. Stay flexible and embrace teachable moments.

Based on Chapter 4, identify your key takeaways. What is directly applicable to your context? What could be a stretch for you in the moment? What are some future goals or steps you wish to take?

_____
_____
_____
_____

CAPTAIN'S LOG: FINAL ENTRY

Collaborative Assessment and Reflection in Dual Language Programs

5

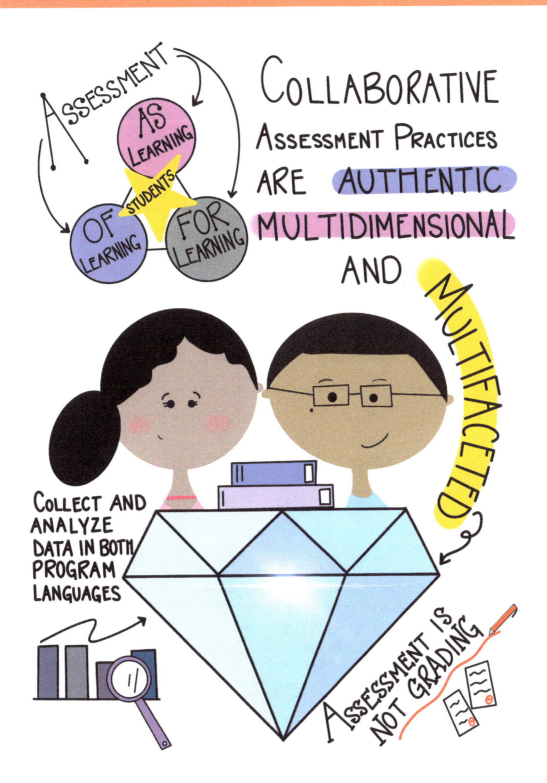

> *"Good assessment is not primarily about looking backward to what a student learned, but [is centered] on looking forward to what a student is ready to learn next. We need to assess multilingual learners in the context of their whole universe of abilities and possibilities—across languages."*
>
> —Dr. Jeremy Aldrich, Director of Teaching and Learning,
> Harrisonburg City Public Schools

MISSION CONTROL

Collaborative planning and collaborative teaching, as we learned in Chapters 3 and 4, are essential components of dual language programs regardless of the model of instruction. Collaborative assessment, the topic of this chapter combined with in-depth reflections, brings us to complete the instructional cycle. We've established that partnering teachers and other members of the school community collaborate for the sake of their multilingual learners. This chapter, parallel to Chapter 3, defines the *who, what, where, when, how,* and *why* of collaborative assessment and offers actionable recommendations and tools to support co-assessments in the dual language context. We recognize the topic of assessment includes many layers, ranging from student assessment, teacher assessment, and program evaluations. We begin here in this chapter with a focus on student assessment to then expand more toward the teacher, administrator, and program evaluation aspects in Chapter 6. More specifically, the fundamental goals of Chapter 5 are to:

1. Define the essential elements of collaborative authentic assessment in the dual language classroom

2. Make connections to the four pillars of dual language education in collaborative authentic assessment practices

3. Distinguish between collaborative authentic assessment *as, for,* and *of* learning in the dual language context

EXPLORATION

As we prepare to launch our exploration into the topic of collaborative authentic assessment, let's return to the perspectives of the student and her teachers in the Vietnamese–English fourth-grade dual language classroom we learned about in Chapter 3, looking at this topic from a shifted glance. We wish to elevate these voices again, now showcasing them through the lens of collaborative assessment and *why* it is so important for multilingual learners' success. As you read some more about Minh and her partner teachers' experiences, we invite you to consider their connections to your contexts as well as to some key research findings.

Through a Student's Eyes

People ask me why I love going to school. I tell them that it's because I am excited to see my friends, and even when I am a bit nervous in class, my teachers make me feel clever and smart, just like the meaning of my name. My teachers ask my class to work hard, and they are always helping us show ourselves and each other all about our learning in English and in Vietnamese by asking us to complete different types of assignments. For my classmates who speak Spanish, my teachers include us all in using all our languages together. They remind us to think about the ideas we're learning and what the ideas sound like and look like in English and all the other languages we can think about. We write together, we read together, and we help each other by explaining our ideas in all our languages. Our teachers give us daily goals for learning, and we have many chances to talk about the goals during class and then tell everyone what we learned at the end of the classes—and we are asked to explain how we know we've learned the goals. When I go home every day, I can tell my parents what I learned in both English and Vietnamese. We have tests in both languages and they're hard, so I have to study. The tests and other kinds of quizzes are better for me when I remember activities we did in class. We don't have to memorize words, and my teachers are always reminding us that we need to be active in class, so we don't memorize ideas just for the day of the test. Sometimes when I'm taking a test, I imagine what I worked on with my friends in class, what the teachers had us do, and most of all what we explained at the end of class every day and how we could show what we learned.

Here is a brief description of how Minh and her classmates are involved in the assessment process:

Because Minh enjoys that she gets to use both her languages at school, she is more confident when she can express her learning via a variety of assessment tools in English and Vietnamese, even while she has assessments that are written in one language at a time. Since Minh reads and writes in Vietnamese with just as much confidence as she does in English, she demonstrates learning in richer ways when she is encouraged to tap into both languages rather than only one, especially as she develops more metalinguistic awareness of Vietnamese and English. When she is assessed in any of the content areas, with formative and summative assessments, she more deeply explains her learning when there is an additional layer of the assessments that offer her time and spaces to describe her discoveries, linking the depths of meaning in her two languages for her learning. Our classroom's lesson activities and their assessments include frequent spaces/ways for students to monitor their own language and content learning in both program languages.

We emphasize that Minh is developing and demonstrating metalinguistic awareness about her own and her classmates' languages both intuitively and through her participation in a dual language program. We invite you to reflect on *why* it is so crucial to support an authentic, multilingual approach for assessing language and content development in both of her languages.

CAPTAIN'S LOG

(Continued)

(Continued)

_____

_____

_____

_____

Through the Educators' Eyes

As Minh's fourth-grade partner teachers, we dedicate a significant amount of time to discussing assessments. During our weekly collaborative planning time, we work with a part-time bilingual teaching assistant and the third-grade looped-in teachers, and we talk about the assessments we've planned to use, and we collaborate about the students' outcomes on prior lessons, comparing notes. We have in-depth conversations about students' progress in the core content areas across the two languages, as well as in their cross-cultural understandings and critical thinking. Because we have planned ways to infuse our students' cultural heritage in the curriculum and are attentive to their bicultural identities, we are committed to discussing how the students' outcomes are reflective within the assessments. We strategically make time to analyze our students' input based on the learning goals they set for themselves. We greatly value this development of their self-reflective skills and use their voices as serious assessment data for decision making.

Since our planning is carved out to specific days and times, we maximize the work by examining our formative student data before we meet so we can review the appropriate curriculum and scope and sequence guides very specifically. Every planning session begins with our brief classroom celebrations based on the assessments we brought to life from our prior planning session. Then, and only then, can we take a deeper dive into the upcoming lessons, based on what the students demonstrated for learning and reshaping multidimensional lesson activities to meet their needs, including students' oracy development in both languages. This is possible because we consistently and deliberately work with the classroom protocols we created that bridge the content-area learning. With regard to collaborative assessments, we discuss the successes and room for change in the self- and peer assessment and goal setting where the students are regularly engaged. We purposefully discuss the students' outcomes from the decisions we made in prior planning regarding the development of content, language, biliteracy, cultural, and critical consciousness. For us to shape and reshape the ways we measure our students' multilingual demonstrations of their new learning through key activities, tasks, and projects, collaborative assessment is an integrated part of the conversations. We simply can't plan without discussing assessments, and vice versa. And since we use a shared Google Drive on our own when we're apart, we log the assessment outcomes and assessment goals to be used in every collaborative planning session.

Minh's teachers discuss the importance of in-depth collaborative conversations about assessments with each other, other teachers, and teaching assistants. They also express the significance of including students' input and self-reflections. As you make the connections to collaborative assessment through these educators' eyes, we invite you to reflect on *how* you might include students' insights and self-reflection in your own collaborative assessment practices.

CAPTAIN'S LOG

_____

_____

_____

_____

WHAT THE RESEARCH SAYS

We want to emphasize the impact of including students in the collaborative assessment processes described by Minh and her teachers on academic and linguistic gains. We further acknowledge their mentions of the students' use of their full linguistic repertoires within the assessment processes. Margo Gottlieb (2021) explains why assessment practices, in addition to academic and linguistic growth, are important for contributing to social justice and equity for multilingual learners:

> *Multilingual learners deserve relevant and fair assessment that generates useful information for improving teaching and learning in linguistically and culturally sustainable ways. Anything less is not equitable, just, or worthwhile. We assert that what is largely missing has been an educational system that embraces assessment in multiple languages. When multilingual learners can show their full linguistic and academic repertoires that are recognized across classrooms, schools, and districts, we enhance their opportunities for success in school and beyond. (p. xxvii)*

Expanding on your previous Captain's Log reflections and considering Gottlieb's research, what are your ideas and opinions regarding students' use of their full linguistic repertoires within the assessment processes and the connection to equity?

Ready to Launch the Exploration

We continue to affirm that collaboration within the full instructional cycle is a non-negotiable for dual language programs to transform, grow, and thrive for multilingualism. In this portion of Chapter 5, we will explore the parallel key questions we asked about collaborative planning in Chapter 3 as they now arise related to collaborative assessment—*who, what, when, where, why,* and *how*—to ensure impactful program transformations based on comprehensive, holistic, and multidimensional assessment outcomes that authentically measure students' learning. We will close our exploration with the strategic importance of reflecting on collaborative practices in the dual language context.

Who Collaborates With Whom?

We've been learning how partner teachers work closely together and that their collaboration involves several educators in the dual language context. Some collaborations may be regularly scheduled and sustained; others may only occur occasionally or on an as-needed basis. Consider the following list and reflect on your ideas. Ask yourself what *collaborative assessment practices* might look like, sound like, and feel like in each of the scenarios when dual language partner teachers collaborate with:

- Each other and other teacher partnerships
- Teaching assistants or other paraprofessionals who work in their classrooms
- Other grade-level teachers (at the elementary level)
- Other grade-level and/or content teachers (at the secondary level)
- Other dual language educators
- Students
- English language development (ELD) specialists
- Special education teachers
- Instructional coaches
- Instructional leaders and administrators
- Parents or guardians
- Community liaisons or other members of the larger linguistic community

As we've learned, even though we implement common dual language frameworks, collaboration is unique in every situation. Each of the educators involved in the collaborative assessment processes will interact with the assessment outcomes in different ways for different purposes. For example, teaching assistants may concentrate on linking effective and efficient classroom resources that directly address multilingual learners' needs based on formative and summative assessment data. Pivoting our thinking to the roles of instructional coaches, special educators, ELD specialists, and other program teachers, collaborative assessment may hone in on common formative assessment outcomes. It's critical to collaboratively analyze whole-group progress as well as to look for patterns in students' work. That way, dual language educators can truly identify what each student needs as well as inform the next steps in learning. Kristina Robertson and colleagues (2022) guide us to remember the connection between collaborative instructional goal setting and assessment data analysis:

> Setting goals and engaging in data analysis [is the way] to inform instruction. The saying goes "What gets measured gets taught," and there's an element of truth to this. In a collaborative team, it's important that both teachers understand the instructional goal and performance expectations as well as how they will use the student work (data) collected to revise instructional practices or reteach concepts. (p. 184)

From another perspective, collaborative assessment with students and parents solidifies two-way dialogue about the children's progress mentioned in Chapter 3, describing multidimensional measures where the students play an integral role in the authentic assessment processes. With that said, in the context of dual language programs and other spaces where we work with multilingual, multicultural communities, we must also remember that there are special cultural nuances within the collaborative assessment processes, some we may not have ever considered. For example, in today's era of technology, how often would we think it was completely normal to have a parent–teacher conference whereby we're sharing student assessment results that also include note-taking on a laptop? Shane Safir and Jamila Dugan (2021) explain the importance of mindful listening:

> Know your audience. If uncertain, ask the person, "Do you mind if I take notes once in a while? Would a computer be distracting?" If real-time notes aren't appropriate, practice mindful listening and set aside ten minutes after the session to jot down some key points. Listen for emotional peaks, which may be revealed through upticks in volume or shifts in tone and body language. (p. 72)

When we are critically conscious about collecting, analyzing, and reporting data to students and parents, we think about the relationships and what they require for collaborative, authentic assessment.

What Is Collaborative Assessment in Dual Language?

Much like we did in Chapter 3 where we defined collaborative planning, we are going to define collaborative assessment for our purposes: It is a process that supports the authentic, multidimensional, standards-aligned measures of language and core content curricula alongside developing cultural and critical consciousness. In this way, dual language educators and other collaborating educators (such as special education teachers, teaching assistants, paraprofessionals, instructional specialists, and others) have true opportunities to coordinate and refine their plans for instruction and assessment (Honigsfeld & Dove, 2022).

Key layers within collaborative assessment include two features that correspond to the overarching theme of this book—transforming dual language programs for equity. These two features are reimagining systems of assessment to be transformative as well as changing our mindsets to be certain our assessments in dual language address systemic reform (Gottlieb, 2021, 2022).

CAPTAIN'S LOG

We fully embrace the ideas Margo Gottlieb (2022) presents on shifting mindsets within the collaborative assessment processes. Reflect on the following ideas we gleaned from current research confirmed by our research and site-based work with collaborating dual language educators. As you reflect, we invite you to think about how you see your own practices aligning, either now or in the future. Collaborative assessment is:

- A direct reflection of the principles of multilingualism and multiculturalism
- Aligned with an expression of the school's and district's mission, vision, and values
- A joint commitment to authentically assessing excellence in both languages, one that seeks feedback from students, family members, teachers, and other school leaders
- Inclusive of scaffolded assessments that are parallel to instructional resources and bilingual supplementary materials
- A way to critically listen to each other, continuing to build a trusting professional relationship whereby you leverage authentic assessment practices of what multilingual learners know and can do
- The use of community and multicultural students' funds of knowledge to establish shared goals, learning intentions, and measurable outcomes for all students
- An endeavor among educators to ensure that grade-level standards are met while equity of languages and cultural understandings are addressed
- An opportunity to leverage multilingual learners' assessment in multiple languages
- Creating a qualitative rubric for multidimensional assessment that is founded on all students' equitable development of content-based academic, linguistic, and sociocultural competence in more than one language

What additional ideas might you add to the list?

_____
_____
_____
_____

We can probably all agree that our students demonstrate extraordinary learning and language use in dual language classrooms. We can probably also agree that there are countless, genuine, and multidimensional data that cannot be portrayed through test scores, reading levels, or other numeric forms of assessment data. Rather, we must be attentive to capturing the rich, descriptive language our students use in our classrooms, their communities, and beyond. In Figure 5.1, we offer an adapted version of Gottlieb's (2022) qualitative rubric designed to capture students' vivid and resonant use of multiple languages. As you reflect on the dimensions of language, think about how they emerge in dual language classrooms.

Figure 5.1 Multidimensional Assessment of Classroom Language Use in Dual Language Classrooms

DIMENSIONS OF LANGUAGE	EVIDENCE OF INFLUENCE OF PARTNER LANGUAGE 1 ON PARTNER LANGUAGE 2	EVIDENCE OF TRANSLANGUAGING	EVIDENCE OF INFLUENCE OF PARTNER LANGUAGE 2 ON PARTNER LANGUAGE 1	EVIDENCE OF STUDENTS' METALINGUISTIC AWARENESS
Discourse • Directionality of writing • Cohesion of thoughts • Expressive language organization • Cross-linguistic/curricular representation of ideas • Linear versus circular thinking and coherence of ideas • Cultural patterns of dialogue				
Sentence • Syntactical order in both program languages • Complexity of structure in both program languages • Connective language in both program languages/prepositional phrases				
Phrase/Word • Cognates and false cognates • Multiple meanings • Idiomatic expressions and when they are appropriate for use • Collocations				

Source: Adapted from Gottlieb (2022, p. 136)

CAPTAIN'S LOG

1. How are the three dimensions of language developed and represented in your dual language classrooms?

   _____
   _____
   _____
   _____

2. Why are translanguaging and students' metalinguistic awareness so important in terms of collaborative assessment?

   _____
   _____
   _____
   _____

WHAT PRACTITIONERS SAY

Julianne Foster, the dual language coach at Brown Station Elementary School in Montgomery County Public Schools in Maryland, emphasized the importance of monitoring student growth across languages through collaborative practices with protected time:

The strength of our dual language program comes from its multiple and varied forms of teacher collaboration. In a week, a classroom teacher meets multiple times with their collaborative partners: teachers delivering instruction in the same target language; teachers facilitating in the partner language, but with whom they share students; and language and content specialists. As a school, we take special care in designing our school schedule to allow time for these meetings, and we set a purpose for each meeting. In general, the meetings are centered on discussing students' progress toward learning goals, anticipating obstacles to learning content as well as language, and dedicating time and instruction to making explicit language connections for our students. Throughout these conversations, we establish expectations of one another as they relate to preparing to meet students' needs.

Scheduling can make it or break it for many teachers when it comes to teacher collaboration. How can your school ensure protected time for teachers to work together?

When and Where Does Collaborative Assessment Take Place?

In Chapters 3 and 4, we established that consistent collaboration within the instructional cycle must be frequent and intentional. When dual language teachers have the opportunity to regularly work together with each other and with other program stakeholders for sustained amounts of time, they are able to carefully examine many forms of student data. When collaborative assessment time is protected, just as with collaborative planning time, teachers make connections between the established classroom/program goals, their collaborative efforts, creativity, and professional commitment to the goals of dual language education. In these ways, they can interact with the data, look for congruency between goals and outcomes, and ultimately make data-informed decisions. Some decisions may impact classroom instruction while others are reported more at the programmatic level. In both instances, the collection, analysis, and use of data must be recognized and appreciated for how the data may be used. For effective collaborative assessment, you may consider these options for *when* the collaborative assessment can take place:

- During the school day, throughout the classroom instructional cycle
- During collaborative planning for lessons and units, as well as quarterly and annual strategic planning sessions
- In the course of using appropriate technology tools and creative ways to meaningfully enhance communication
- With professional learning communities (PLCs)
- In the course of parent–teacher, student–teacher, and student–student conferences and conversations
- As an integral part of school-based professional development days

WHAT THE RESEARCH SAYS

The *Guiding Principles for Dual Language Education* (Howard et al., 2018) steer us toward teachers' and staff's needs for ongoing professional development opportunities in assessment and accountability. Exemplary-level practices are described as

> [o]ngoing professional learning experiences (e.g., workshops, data team meetings, professional learning communities [PLCs]) [that] are coordinated at the program and district level and are provided on assessment topics aligned with program goals to help teachers and administrators inform instruction, identify and communicate program outcomes, and plan for continual improvement. (Howard et al., 2018, p. 80)

What type of systematic processes are in place in your school to continually update and improve professional learning activities?

Collaborative Assessment Essentials

In Chapter 3, we explored a content-embedded linguistic angle of collaborative planning and suggested you plan to address four specific developing needs dual language learners have in your classrooms. Let's revisit them and extend our thinking by adding on the collaborative assessment considerations that go with each of the four. We invite you to stretch your brainpower a bit as you think about collaboratively assessing the following:

1. *Language progressions*—How are you measuring levels of proficiency that are represented in your classrooms? How are you measuring when your students learn language, in terms of both general language acquisition and discipline-specific academic language and literacy development in both program languages?

2. *Language demands*—How are you measuring the linguistic expectations and opportunities in both program languages that you embedded within specific texts and tasks with which your students engaged across the core content classes?

3. *Language scaffolds*—Within your assessment tools, how are you mirroring the specific representations and instructional strategies you used to help students gain access to the core concepts as well as to the languages they needed to learn?

4. *Language supports*—How are you measuring your classroom and school organization you coordinated to support students in continually building a deep understanding of both program languages across the content areas?

In the dual language context, this framework needs to be expanded to ensure you are assessing (a) equitable language and literacy development in both languages, (b) grade-level core content attainment, (c) cultural competency, and (d) critical consciousness. In order to apply these important considerations for dual language classes, we have created an assessment template incorporating this critical framework that can be used when jointly planning/replanning instruction, when you are collaboratively assessing instruction, and when you're having collaborative data discussions (see Figure 5.2).

Figure 5.2 Integrated Focus on Assessing Your Dual Language Teaching

FOCUS	KEY QUESTIONS	ASSESSMENT NOTES/MULTILINGUAL SOURCES OF EVIDENCE
Language Progressions	What are the outcomes in terms of language progressions our plans addressed?	
	What language progression patterns do we notice about the language learning standards we targeted and assessed?	
Language Expectations and Opportunities	What student outcome patterns do we notice about the content standards we targeted and assessed in terms of high expectations?	
	What academic language—general and subject-specific—is embedded in the target content, and how did we measure it?	
	What opportunities did we measure from our students as they practiced the four key language uses (narrate, inform, argue, explain)?	
Language Scaffolds	What multilingual scaffolds are needed to support measuring language and content comprehension through interpretive modes of communication (listening, reading, viewing)?	
	What multilingual scaffolds are needed to support measuring language and content through expressive modes of communication (speaking, writing, visually representing)?	

(Continued)

(Continued)

FOCUS	KEY QUESTIONS	ASSESSMENT NOTES/MULTILINGUAL SOURCES OF EVIDENCE
Community and School Language Supports	*How can we note the school-based supports we tapped into for this unit of study?*	
	How can we note the out-of-school, community-based supports we tapped into for this unit of study?	
Cultural Competence	*How effective were the materials we selected to help students develop cross-cultural competence? What evidence can we describe?*	
	What evidence do we have of learning tasks and activities that actively engaged students to demonstrate cross-cultural competence in both program languages?	
Critical Consciousness	*How can we show we have ensured that both program languages are given equitable attention and language status? What evidence can we share?*	
	How have we measured aspects of critical consciousness we wove into the lesson content and/or materials? What evidence can we share?	
	How have we measured opportunities we planned for our minoritized dual language learners to serve in linguistic leadership roles? What evidence can we share?	

CAPTAIN'S LOG

1. What other professional priorities do you have for collaborative assessment? How do you jointly determine these professional goals?

   _____
   _____
   _____
   _____

2. How will you plan to discuss moments when you notice patterns in the data that reveal potential inequities in a lesson, especially when you disagree with your collaborative partner(s)?

   _____
   _____
   _____
   _____

NAVIGATION SYSTEMS

So far in the book, we have called attention to the numerous, rich dimensions and complexities that multilingual learners bring to our classrooms. We've strongly established the need for collaboration and how it enriches dual language education. In this section of Chapter 5, we will continue to honor and leverage multilingual learners' languages, cultural identities, and academic growth in collaborative assessment. The research systems we use to guide us further are based on Margo Gottlieb's (2021) three types of assessment. They are *assessment as learning*, *assessment for learning*, and *assessment of learning*. A critical aspect of these three types is that they all keep students' assets at the core of the processes, reinforcing our focus on equity and empowerment.

In assessment *as* learning, students are the frontrunners of their own learning. From a collaborative perspective, they also work with each other in leadership roles to establish shared goals for progress. Within assessment as learning in dual language programs, students can describe their learning and express their needs for growth in content and both program languages. Assessment as learning also ensures they can actively participate in self- and peer reflections. When students actively participate at this level, they can accelerate the co-creation of opportunities to build linguistic, academic, cultural, and critically conscious abilities in both languages.

(Continued)

(Continued)

In assessment *for* learning, dual language learners build on their assessment *as* learning by including teachers in their discussions to make collaborative decisions regarding multilingual assessments. Some examples include the use of students' work samples, multilingual task development, multilingual rubrics, and other options to indicate criteria for success, as well as other multilingual classroom data sources. Assessment *for* learning, combined with assessment *as* learning, typically represents what many educators commonly label as formative assessments. In the context of dual language education, these formative assessment opportunities are unique in that they measure content and language development in *both* program languages.

Finally, assessment *of* learning in dual language education bridges classroom multilingual assessments outward to include other teachers, paraprofessionals, and additional educators (grade-level teams, content-specific department teams, coaches, facilitators, administrators, etc.). The assessment of learning usually represents what we more commonly think of as summative assessments in both program languages. Figure 5.3 represents these three layers of multilingual assessment with the dual language learners and their assets as the central stars.

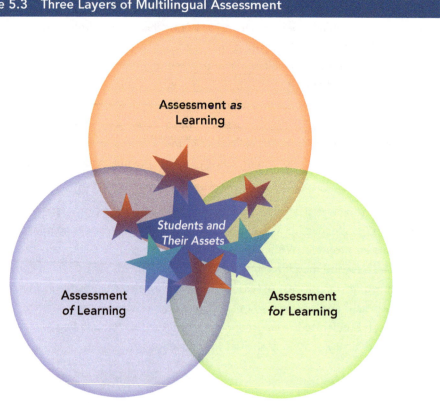

Figure 5.3 Three Layers of Multilingual Assessment

When assessment *as*, *for*, and *of* learning is collaborative, the outcomes aim to ensure a multidimensional approach to assessment practices embraced not only by dual language educators but by their students as well. When an equity lens is used and you systematically examine how you assess your students and what assessment tools and measures you use to determine what your students can do, and when you invite your students as collaborators into the assessment process, they can practice their agency and develop their learner autonomy. For example, Jaclyn Ewing and María Cristina Youtsey, fifth-grade dual language teachers at Mechanics Grove Elementary School in District 75 in Illinois, offer their students frequent opportunities to use anchor charts that not only scaffold language use and biliteracy development but also invite their students to self-assess and reflect on their own learning (see Figures 5.4 and 5.5).

Figures 5.4 and 5.5   Scaffolded Sentence Frames to Support a "Stop and Jot" Activity Complete With Self-Assessment and Reflection Opportunities

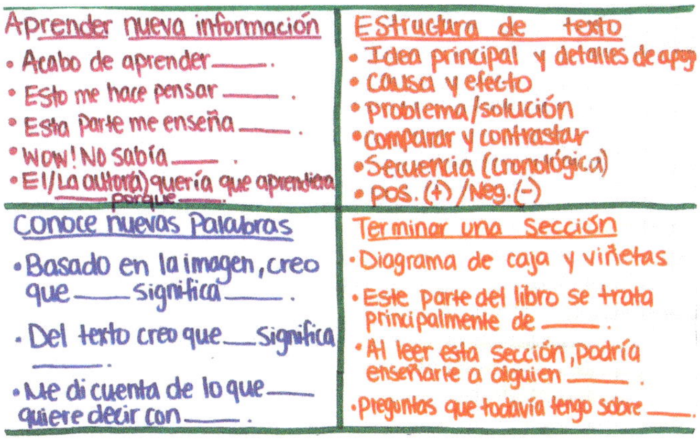

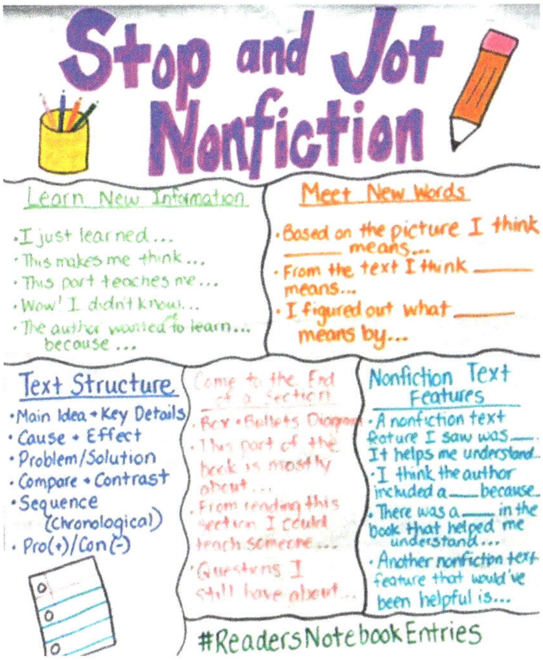

Source: Jaclyn Ewing and María Cristina Youtsey. Used with permission.

We invite you to apply some of the ideas you've learned about assessment *as*, *for*, and *of* learning in dual language education. Use or adapt the tools in Figures 5.6, 5.7, and 5.8 as a collaborative protocol of "look fors" in lesson activities to identify ways for dual language learners and their educators to monitor linguistic and academic development across partner languages. As you read the listings in the "assessment *as*, *for*, and *of* learning" columns, think about how you would create pathways for these ideas to take place in your lessons, in both program languages. You might consider using this tool alongside a lesson plan you're developing, or even some unit plans if you want to start using the protocol across multiple plans. As you use the protocols, we want you to feel empowered to show your creativity by noting ideas that best align with your classrooms and students.

Figure 5.6 A Collaborative Protocol of "Look Fors" in Lesson Activities

ASSESSMENT *AS* LEARNING	PARTNER LANGUAGE 1	PARTNER LANGUAGE 2
When and where are students asking and answering questions with each other, with spaces for translanguaging, in the instructional cycle?		
Why and where are students self-/peer assessing? How are they making connections and building metalinguistic awareness?		
How are students using their own/their peers' assessment information for new content and language learning in both partner languages?		
Add Your Own Questions to Enhance This Protocol		

Figure 5.7 A Collaborative Protocol to Co-Design Assessment Tools and Measures

ASSESSMENT *FOR* LEARNING	PARTNER LANGUAGE 1	PARTNER LANGUAGE 2
Partner teachers collaborate to co-design and collaboratively analyze concurrent assessments/outcomes aligned with lesson goals and activities in both program languages.		
Partner teachers collaborate to co-create *common* assessments used to measure language and content development in both program languages.		
Partner teachers collaborate with students to co-create *common* assessments used to measure language and content development in both program languages.		

Add Your Own Questions to Enhance This Protocol

Figure 5.8 A Collaborative Protocol to Review Existing Assessment Results

ASSESSMENT OF LEARNING	PARTNER LANGUAGE 1	PARTNER LANGUAGE 2
Partner teachers collaborate to review multilingual learners' (MLs') outcome data on school-based (programmatic) assessments that measure language and content development in both program languages.		
Partner teachers collaborate to review MLs' outcome data on local assessments that measure language and content development in both program languages.		
Partner teachers collaborate to review MLs' outcome data on state assessments that measure language and content development in both program languages.		
Add Your Own Questions to Enhance This Protocol		

Rocio Hernandez, an instructional coach in the Department of Language and Culture in Schaumburg School District 54 in Illinois, shared with us how the district's dual language program is built on a high-functioning professional learning community and what roles collaborative assessment plays in the success of the program. First things first! Rocio also shared with us that School District 54 has a multiyear strategic plan, the 54 Promise, to guide District 54's core work of ensuring whole-child student success. The 54 Promise provides the entire District 54 community clarity around the key district goals and operating priorities that drive the system ahead in the years to come, and it includes four strategic focus areas (see Figure 5.9): (1) supporting whole-child academic and social-emotional success, (2) cultivating innovation in learning spaces and instructional design, (3) recruitment, development, and engagement of exceptional personnel, and (4) facilities and fiscal responsibility. As you view and analyze the four strategic focus areas within the 54 Promise, we invite you to think about how they apply specifically to dual language programs.

LAUNCHED MISSIONS

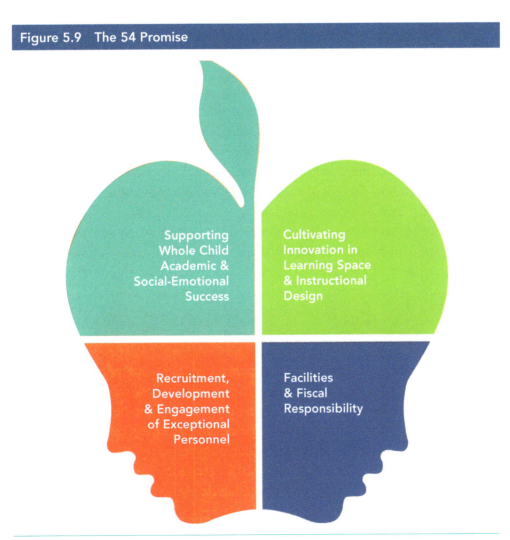

Figure 5.9 The 54 Promise

Source: Rocio Hernandez. Used with permission.

CAPTAIN'S LOG

1. How can you draw connections from each of the four focus areas to the roles collaborative assessment plays in the success of your own dual language program?

   _____
   _____
   _____
   _____

2. How can you make connections between the four focus areas and the four pillars of dual language education?

   _____
   _____
   _____
   _____

To be a successful professional learning community (PLC), Schaumburg School District 54 focuses on three big ideas: collaboration, student learning, and results. A collaborative culture involves the interdependence that exists within a PLC. A PLC meeting is more than teachers getting together to share data—it is a group of individuals who meet to achieve common goals to ensure student learning for their grade level and for the school. Instead of sharing data, District 54 educators respond to data, which requires a sense of mutual accountability and changing classroom practices. As a PLC, District 54 grade-level teams are more than a group of people working together; they are a group of people working interdependently to achieve a common goal for which they are mutually accountable. In a PLC, each educator brings strengths to the team, and to be an outstanding PLC, educators recognize and utilize their strengths.

PLC grade teams set norms or commitments at the beginning of the school year. Of her district's PLC, Rocio shared:

Making commitments to ourselves and each other aligns our values and beliefs, which determines how we choose to treat each other and how we can expect to be treated. Having made such commitments simply reminds us to be highly conscious of our actions and what we can expect from each other as we engage in conversations about our work. It is important to know our purpose, to set norms, and to build consensus for a collaborative culture in our PLC. Teams use communication tools to keep the PLC collaborating and communicating clearly.

Team norms help us live our vision each time we come together. The norms are our commitments to each other during our meetings. Setting norms clarifies direction and purpose, sets a standard of excellence, and inspires commitment. It helps to build psychological safety (a key component to building a collaborative culture) because everyone is on the same page. Teams create a list of three to five norms for meetings. These are revisited every year and as new people join the team. Here are some examples:

- Focus on what's best for students
- Maintain positive tone and words at our meetings
- Refrain from complaining about a problem unless we can offer a solution
- Come prepared for our meetings
- Stay fully engaged throughout each meeting
- Contribute equally to the workload of this team
- Listen respectfully and consider matters from another's perspective

Within our PLCs, we continuously reflect on four critical questions to ensure student success. These four PLC questions help us define and refine what our team is collaborating about:

- What is it we want all students to know and be able to do?
- How will we know if each student has learned it?
- How will we respond when students don't learn it?
- How will we extend for students who have already demonstrated mastery?

In addition, we formulate a team vision, which reminds us all of the purpose of our team and drives behaviors, creativity, commitment, engagement, and determination. We believe that a vision statement is our written commitments to each other as we work together. As such:

- It is clear and concise.
- It is in agreement with the commitments of the team.
- It answers the following questions:
    - Who are we?
    - What do we do?
    - What do we stand for?
    - Why do we do it?

Based on these criteria, we developed the following dual language vision statements:

> Our students will:
> - ☐ Perform academically at grade level in two languages, commensurate with their monolingual English-speaking peers.
> - ☐ Use two languages comfortably and effectively in social situations appropriate for their age level.
> - ☐ Communicate effectively through reading and writing in two languages at a level appropriate for their age.
> - ☐ Demonstrate an appreciation of cultural diversity and develop cross-cultural competence.

This vision well supports our commitment to continue to build a collaborative culture.

Our curriculum was developed *by* teachers in District 54, *for* teachers in District 54. The standards were determined first by answering the four critical questions. After answering these critical questions, teams of teachers select the very best materials to teach each standard. If we truly have a guaranteed and viable curriculum, it means:

- No matter who teaches a given course or grade level, we guarantee that topics identified in the curriculum will be covered in every class.

- Every single student will be taught the same essential knowledge and skills. The execution might look different in each classroom, but the skill/standard will be consistent.

As effective educators, we need to set and hold high expectations for *all* students.

- Standards are the floor. They are only the starting point. How teachers teach the content to ensure all students learn the material is up to them and their PLC.

- Value each instructional minute to get the most out of each subject area. Minimizing downtime and filling each instructional minute ensures students are being exposed to the guaranteed and viable curriculum, ultimately leading to learning.

- Collecting anecdotal notes/data during small-group instruction ensures we're communicating successes (stars) and challenges (wishes) to our students, gathering data to help drive future instruction and to assist in making instructional decisions to ensure best practices are in place.

- Utilizing curricular resource guides ensures that instructional supports are in place for literacy and math instruction. These guides aid in scaffolding and differentiating instruction to best meet the needs of *all* learners.

As a PLC, we utilize common formative assessments. After implementing the guaranteed and viable curriculum, assessments are given to determine if student learning has taken place. We examine student data and reflect on current and future teaching practices. Analyzing student performance helps to ensure all students are on the path to mastery. Our assessments:

- Inform students of the next steps they must take in their learning.

- Inform each teacher of individual students who need intervention because they are struggling to learn or who need extension because they are already proficient.

- Inform each member of the team of their strengths and weaknesses in teaching particular skills so each member can provide or solicit help from colleagues on the team.

- Inform the team of areas where many students are struggling so that the team can develop and implement better strategies for teaching those areas.

Common formative assessments are key to knowing each student and informing our next steps in learning. Within our PLC grade-level teams, we utilize common assessments to identify students' areas of strengths and goals. The PLC creates the assessments collaboratively, and these types of assessments help with grouping for acceleration along with planning differentiated lessons.

CAPTAIN'S LOG

1. What stands out for you regarding the role of PLCs in the Schaumburg School District 54 dual language program?

   _____
   _____
   _____
   _____

2. What did you notice about the use of common formative assessments?

   _____
   _____
   _____
   _____

STAYING THE COURSE

As we come to the conclusion of Chapter 5, we share a set of the Core Beliefs and "Let's Agree" Statements regarding collaborative assessment. Remember, as in the prior chapters, these concepts and beliefs are what keeps us safely connected to the notion that we must stay on the course of empowerment, equity, heart spaces, and strength for all dual language programs.

Core Beliefs

- Multilingual learners are intellectuals.
- Collaborative assessment practices must be authentic, multidimensional, multifaceted, and aligned with the four pillars of dual language education.
- Well-crafted dual language programs require collaborative assessment frameworks to support measuring what *all* multilingual learners *can do*.

"Let's Agree" Statements

Let's make a commitment for collaborative assessment to be recognized and enacted as a student-centered endeavor, and as such, let's embrace the following:

1. Collaborative assessment processes first include students' voices.
2. Collaborative assessment processes must also include dimensions of critical consciousness.
3. Authentic assessment in dual language classrooms is ongoing and must involve students, families, and communities.
4. Collaborative assessment is multidimensional and multifaceted.
5. Collaborative reflection is a key component of understanding dynamic multilingualism.

Collaborative Reflection

As we transform our collaborative practices in dual language education to be truly multidimensional, we must also shift our actions to increase our collaborative reflections. Biliteracy development is based on the intertwining of both languages, a process we all agree to describe as deeply complex. Kathy Escamilla and colleagues (2014) remind us that collaborative zones/trajectory approaches to classroom language and content development are highly beneficial and require teachers' ongoing reflection regarding students' momentums and movements within the zones and trajectories. In agreement, Stephen Brookfield (2017) advises the use of regular, disciplined, critical reflection. We invite you to try out the four-lens approach to reflection or devise different approaches to support your efforts with your collaborative team members and teaching partners in order to fully integrate reflective inquiry into your collaborative assessment practices. For reflection to be continual, its documentation needs to be easily and readily accomplished. As you begin to consider how your reflective practices will take shape, you may wonder what types of strategies are needed to make ongoing reflection a success. Brookfield suggests that we view what we do, and we form assumptions about the teaching–learning process that takes place in our classrooms, through four different lenses. We've adapted them for the dual language context:

The students' eyes:
- What are the students seeing and experiencing as they assess their own multilingual/multiliteracy development?

Our colleagues' perceptions:
- What are our colleagues seeing and experiencing within the collaborative assessment processes that are reflective of sociocultural competencies?

Our own personal experiences:
- What have we experienced in the past that is similar to or different from what our multilingual learners experienced? What connections can I make to my own sense of critical consciousness?

Relevant theory and research:
- What do related educational theory and research have to say about these experiences as they align with all four pillars of dual language education?

After thinking about these four lenses of in-depth professional reflection, what do you see as your current strengths in your own reflective practices? In what ways would you like to increase your personal and professional reflections? And finally, how will you weave in collaborative reflection with your colleagues?

Chapter 5 has facilitated our learning about many collaborative assessment processes in dual language programs. To strengthen collaborative practices, it's important to generate practical ideas about co-assessment *as*, *for*, and *of* learning in dual language education. See Figure 5.10 for completed examples of actionable steps partnering educators can take to collaboratively assess their multilingual students.

GEAR UP!

Figure 5.10 Actionable Steps for Co-Assessment *as*, *for*, and *of* Learning in Dual Language Education

Ideas for Collaborative Assessment *as* Learning	• Self-select progress on student-friendly standards rubric in both program languages. • Students self-/peer assess using multilingual rubrics in both program languages to measure their ability to independently use new/academic language in a lesson activity/lesson tasks. • Students reflect before, during, and after their work, on their learning and growth toward the lesson goals, both content and language related (*a bit blurry*, *somewhat clear*, *very clear*, *so clear I can explain it to others*, etc.). • Multilingual feedback is timely, purposeful, and strategic, and it enhances self-/peer reflection and students' growth. • Collaborative projects on a certain topic/story/content in either or both program languages allow for making bridged connections. • Students reflect on progress in both program languages whenever possible. • Students self-/peer assess their skills and monitor/share about progress in multilingual ways. • Students create their own multilingual assessments and quizzes/test items/projects for the unit and then have the teacher(s) enact the assessments, bridging both program languages. • Students periodically self-assess "levels of understanding" of content, cultural connections, and critically conscious topics. • Multilingual writing workshops—students share their written work in both program languages and have spaces for translanguaging conversations, to offer each other multilingual *glows* and *grows*. • Teachers give ongoing feedback in both program languages when appropriate while students are working.
Ideas for Collaborative Assessment *for* Learning	• Use universal, clearly understood multilingual rubrics. • Students provide peer feedback (with translanguaging spaces when appropriate) on written books/comics before turning in the final draft. • Learning clearly builds on previous assignments (backward planning) so student examples in either program language can be brought back and reevaluated by peers. • Assessment tightly and transparently aligns with what students learned rather than what students should have learned. • Students help create rubrics in both program languages for scoring. • Pre-assessments allow students and teachers to see where they can improve and what they need to know. • One-on-one and small-group conferences with translanguaging spaces are provided when appropriate. • Consistent multilingual opportunities/checkpoints for feedback are offered in the language of content instruction during projects.

Ideas for Collaborative Assessment *of* Learning	• To allow for multilingual innovation, students should serve as leaders in the collaborative assessment processes to help with designing ways to show what they have learned in both program languages. • Students feel confident to take risks, think creatively, and share in multilingual ways about the ideas and concepts they are learning. • Focus (quantitatively/qualitatively) on what students did well in both content and language development rather than what they did incorrectly. • Conduct "learning walks" where teachers/students see each other's multilingual work. • Engage in the collaborative process of collecting multilingual data on student performance to inform instructional decision making. • Adapt or adjust the flow in both program languages. • Rubrics in both program languages will serve as checklists for teachers/students—and redos are encouraged with spaces for translanguaging when appropriate. • Assessments include directions and rubrics for content and language objectives. • Provide as many project-based options as possible. Language is co-created. • Start with four corners to show where you stand in terms of knowledge or opinions, then engage in discussion and possible shift in corners. • Posttest to measure student and teacher success. • Reflect informally on how a lesson went. • Assessments in both program languages should be a balanced combination of formative and summative throughout the learning experiences.

EL ESPEJO Framework

To further support your learning, we invite you to enhance your collaborative practice through a recently created tool. Margo Gottlieb (2021) reminds us of the need for explicit alignment among curriculum, instruction, and assessment. She developed the Embedded Language Expectations for Systemic Planning, Enacting, and Justifying Outcomes (EL ESPEJO) framework, which is a "linguistically and culturally sustainable curricular model that exemplifies the interplay among content, language, and culture" (p. 65). We believe it's an ideal option for you to add to your tool kit for practice.

In this framework, unit planning intentionally *mirrors* lesson planning dimensions while making deliberate connections to assessment *as*, *for*, and *of* learning, hence the name EL ESPEJO, which means *mirror* in Spanish. With the use of this framework, we are able to see how lessons build on one another with both depth and breadth—developing content and multilingualism together. Figure 5.11 is adapted from Gottlieb (2021) to add the dimension of critical consciousness to this framework.

Figure 5.11 EL ESPEJO Framework Adapted for Dual Language Classrooms

Unit Planning Based on a Compelling Question or Theme

Classroom/Grade-Level Products, Projects, or Performances With Use of Multimodalities	Community and Environmental Resources for Learning (Funds of Multilingual Knowledge)	Coordinated Language and Content Standards, Including Disciplinary Practices and Focus Genres	Integrated Learning Goals/Targets for Content and Language With Crosslinguistic and Transcultural Considerations	Language Use Associated With a Socioculturally Relevant, Compelling Question, Theme, or Issue	Language Use for Critical Consciousness (Social Justice and Equity)

Considerations for Assessment *as*, *for*, and *of* Learning

Classroom Learning Tasks and Activities With Multimodal Resources	Student and Family Resources for Learning (Funds of Multilingual Identity)	Coordinated Language and Content Standards	Integrated Targets/ Objectives for Content and Language With Crosslinguistic/Cross-Cultural Application	Oral, Written, Visual, and Digital Engagement With Socioculturally Relevant Compelling Question, Theme, or Issue	Oral, Written, Visual, and Digital Engagement With Critical Consciousness (Social Justice and Equity)

Lesson Planning Based on Key Dual Language Practices

Source: Adapted from Gottlieb (2021)

A mirrored unit and lesson planning approach such as the one promoted by EL ESPEJO ensures consistent navigation and systemic alignment of the planning processes while also deepening critical consciousness with both the teachers and their students.

In addition to the EL ESPEJO tool from Figure 5.11, we invite you to co-develop and add further items to your own collaborative assessment and reflection tool kit items.

- Protocols for collaboratively assessing student data
- Tools for co-designing assessments with the students
- Tools for students to use with each other to measure their own learning in both program languages
- Protocols for sharing examples of student assessments with other teachers and administrators both in and apart from the dual language program
- Multilingual tools for sharing examples of students' assessment data with parents

Investing time into in-depth conversations with your partner teacher and other collaborating educators will also result in engaging in a range of highly impactful professional activities. Why does it matter? Your collaboration will contribute to job-embedded, ongoing professional learning and shared ownership of the work by virtue of:

- Collecting and analyzing formative and summative student data in both program languages to inform planning and instruction
- Strategically planning your instruction based on monitoring student growth
- Reflecting on the teaching–learning process that took place in the class
- Negotiating the taught curriculum so that it integrates dual language and literacy development with culturally and linguistically responsive and sustaining content instruction as well as critically conscious topics and projects
- Collecting and analyzing data about teachers' own effectiveness and impact on student learning, dual language oracy, and literacy development in both program languages
- Considering and frequently celebrating each other's strengths as collaborative instructional partners

As we wrap up the Gear Up! portion of Chapter 5, we share the ideas of Shera Simpson and Elizabeth Howard (2021). They remind us that teacher collaboration in the dual language context is necessary to establish ways "to leverage our respective strengths, address our respective challenges, and integrate our different working styles in order to provide a cohesive, engaging, and effective classroom environment for our students" (p. 1). Let's take these reminders of strength through collaboration with us as we Tune In! to additional resources that may support your work, helping you keep equity in action as you move forward in transforming dual language education.

Here are some key links to books, articles, reports, and organizations to support your collaborative assessment endeavors as you *aim for the stars*:

Books

Brookfield, S. (2017). *Becoming a critically reflective teacher* (2nd ed.). Jossey-Bass.

Calderón, M. E., Dove, M. G., Staehr Fenner, D., Gottlieb, M., Honigsfeld, A., Ward Singer, T., Slakk, S., Soto, I., & Zacarian, D. (2020). *Breaking down the wall: Essential shifts for English learners' success*. Corwin.

Escamilla, K., Hopewell, S., Butvilofsky, S., Sparrow, W., Soltero-González, L., Ruiz-Figueroa, O., & Escamilla, M. (2014). *Biliteracy from the start: Literacy squared in action*. Caslon.

Gottlieb, M. (2021). *Classroom assessment in multiple languages: A handbook for teachers*. Corwin.

Gottlieb, M. (2022). *Assessment in multiple languages: A handbook for school and district leaders*. Corwin.

Web-Based Resources

Foltos, L. (2018, January 29). Teachers learn better together. *Edutopia*. https://www.edutopia.org/article/teachers-learn-better-together

Paul H. Brookes Publishing. (2022, February 24). Screening and assessment of dual language learners: Four essential resources. *Brookes Blog*. https://blog.brookespublishing.com/screening-assessment-of-dual-language-learners-4-essential-resources

TUNE IN!

Consider the following practical tips for implementing collaborative assessment practices:

10. Showcase your students' multilingual, multicultural work and celebrate them often.
9. Remember: Assessment is not grading.
8. Always define students in ways that go far beyond their test scores, language levels, and other numbers.
7. Recognize students' unique talents and gifts, rather than their identifying deficiencies.
6. Remember it is never too late to learn new things.
5. Try new ways of capturing all the knowledge, skills, and language your students have developed.
4. Collaboratively develop multilingual assessment tasks, tools, and measures.
3. Collaboratively administer multilingual, multidimensional assessments.
2. Collaboratively interpret data and make sense of students' multilingual progress together as you reflect on your next steps.
1. Keep your students' *star assets* at the core of your collaborative assessment and reflective practices.

COUNTDOWN TO LAUNCH

CAPTAIN'S LOG: FINAL ENTRY

Bringing you back to the Mission Control messages you had at the beginning of the chapter, let's reflect on your takeaways and new ideas as you prepare to take off from Chapter 5. Your final entry offers you a space to log your own thoughts and voice for future use, especially while sharing the information with others.

1. What are a few new key essential elements of collaborative assessment *as*, *for*, and *of* dual language learning you want to implement? What are two actions you can take right away?

   _____
   _____
   _____
   _____

2. How will you transform your collaborative assessment and reflection practices to be aligned with the four pillars of dual language education?

   _____
   _____
   _____
   _____

Collaborative Leadership Support for Dual Language Programs

6

"The final stage of equity-centered transformation is to move on your emerging ideas with a mindset of courage."

—Shane Safir and Jamila Dugan

MISSION CONTROL

Dual language programs get established, grow, and thrive only with a range of stakeholders' commitment and hard work. District and school administrators, coaches, and other instructional leaders play a pivotal role in the success of dual language initiatives. The fundamental goals of Chapter 6 are to:

1. Explore three types of collaborative partnerships teachers and administrators form to make transformative decisions in dual language programs

2. Identify and map out teachers' and administrators' essential roles in establishing a collaborative approach to transform dual language programs

3. Establish connections to the four pillars of dual language education in collaborative leadership practices

EXPLORATION

Before we launch our exploration into collaborative leadership practices, let's look at this topic from the perspectives of a dual language teacher and an administrator. In the previous chapters, we've explained that collaboration in dual language programs takes shape in many different configurations. In this example, a grade-level team of seventh-grade teachers are paired to work collaboratively. They deliver different content subjects via different program languages. Yet, their students' successes are dependent on their collaborative teacher leadership practices to bridge content and language development. Karen Beeman and Cheryl Urow (2013) remind us that *The Bridge* is "the instructional moment when teachers help students connect the content area knowledge and skills they have learned in one language to the other language" (p. 4). In the following vignette, Katie demonstrates teacher leadership as she makes a specific reference to bridging as a part of her grade-level team's collaborative discussions.

Through a Teacher's Eyes

My name is Katie, and I'm a seventh-grade math teacher in a K–8 Spanish and English dual language school in Virginia. I teach my classes in English, and I work with a partner teacher who delivers his instruction in science in Spanish. When I think about the ways in which our school teams make decisions, I cannot imagine any of us working well without each other. We have regular grade-level team meetings to discuss big ideas we're teaching, as well as the kids' needs based on how they are working in all our classes, and then we drill down to other important details such as bridging curricular topics, and language and literacy practices across both Spanish and English. We discuss instructional strategies that point our students to thinking about the knowledge and skills they learned in English to make direct connections between knowledge and skills in Spanish, and vice versa—across the subject areas. We have regular meetings with other teachers in our professional learning communities (PLCs), the instructional coaches, and our administrators so we can be sure we're really complementing each other's instruction without being repetitious. We're very fortunate to have an administrative team that asks us for our input and makes program decisions with us in mind. We also get a lot of information from the administrative team about things we can't really control, like the state mandates for testing, but we do work together to do what we can for our students. Our collaboration is critical for the program. I feel like I'm a leader and that my professional skills are valued. And I also feel encouraged to share my ideas with everyone. We all work together, even when we disagree. We also work together to keep detailed examples of student data. That makes the conversations with kids, parents, and other administrators organized and clear. We have to collaborate to do all of the work we do well.

WHAT THE RESEARCH SAYS

In a study on successful leadership practices, Victoria Hunt (2011) found the following to be true, especially with regard to teachers supporting other teachers:

> Collaborative leadership is the reason many dual language programs last and continue to develop. Principals support teachers, teachers support their principals, and teachers support other teachers. . . . When a principal leaves the school, and leadership changes, it is the collaborative work of the teachers that maintains the program. Creating avenues for leadership to move beyond the principal is critical in promoting the enduring success of a dual language program. (p. 203)

In what way(s) may Katie's experiences be affirmed by this seminal research about the role of teachers as leaders with each other?

Through an Administrator's Eyes

My name is Joseph, and I'm a dual language school principal in a K–8 Spanish–English program on the western side of Virginia. I have been in a leadership role for nearly 10 years and have learned a lot about the importance of making decisions together with many different leadership teams, starting with our students and their families. By the time they reach the end of eighth grade, the students in our program are very different kinds of learners and thinkers. Putting it simply, they are deeply involved in problem solving, not only within the curriculum at our school, but also as actively involved leaders for the program itself. I heavily rely on all the students' input and the insights I gain from their families about why our program exists, what changes we need to make, and how we can always look at program growth to meet their needs. That's why we're here, after all—for the students, their families, and our communities. Over time I've had some challenging conversations. In working closely with my teachers, my leadership teams, the district, and the state, I've learned how to shift my conversations to promote dual language, keeping equity as a part of the dialogue. Having the support of many educator leaders is why I stay in my role. I still get some pushback from stakeholders, especially about funding. Whenever I have to answer hard questions about the program decisions (whether I trust my teachers to make them, make them collaboratively, or make them administratively), I can talk numbers, and I have data readily accessible, but I am also intentional about sharing students' voices that more authentically represent their experiences. All this makes the dialogue impactful and transformational.

CAPTAIN'S LOG

1. How do Katie's and Joseph's expertise and experiences contribute to a collaborative approach to dual language leadership?

   _____
   _____
   _____
   _____

2. What are some ideas you have about addressing difficult questions with stakeholders?

   _____
   _____
   _____
   _____

Figure 6.1 presents a few examples of how we can work together to shift our own dialogues, much like Joseph in the vignette expressed. In what ways can you begin to shift your dialogues and conversations with program stakeholders? How can we keep the students and their families at the core of decisions made on all levels?

Figure 6.1 Transforming Dialogues With Parents and Other Stakeholders

TOPIC	WHAT LEADERS MAY FREQUENTLY HEAR	TRANSFORMED DIALOGUES
Literacy Development (Bi/Multi)	It's taking too long for my child to learn two languages. The dual language program is holding him back, and he's behind in reading English.	It's very common for parents to be concerned about their child's progress, and we can probably all agree that we want our children to progress in their learning. When our kids are becoming biliterate, the processes take additional time, which isn't a negative thing. Dual language students really show their academic and social gains as they approach the upper elementary grades and even more so into middle and high school. Learning new content via two languages takes time.
School Attendance	So many kids from minoritized populations have excessive absences from school. They're at such high risk for dropping out.	Research tells us that kids enrolled in dual language schools, especially when they are from all kinds of cultural, socioeconomic, racial, and linguistic backgrounds, tend to come to school regularly, reducing the numbers of absences. The students tend to want to be at school in an environment where they feel they are thriving—and are encouraged to be multilingual.
Hiring Teachers	There is a national shortage of bilingual teachers, and it is nearly impossible to hire sufficient teachers to build the dual language program.	Let's think about all our bilingual community members, paraprofessionals, current high school students, and others. How can we recruit them to work with us in dual language schools? What supports would they need for certification purposes? Who are the stakeholders we need to involve in our conversations?
Curricular Materials	We don't have enough funding to purchase books in English and Spanish.	It would be more cost-effective if we purchased materials in both program languages that complement each other rather than buying twice the numbers of books. In this way we can support bridging practices in our program. We can also be innovative by facilitating opportunities for our secondary dual language students to create community-based, authentic materials for us to use in our schools. In this way they have options to showcase their bi/multilingual writing skills, artistic talents, and stories to embrace community assets.
Limited Space in Dual Language Programs	The spaces in dual language programs should be held for the kids who are serious about school—for those who are already high flyers.	Research tells us that all kids benefit from dual language education. Therefore, we really need to think about the students in our communities with the most needs. How can we focus on program expansion so we can offer dual language to everyone?
Program Length	We don't have enough teachers to even think about expanding into secondary school. Let's just end the program after the fifth grade.	Research tells us that building secondary options is critical for students' continued successes and deepened multilingualism. What can we do early on for vertical planning to build in secondary options?

Ready to Launch the Exploration

As we continue to unpack leadership practices in dual language, we'll acknowledge the many stakeholders whose willingness to collaborate and coordinate efforts may lead to successful program implementation. We will also explore the types of decisions teachers and administrators make to transform dual language programs and delve into collaborative practices that foster shared leadership. From the beginning of the chapter, we want to honor the complexities of collaborative decision making and distinguish among different levels and types of leadership necessary to support a collaborative approach to dual language programming. Furthermore, we recognize the importance of this incredibly hard work for the benefit of the multilingual learners in the tens of thousands of classrooms and thousands of schools and communities. As we read further, the chapter's navigation systems will identify and map out teachers' and administrators' essential roles in establishing a collaborative approach to transform dual language programs.

WHAT THE RESEARCH SAYS

Kate Menken (2017) notes that leadership for dual language education "is not concentrated in only one individual, but includes teams of administrators, instructional staff, parents and families impacting decisions which value bilingualism and multicultural perspectives" (p. 2).

Similarly, John DeFlaminis and colleagues (2016) also suggest mutual interdependence among multiple members of a school community to be leveraged by the school principal:

> *The expectation that principals be content experts across all disciplines, not to mention the accompanying pedagogical approaches particular to each subject and field of study, is unreasonable. In reality, principals must know instruction, but they also must be able to tap into the knowledge and expertise of other educators.* (p. xvi).

What is your experience with leadership roles and responsibilities in dual language programming? In what ways can collaborative leadership leverage multiple school community members' knowledge and expertise?

When we think about the many stakeholders and their varying roles, we also think about the levels of decision making in the mix. For example, school boards of education are charged with making large, budgetary decisions and perhaps even making the final decision of whether the dual language programs are maintained, expanded, or, sadly, eliminated. Human resources departments work with administrators to address the complexities of the staffing and personnel, which is a significant undertaking given the unique pedagogies dual language teachers will implement and the shortage of dual language teachers nationwide. In Figure 6.2, we capture a small example of the many stakeholder intricacies of participation in dual language decision making. As you look at the figure, we invite you to reflect on what roles each plays in your program. What other details might you add?

Figure 6.2 Stakeholders in Dual Language Programs

Families: Sharing and addressing successes and concerns

Other Dual Language Administrators: Engaging in professional learning at local, state, national, and international conferences

Community Members: Ensuring transparency about the benefits of the program

Federal Agencies: Reporting for programmatic funding

School-Level Teams: Contributing input for scheduling, curricular materials, and assessments

Multilingual Students

State Education Agencies: Relaying programmatic needs based on holistic evaluations

District-Level Coaches: Supporting multilingual learners via data-informed practices

Local Boards of Education: Reporting and justifying goals to maintain or expand the program

Human Resources Departments: Hiring personnel and finding the best fits for the program

CAPTAIN'S LOG

1. Consider the stakeholders presented in Figure 6.2. How do they contribute to the administrative and collaborative decisions that are made in your dual language program?

   _____
   _____
   _____
   _____

2. How can existing curriculum, instruction, and leadership capacities be used to make the school a more effective and nurturing place for all?

   _____
   _____
   _____
   _____
   _____

Decisions, Decisions, and More Decisions!

Did you know that a recent study in psychology (Nolte et al., 2019) indicates the average person makes nearly 35,000 decisions every day? Alyson Klein (2021) also recently cited some seminal research that suggests that teachers make at least 1,500 decisions daily. Either way, that is a lot of decisions! How about *collaborative* decision making? What would you tell others about the numbers of and types of collaborative decisions you make every day at school? Some decisions may feel very comfortable and almost automatic, such as deciding to use bilingual anchor charts to support a lesson. Other decisions may feel a bit more thought-provoking, or even like rocket science at times, similar to NASA's Mission Control Center team when they collaboratively decide many things about two rockets' trajectories while avoiding a collision.

WHAT PRACTITIONERS SAY

Gloria Cho, K–8 department head in the Brockton (MA) Public Schools' Department of Bilingual–ESL Services, shares her insight on the many decisions that have to be made within the context of a dual language program and the importance of collaboration among school and district leadership and a range of other stakeholders:

The ongoing collaboration between the district and the school leadership is a key factor to ensure that research-based approaches in programming, curriculum and instruction, professional development, teacher recruitment, lottery and registration procedure, family engagement, and any other ongoing tasks are planned and structured with consideration of the building context. For example, I and Natalie Pohl, who is the principal of the Manthala George, Jr. Global Studies School, meet weekly with the building leadership team that is comprised of the principal, assistant principal, literacy coach, language acquisition coach, and science, technology, engineering, and mathematics (STEM) coach, as well as district administrators such as the director of Title I services, to discuss data, instruction, needs for support from the district, protocols, and any other weekly agenda co-created among the team members. In addition, both the department head and the principal attend the state organization's dual language leadership network, conferences, and professional development to align the knowledge and current practices to reflect on and plan the next steps together. The budget allocation and logistical support for conferences, professional development, recruitment, and lottery, as well as purchasing online and physical materials, are provided by the bilingual department leadership team such as the director, the coordinator, and the assessment specialist. The lottery process requires close collaboration between the parent information center that oversees district-level registration and the bilingual department, as they share registration and transportation data. Any changes in enrollment are communicated among the school building, the bilingual department, and the parent information center. The school secretary and the bilingual department secretary document the forms and changes in our student data system under the supervision of the bilingual coordinator. Finally, the kindergarten screening and subsequent parent orientations cannot be done without the bilingual community facilitators and advocates who contact and communicate with multilingual families as well as the kindergarten teachers who meet the parents and screen the students. It truly takes a village.

Gloria discusses the many logistical challenges and possible solutions surrounding her district's dual language program. What works for you in your context?

We can probably all agree that self-reflection of our own teaching and learning may present areas where we would like to change our practices and grow in our own capacities. Even with the willingness to move forward, sometimes making transformations to our practices is difficult. Shane Safir and Jamila Dugan (2021) remind us that change can feel challenging, sometimes even downright hard. Even so, collaborative decision making is especially crucial for programmatic transformation through equity, changed pedagogies, and strategies for program-wide progress. Dual language teachers, administrators, students, parents, community members, and other stakeholders make decisions about many program-related aspects—all with many pieces and moving parts. Chapter 6 aims to guide you to explore a range of transformative decisions teachers and administrators make in dual language programs using three types of leadership adapted from Douglas Reeves's (2020) work (see Figure 6.3).

1. Teacher Leadership: Partnering teachers collaborate.
2. Collaborative Leadership: Partnering teachers and administrators collaborate.
3. Administrative Leadership: Administrators collaborate with stakeholder input.

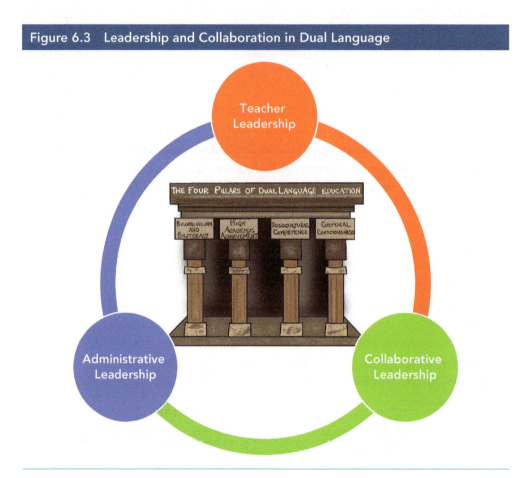

Figure 6.3 Leadership and Collaboration in Dual Language

The first of the three types of collaborative leadership (Reeves, 2020) we are adapting for making transformative decisions in dual language programs is *Teacher Leadership*. As teachers collaboratively plan, teach, assess, and reflect, they are making numerous important decisions with each other, especially about how to adapt the curriculum, create corresponding instructional materials, engage students actively in the teaching–learning cycle, and contribute authentically to the holistic program evaluation. The second type is *Collaborative Leadership* where teachers and administrators make decisions together by learning with and from all stakeholders and jointly shaping the program based on ongoing progress monitoring. The third, *Administrative Leadership*, refers to curricular, fiscal, and staffing decisions that school and district leaders have to make based on local, state, and federal guidelines and policies with input from all stakeholders.

Teacher Leadership: Teachers Making Decisions With Teachers

In partnerships where dual language teachers are strategically paired to work together, either in the same classroom or in parallel classes, the collective decision-making processes are beneficial in so many ways, starting with modeling collaboration for their students. We know that well-crafted dual language instruction is not only transformational for the participating students and teachers; it may also contribute to a vehicle for school-wide and systemic reform. And we also know that collaborative teaching and learning is one of the most important strategies dual language teachers use in the classroom for the co-creation of language and content concepts (Thomas & Collier, 2017). These findings help us focus on teachers serving as critical role models for multilingual students. For these reasons and more, we honor their impact as teacher leaders in classrooms, schools, and communities. When collaborating teachers have regular, in-depth conversations, they make informed decisions with each other in very different ways than teachers who might only have the chance to periodically communicate with each other via emails or sit next to each other during staff meetings every now and then. When teachers collaborate, they put their heads together, leading to double the brain power, double the innovative thinking, and double the careful considerations to make valuable decisions for their students' learning (Lachance, 2020). Let's explore some specific ways dual language partner teachers make decisions about curriculum, instruction, and assessment practices together while building agency for leadership.

Engaging in Transformative Collaborative Conversations

Dual language partner teachers and co-teaching pairs make collective decisions toward what we refer to as *multidimensional teaching and learning*, in which the curricular and instructional transformations grow. When we say multidimensional teaching and learning, we are referring to instructional design that is built on the four pillars of dual language education while also facilitating students' active engagement with each other and with the content (Fredricks, 2014). Activities that are project-based and have group-worthy tasks to substantiate co-created learning are nonnegotiables for multilingual students' development. As a result, students are actively participating in a rich curriculum rather than simply surviving daily instruction, or observing it as an outsider, and feeling like they are being linguistically and culturally flattened (Guerrero & Lachance, 2018).

Consider how you engage in critical conversations and how you work toward curricular and instructional transformations. Sincere, in-depth discussions with each other build communication that leads to shifting your discourse for collective outcomes. As partner teachers, you may have daily discussions, some that are quick and others that take more time. There are other occasions when your conversations will extend beyond your classrooms to be shared with others who are a bit more separate from your close partnership. For example, you may have opportunities to strategically carve out time for discussions with grade-level teams, explaining and describing the curricular decisions you've made for them to consider. An even greater extension to propel your teacher agency leadership is to share your work with members of your PLCs (see Launched Mission later in the chapter).

We invite you to explore the list of discussion prompts in Figure 6.4 to jump-start decision-making discussion. Feel free to add some of your own examples that relate to your context. Remember, you may be as creative and innovative as you wish when you think about the information and examples of the collaborative decisions you want to make and share, how you want to share them, and with whom.

Figure 6.4   Discussion Prompts for Teachers' Collaborative Curricular and Instructional Decisions

How have we included lesson activities with culturally and linguistically rich curricular materials that uphold high standards?

_____

_____

_____

_____

What did we strategically decide to change about our daily routine to increase students' use of their full linguistic repertoires?

_____

_____

_____

_____

What are some examples of how we have increased the ways and frequencies in which our students write collaboratively using both program languages? How can we showcase students' work samples?

_____

_____

_____

_____

What decisions can we make/have we made together about our daily lessons to increase opportunities for students to actively use their languages in new ways with each other?

_____

_____

_____

_____

What more do we need to think about so that students are more actively engaged with connecting curricular topics to bridge languages, rather than simple repetition of the same lesson topics in both program languages?

_____

_____

_____

_____

When do we have opportunities to share ideas/examples from our curricular and instructional decisions with grade-level team partners? How should we best leverage collaboration time?

_____

_____

_____

_____

When do we have opportunities to share ideas/examples from our work with PLCs? How may it be different than what we shared with our grade-level teams?

_____

_____

_____

_____

How will we offer our grade-level teams and/or PLCs transferrable ideas from our collaborative progress?

_____

_____

_____

_____

Which school-wide initiatives can we help advance? How can we leverage our collaborative expertise?

_____

_____

_____

_____

(Continued)

(Continued)

> Add your own discussion questions here:
>
> • _____
>   _____
>   _____
>   _____
>
> • _____
>   _____
>   _____
>   _____
>
> • _____
>   _____
>   _____
>   _____

There are no limits on what you can explore and discover when you collaboratively discuss your ideas with each other. However, you may experience feelings of vulnerability when discussing your experiences and sharing your personal and pedagogical beliefs. Shane Safir (2017) reminds us that trust is fragile. Building relational trust within collaborative partnerships is essential for program success. In *Atlas of the Heart,* Brené Brown (2021) guides us in a parallel way regarding emotions and trust in professional relationships. She especially emphasizes elements of trust in a relationship such as nonjudgment, integrity, generosity, reliability, and accountability. She says, "I believe with an adventurous heart and the right maps, we can travel anywhere" (Brown, 2021, p. xxvii). With these ideas in mind, we invite you to reflect on what you believe to be important discussion norms to consider as you keep your conversations heart-centered and sincere (see Figure 6.5).

Figure 6.5 Conversations From the Heart

Examine Figure 6.5 more closely. Which of the conversation norms in the heart would you identify as your top five priorities? Which additional norms might you add that aren't shown in the heart?

1. _____
2. _____
3. _____
4. _____
5. _____
- _____
- _____

CAPTAIN'S LOG

WHAT THE RESEARCH SAYS

Think back to Chapter 5, where we explored the importance of listening to students from Shane Safir's (2017) research regarding viewing students as intellectuals. She reminds us:

> As educators, we need to listen to our students as intellectuals. New teachers often focus on getting to know things about their students' personal lives, which is important, but the student-teacher relationship is fundamentally an intellectual enterprise. . . . We are aiming to practice attention to nonverbal cues, mature empathy, and affirmation, not the pobrecito syndrome. (p. 170)

In what ways are your relationships with your students showcasing them as intellectuals? How do you listen to your students? And what do you listen for when they share?

Collaborative Leadership: Teachers Making Decisions With Administrators

Partner teachers not only have collaborative discussions with each other; they extend their work, curricular transformations, impactful instructional and assessment practices, and holistic program evaluation by sharing their journey with others, including administrators, instructional coaches, and other school leadership teams. We recognize the importance of teachers' self-reflections with their peers, with coaches, and especially with administrators. With these trusting relationships, teachers are empowered to make decisions with administrative teams. The collaborative instructional cycle consisting of collaborative planning, teaching, assessment, and reflection also requires collaborative leadership support. See Figure 6.6 for a summary of the four key collaborative practices, each aligned with key teacher and leader activities, adapted from Andrea Honigsfeld and Jon Nordmeyer's (2020) recent work.

Figure 6.6 Key Collaborative Instructional and Leadership Actions

	WHAT COLLABORATIVE TEACHER PRACTICES LOOK LIKE	WHAT COLLABORATIVE LEADERSHIP SUPPORT LOOKS LIKE
Collaborative Planning	• Co-develop instructional routines and strategies based on the content subjects and their program languages of delivery • Prepare unit/lesson plans with socioculturally relevant, measurable, and rigorous content/language objectives in both partner languages • Ensure all lessons have spaces for students to demonstrate multilingual leadership and critical consciousness development • Design multilingual formative and summative assessment measures	• Provide common planning time, which may be rotational if needed, to support various groupings of content teachers and common language delivery teachers across different subject areas • Establish school-wide norms and expectations for co-planning • Ensure all teachers have the necessary curricular materials and instructional tools to promote linguistic equity

	WHAT COLLABORATIVE TEACHER PRACTICES LOOK LIKE	WHAT COLLABORATIVE LEADERSHIP SUPPORT LOOKS LIKE
	• Ensure lessons and their assessments facilitate, promote, and demonstrate linguistic equity • Select and make spaces for instructional accommodations and accelerations based on students' academic and linguistic needs in both program languages	• Provide ongoing professional development, coaching, and support to maximize collaborative planning
Collaborative Teaching	• Co-deliver differentiated, bridged instruction to scaffold learning in both program languages across the content areas • Share ownership of instruction through intentional multilingual student grouping and multilingual teacher roles • Demonstrate co-equal partnerships by selecting and adapting a variety of co-teaching models, aligned with the dual language program type and language allotment • Build in activities for purposeful, dynamic multiliteracy development	• Create a manageable and flexible schedule that allows for a variety of in-class support configurations • Build multilingual staffing ratios and relationships to support co-teaching partners • Engage multilingual counselors, teachers, and other key personnel in determining class composition based on the program type and language allotment • Provide professional development, coaching, and support to build collective horizontal and vertical efficacy
Collaborative Assessment	• Develop, administer, and evaluate the outcomes of multilingual formative and summative assessment measures • Set goals for (and with) students for the development of dynamic bilingualism • Use assessment data collaboratively with colleagues, families, and students • Jointly analyze student data to identify areas for growth or targeted supports	• Identify additional time devoted to data collection and analysis • Provide all necessary multilingual assessment materials and tools • Sustain professional development, coaching, and support for school-wide assessment literacy and evidence-based assessment practices
Collaborative Reflection	• Collectively examine the effectiveness of the collaborative instructional cycle, with an intense focus on content and language development in both partner languages • Discuss the impact of collaboration on both students' multilingual learning and teachers' pedagogical knowledge, skills, dispositions, and critical consciousness • Regularly engage in reflection *in* action and reflection *on* action (Schon, 1990)	• Engage in collaborative reflection with teachers • Provide systematic support and a school-wide commitment to improve horizontal and vertical collaboration • Integrate a process of reflecting on new learning and applying new collaborative practices • Showcase successful partnerships and practices in multilingual ways, including students' artifacts when possible

Adapted from Honigsfeld & Nordmeyer, 2020, p. 26

Teachers and administrators have a joint responsibility to implement the collaborative instructional cycle, especially when considering overall program effectiveness. Teacher commitment is critical and leadership support is instrumental in ensuring that dual language classrooms are a safe place for developing shared ownership of dual language pedagogies, multilingualism, and evidence-based best practices for content and language integration. Linda Darling-Hammond and colleagues (2017) found that "collective work in trusting environments provides a basis for inquiry and reflection into teachers' own practices, allowing teachers to take risks, solve problems, and attend to dilemmas in their practice" (p. 10). Leaders' engagement in similar practices and their support for teachers to enhance their collaborative collective efficacy—the shared belief that together they can achieve success with multilingual learners—increases.

Shared Decisions for Curricular and Instructional Transformation

Let's take a closer look at the curricular and instructional decisions made for cross-disciplinary approaches and the inclusion of thematic connections in dual language classes through collaborative practices. Let's also explore the types of joint decisions that are made about vertical and horizontal alignment to link the content curricula across languages, including scope and sequences, resources (books, classroom materials, the use of digital tools), and the assessment processes we discussed in Chapter 5.

WHAT THE RESEARCH SAYS

Strand 2: Curriculum of the *Guiding Principles for Dual Language Education* (Howard et al., 2018) tells us about the high level of importance given to the fundamental need to make collaborative decisions for curricular transformations. Current research indicates most curricula, and their corresponding assessments, are still designed without an intentional focus on the needs of multilingual learners, starting with the programmatic foundations for multiliteracy development. Keep the following in mind:

> *Thus, adaptations may need to be made to the curriculum and associated assessments. For example, the curriculum should provide a scope and sequence for initial literacy development in the partner language that specifically addresses the literacy skills needed to read and write in that language rather than simply mirroring the teaching of English literacy. This scope and sequence should also include biliteracy development, not simply literacy development for each language individually.* (Howard et al., 2018, p. 33)

How does the scope and sequence of the curriculum in your dual language program compare to the general education curriculum?

Let's bring instructional coaches, administrators, special educators, and other school leadership team members into the conversations. When you hit a topic that seems prickly (and you will!) and you agree that your discussions should move forward a bit more intentionally, take your time to listen to each other and make informed progress. Working together with each other as peers while recognizing hierarchical dynamics to communicate with administrators may sometimes make you feel vulnerable. From that perspective, the discussion prompts in Figure 6.4, enhanced with your personal notations, are to help serve and guide your explorations with an informed trajectory. We offer additional prompts in Figure 6.7 to continue your collaborative leadership work for curricular and instructional transformation.

Figure 6.7 Collaborative Leadership Discussion Prompts

As we discuss how the teachers transformed lesson activities with culturally and linguistically rich curricular materials that uphold high standards, we have discovered the following ideas about using textbooks, digital tools, and other materials to enhance learning:

_____

_____

_____

_____

As we discuss what teachers did to increase students' use of their full linguistic repertoires, we have discovered the following needs with regard to bilingual classroom materials, digital tools, and bilingual resources:

_____

_____

_____

_____

Here are some ideas about showcasing students' work samples across the curriculum:

_____

_____

_____

_____

(Continued)

(Continued)

To collaborate further and examine horizontal alignment, here are some ideas we have for instructional teams and coaches to ensure students are actively using new language in new ways with each other across the curriculum:

_____

_____

_____

_____

Here are some examples of how our program leverages thematic curricular topics to bridge languages, rather than offering a simple repetition of the same lesson topics in both program languages across grade levels and content areas:

_____

_____

_____

_____

Here are ways we will schedule and shape grade-level teams' and PLCs' collaboration:

_____

_____

_____

_____

Here is how we will integrate school-wide initiatives so they complement and leverage our dual language program decisions:

_____

_____

_____

_____

Add your own discussion prompts here:

- _____

_____

_____

_____

- _____
  _____
  _____
  _____
  _____

- _____
  _____
  _____
  _____
  _____

WHAT PRACTITIONERS SAY

Michael Rodríguez, executive director of Dual Language Education of New Mexico, is a former dual language school principal in Albuquerque. As he reflected on his time as a school administrator practicing collaborative leadership, he shared the following:

> *Where I last worked, we had a K–8 program, and we asked ourselves what's the best curriculum that's going to get us there [to curricular transformations]. So, we created the curriculum to really be connected. The teachers and the instructional coach met weekly and tweaked the curriculum at the end of every unit. They added in resources such as multilingual books and were careful and intentional in including multiple perspectives of history or science. Making connections between the different resources and visuals around the room was critical. The kids must have resources at their fingertips for both the partner language and the content that they are learning. The teachers, coaches, and administrators all came together to ensure accountability for the alignment from kindergarten through eighth grade. That continuity and alignment that happens is where [curricular transformation] comes in. The administration has control over the timing of the master planning and really must consider the best approach to meet the material, resource, and time needs of the program, especially as they're developing curriculum.*

How did the teachers' and instructional coaches' practice of including multiple perspectives on history and science contribute to their critical consciousness?

Administrative Leadership: Administrators Making Decisions Based on Stakeholder Input

All educators understand that some decisions will have to be made at the school or district administrative level. Administrative teams make numerous decisions about dual language programming with input from community members, parents, students, and other educational entities such as boards of education and state departments of education. Dual language school principals wear so many hats! They are regularly asked to describe the dual language program's success and at the same time justify the decisions they're making with local, state, and even federal stakeholders, especially when it comes to funding. This is no easy task, especially as administrators also consider the complexities linked to hiring multilingual personnel for their dual language programs. If you're a current dual language educator, take a moment and think about when and how you were hired for your role. What types of questions were included in the hiring processes? What staffing challenges are you aware of in your context? Dual language educators continue to confirm that we still have a nationwide critical shortage of highly qualified dual language teachers—so much so that the shortage contributes to growth barriers within the dual language education arena. How might increased collaborative practices help to address these challenges and barriers?

Administrators must rely on decades of research that confirm well-crafted dual language programs depend on leadership that is truly collaborative (Menken, 2017). Administrators make data-informed programmatic decisions when they deliberately and consistently consider input from teacher leaders and collaborative leadership practices.

WHAT PRACTITIONERS SAY

See how David Kauffman, EdD, founder of Kauffman Education LLC and former executive director of multilingual education in a large, urban district in Texas, emphasizes the importance of school district leadership decisions:

School districts must ensure that curriculum and instructional materials fully align with the dual language program. Content courses taught in the partner language (e.g., Spanish) should include equitable resources that do not rely on the teacher to translate. To facilitate content team collaboration, the scope and sequence of the content class taught in the target language should have approximately the same timeline of the class taught in English. The content curriculum guides for both languages should include language objectives integrated with content objectives. Time should be built in at the end of each unit for bridging to the other program language, with guidance provided regarding bridging vocabulary and strategies for metalinguistic analysis.

One of the most powerful systemic changes a district can make is the shift to designing first for dual language, rather than starting with monolingual English curriculum and instruction. The latter approach typically leaves it to the district's bilingual/multilingual education team or even the dual language teachers themselves to adapt everything in isolation from their colleagues. Co-designing dual language curriculum and instruction, then adapting to monolingual English where needed, facilitates greater collaboration among teachers.

Based on his decades of experience as a school and district leader, David asserts the need for collaborative approaches to program design and alignment. How would his approach support your program?

We invite you to log connections to the four pillars of dual language education in Figure 6.8 as they align with collaboration and leadership.

CAPTAIN'S LOG

Figure 6.8 The Four Pillars of Dual Language Education for Collaboration and Leadership

THE FOUR PILLARS OF DUAL LANGUAGE EDUCATION	TEACHER LEADERSHIP	COLLABORATIVE LEADERSHIP	ADMINISTRATIVE LEADERSHIP
Bilingualism and Biliteracy			
Grade-Level Academic Achievement			
Sociocultural Competence			
Critical Consciousness			

The Need for Holistic Program Evaluation

Research guides us to think about holistic program evaluation that is multifaceted and multidimensional, embodying the authentic ways in which we assess students *as, for,* and *of* learning (Gottlieb, 2021). Holistic dual language program evaluation as a process requires input from various stakeholders about different measures of success. Virginia Collier and Wayne Thomas (2018) prompt our thinking regarding these academic, linguistic, and sociocultural successes in dual language education, and the need to not only measure them within your program but also be prepared to share them with other stakeholders. We encourage you to think about these different research-based aspects of measuring success to showcase in your dual language program's holistic program evaluation. As you think about each portion and the collaborative input within each of the "look fors" in Figure 6.9, make some connections to your own context. What patterns are you noticing from the input data you're beginning to gather? How might you use these data from a holistic approach for ongoing program growth? The goal of collecting information here is to help you make further collaborative leadership decisions for effective holistic program evaluation, reporting, and ongoing program design.

Figure 6.9 "Look Fors" in Holistic Program Evaluation

ACADEMIC SUCCESSES	TEACHERS' INPUT	INSTRUCTIONAL COACHES' INPUT	ADMINISTRATORS' INPUT	OTHER SCHOOL LEADERSHIP INPUT
Classroom Formative/Summative Assessment Results				
School/District Benchmark Outcomes				
State-Level Test Scores				
Portfolio Assessments				
Students' Graduation Rates (if applicable in secondary programs)				
Add your own: _____ _____				
Add your own: _____ _____				
Linguistic/Cognitive Successes				
Common Assessments in Program Language A				
Common Assessments in Program Language B				
Students' Increased Problem-Solving Skills				
Students' Increased Creativity				
Students' Increased Metacognition				
Add your own: _____ _____				
Add your own: _____ _____				
Sociocultural Successes				
Students' Willingness to Collaborate				

(Continued)

(Continued)

ACADEMIC SUCCESSES	TEACHERS' INPUT	INSTRUCTIONAL COACHES' INPUT	ADMINISTRATORS' INPUT	OTHER SCHOOL LEADERSHIP INPUT
Students' Higher Attendance Rates				
Fewer Disciplinary Issues				
Students' Abilities for Conflict Resolution (in classes and at school in general)				
Add your own: _____ _____				
Add your own: _____ _____				
Critical Consciousness				
Students' Abilities to Identify and Disrupt the Language of Inequality				
Students' Abilities to Promote Linguistic Equity Within and Outside of the Dual Language Program				
Teachers' and Students' Collaborative Practices for Shifting Dialogues to Be Critically Conscious With Others				
Educators Collaborating With Stakeholders, Demonstrating Shifted Dialogues, and Demonstrating Critical Consciousness				
Add your own: _____ _____				
Add your own: _____ _____				
Overall Patterns From the Input				
Potential Connections to Programmatic Design				

WHAT THE RESEARCH SAYS

In preparation for this book, we asked Wayne Thomas and Virginia Collier (personal communication, December 21, 2021) to comment on their longitudinal research in the context of collaborative leadership and the continued need to involve students in dual language schools' programmatic decisions. Here's some of what they shared:

We still have opportunity gaps and achievement gaps. Multilingualism creates a better school experience as long as the students are given the roles they deserve in the decision-making processes. Multilingual students approach things from a more socially just position. Students from poverty in dual language programs, from all ethnicities including white students, bring up overall school success. We've seen so many cases in which, all of a sudden, principals want dual language at their schools because they see the "kids from poverty" data. Even in Title I, Head Start, and other programs that were [and are] heavily funded, our data show that nothing closes the achievement gap like dual language programs. So, principals really need to keep the students involved in the decisions with others and be sure to include the students' messages to upper leadership. That's what really justifies the programs.

Reflect on how these insights complement Joseph's message from the chapter opening vignette.

Creating a culture of collaborative leadership in dual language programs depends heavily on shared visions and goals. Based on research and practitioners' experiences, we offer these ideas in Figure 6.10 to help you develop and apply your own navigation system for common understandings, shared visions, and shared goals. As you think about these facets to complete the blank portions next to each idea, consider and note the essential roles that students, teachers, administrators, and other stakeholders have within the collaborative processes.

NAVIGATION SYSTEMS

Figure 6.10 Navigation System for Your Common Understandings, Shared Visions, and Shared Goals

FEATURES	WHAT IT IS	WHAT IT MEANS FOR MULTILINGUAL LEARNERS (MLS)	YOUR IDEAS AND NOTES ABOUT THE CONNECTIONS TO VERTICAL AND/OR HORIZONTAL PROGRAM MAPPING
Shared Program Vision and Mission	Clearly agreed-upon desired outcomes, shared values, and goals that place leveraging all students' successes at the program's core	A culturally and linguistically responsive and sustaining school in which MLs are fully included	
Shared Goals to Serve the Community	Critically analyzing the community and the program participants	Ensuring equitable access to dual language education	
Common Understandings of a Culture of Collaboration Across the Program and the School	A clear and intentional program structure with nonnegotiables aligned with the benefits of the three types of collaborative leadership (Teacher, Collaborative, and Administrator)	Students learn in an environment where they are surrounded by collaborative educators who leverage MLs' assets	
Shared Vision of Dynamic Multilingualism	Clearly agreed-upon desired outcomes, shared values, and goals that leverage MLs' language processing and how it differs from monolingual literacy (Escamilla et al., 2022; National Clearinghouse for English Language Education, 2022)	MLs are learning in classrooms with strategically coordinated alignment in literacy instruction in both program languages—with authentic topics and sequencing to each language	
Collaborative Curriculum Development	Through curriculum mapping and coordinated curriculum development, program coherence is established	Curricular adaptations and modifications consider MLs' linguistic and academic needs, including spaces for students' translanguaging with named and unnamed languages (García, 2020)	
Shared Instructional Practices	Planning, implementation, and assessment practices are coordinated	Differentiated instruction, academic and linguistic scaffolds, and social-emotional supports are designed and implemented with MLs' language and literacy development in mind	
Shared Vision and Goals for Vertical Planning	Clearly agreed-upon desired outcomes, shared values, and goals that facilitate effective literacy vertical mapping from one grade level to another	MLs experience cohesive instructional alignment to maximize the development of content and language progression in both program languages	
Student-Centered Approach	Instructional focus is on the needs of the learner; students develop their own understanding through active learning techniques	MLs are able to build their background knowledge and complete self-selected projects at their own level of linguistic ability	

FEATURES	WHAT IT IS	WHAT IT MEANS FOR MULTILINGUAL LEARNERS (MLS)	YOUR IDEAS AND NOTES ABOUT THE CONNECTIONS TO VERTICAL AND/OR HORIZONTAL PROGRAM MAPPING
Common Understanding of the Program Structure and Time Allotments	A common agreed-upon implementation of the program's instructional time allotments and corresponding languages of instruction	MLs' content and biliteracy are developed to higher degrees	
Shared Definition of Program Success	Clearly agreed-upon outcome and shared understandings of what students' successes are, representing a wide range of both in-school and out-of-school experiences, ways for students to share their stories	MLs are given equitable opportunities to share their voices as authentic representations of a wide range of individual and program successes	
Common Understanding of Holistic Program Evaluation	Clearly agreed-upon measures of the desired outcomes, shared values, and goals as defined by program success	MLs are afforded ample opportunities and equitable systems to show their progress, in content and both program languages	
Shared Vision for Reporting Student and Program Successes	Ensuring program evaluation reports include a well-balanced combination of qualitative and quantitative data representing students' in-school and out-of-school successes	Students may showcase their wide range of successes in content development and multilingual, multicultural progressions	
Shared Goals for Program Improvement	Clearly agreed-upon, data-informed, and actionable steps that address what you want to improve upon—based on the results of your desired outcomes, shared values, and goals as defined by program success	Students are given access to a program that grows toward authentically meeting their needs, as well as the needs of the community with a multidimensional stance on program success	
Shared Goals for Program Expansion	A programmatic focus on building clear pathways for K–12 expansion within/and to grow feeder school patterns	Continued access to dual language education in secondary settings to greatly expand students' long-term academic, linguistic, and sociocultural gains	
Ongoing Shared Professional Learning	Individual teacher learning is integrated into collaborative efforts to enhance all teachers' practice	All faculty understand and implement research-informed and evidence-based approaches to instructing and assessing MLs	
Add Your Own			
Add Your Own			

LAUNCHED MISSIONS

Given the depth of the many layers within collaborative leadership in Chapter 6, we strategically chose to feature more than one example in this chapter's Launched Missions section. The first example is from Carol Rodd, principal at Collinswood Language Academy in Charlotte-Mecklenburg Schools in North Carolina. She shares her experiences with collaborative leadership practices in the Collinswood program as they relate to common understandings of program structures, shared values about multilingual personnel, biliteracy and language status, and master scheduling to impact program success:

> We are intentional in how we use time, people, and resources to create impact for learning with our kids, and so thoughtfully designing common understandings is crucial. Making sure that we have the right structures in place is important for our program's success. If I was giving a new dual language school principal advice, I'd first say it's important to have common understandings and shared definitions of your programmatic aspects. I have found that there are such different interpretations about all the things needed to help students reach high levels of success, starting with bilingualism and biliteracy. I would really encourage folks on the front end of the administrative processes to invest time around common understandings and shared visions.
>
> What does biliteracy look like and sound like, and how does that manifest in the classroom settings in my school? At first, we didn't do that well. I figured we all had some common understandings when we didn't. Our teachers and staff are diverse with various levels of bilingualism, people who are bicultural or not. Even if they are bicultural, maybe they identify as one dominant culture but then have other aspects of their heritage that they identify with. So, hiring becomes quite complex. I have learned how important it is to take time to purposefully create common understandings and common foundations so that we have a common vision of what our program needs and the educators we need to fit the program. A specific example of this is that when we discuss biliteracy we all look at the English literacy standards, and we also look at the Spanish literacy standards, and we compare them, and we see where things are similar and where there are some differences. And it doesn't matter which language—if it's in English or in Spanish, we're going to make sure all the instructional standards are valued so that we give both languages equal status. I discuss it with my team and compare it to a braid where we weave together content and both program languages—and we do that over time.
>
> Everything in a dual language school should be purposeful—for example, the structure of the master schedule, which is a primary tool for principals to impact student learning. We have a common understanding of how we are using blocks of time to make sure that we're having engagement across both languages, not repeating. Some schools repeat A and then B. We really need to avoid repetition. We want to augment and amplify across the curriculum. All these parts of common understandings and shared values are important because otherwise we would create fragmentation and misalignments in our program.

The second example is from the District 54 Department of Language and Culture in Schaumburg, Illinois, which we learned about in Chapter 5. In the context of collaborative leadership and the importance of discussions as part of the collaborative leadership processes, Instructional Coach Rocio Hernandez shares information from her collaborative team, consisting of five members (see Figure 6.11 from left to right). The team members are Ruiyan Xiong—Chinese immersion instructional coach, Sarah LoPresti—Spanish dual language instructional coach, Seika Kobari—Japanese dual language instructional coach, Rocio Hernandez—Spanish dual language instructional coach, and Katie Smith—English learner instructional coach. This collaborative team is proud to have accomplished the following:

- Facilitating and fully supporting high levels of communication and collaboration to maintain consistency with the District 54 Vision of Ensuring Student Success

- Providing ongoing professional development that focuses on best practices to support multilingual learners

- Creating authentic curriculum and multilingual resources for students in Grades K–8 in the Japanese dual, Spanish dual, and Chinese immersion programs

- Developing and supporting multilingual families through various parent and community events

Figure 6.11   District 54 Department of Language and Culture Team

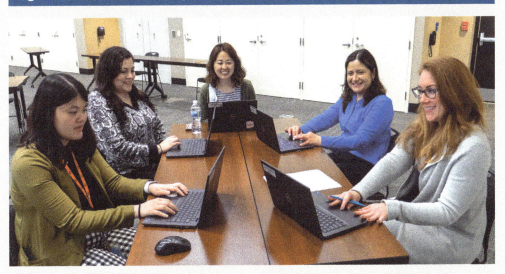

Source: Ruiyan Xiong, Sarah LoPresti, Seika Kobari, Rocio Hernandez and Katie Smith. Used with permission.

We acknowledge that collaborative leadership is complex. We invite you to continue your collaborative leadership work, including the examples of common program structure understandings, shared values about multilingual personnel, biliteracy and language status, master scheduling to impact program success, the importance of in-depth conversations, and any other experiences as they relate to your dual language program.

STAYING THE COURSE

As we come to the conclusion of Chapter 6 and this book, we are ready to share our final set of Core Beliefs and "Let's Agree" Statements. Remember, as in the prior chapters, these concepts and beliefs are what keep us safely connected to the notion that we must stay on the course of empowerment, equity, heart spaces, and shared ownership for all dual language programs.

Core Beliefs

- Multilingual learners' variety of successes are at the core of our collaborative decision-making processes.
- Shared visions and goals for success in dual language programs must be aligned with the four pillars of dual language education.
- Well-crafted, equitable dual language programs require collaborative leadership to support all multilingual learners.

"Let's Agree" Statements

1. Collaborative leadership in dual language programs is essential—dual language educators have superpowers!
2. Program development including curricular and instructional transformations and holistic program evaluation is ongoing and must involve students, families, and communities.
3. Holistic program evaluation is multidimensional and multifaceted.

GEAR UP!

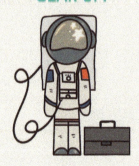

We agree that equitable dual language programs require collaborative leadership to support all multilingual learners. Ayanna Cooper (2020), renowned advocate for multilingual learners, created an eight-question framework in *And Justice for ELs: A Leaders' Guide to Creating and Sustaining Equitable Schools* to emphasize the importance of developing equitable practices. We were inspired by the depth and breadth of these questions and adapted them in Figure 6.12 to serve as a reflective tool for you to use in your own context.

Figure 6.12 Guiding Questions for Creating and Sustaining Equitable Dual Language Programs

1. How many students participate in the dual language program, and what are the language backgrounds (emergent bilinguals, English learners/multilingual learners, etc.)?

2. What is the dual language program model's approach to promote equitable access to dual language education?

3. In which grade levels do you have dual language programs, and what are your plans to expand the program to sustain equitable access to the program from the K–12 perspective?

4. What are the students' language levels, areas of strength, and areas for growth in the partner languages? How are you ensuring both program languages are given equitable linguistic status?

5. How many, if any, students are dually identified (multilingual learners who are identified as gifted and/or have other special education learning needs)?

6. In what ways can you advocate for bilingual paraprofessionals to become certified teachers in the dual language program, leveraging an equitable pathway for them?

7. How many students have reached proficiency in one or both languages? How is proficiency/language progression determined?

(Continued)

(Continued)

8. How are the students monitored once they have exited the dual language program?	
9. Add your own:	
10. Add your own:	
11. Add your own:	
12. Add your own:	

Source: Adapted from Cooper (2020, p. 11)

TUNE IN!

To wrap up the ideas and information from Chapter 6, we've lined up a wide variety of practical tools, resources, and collaborative strategies that enhance collaborative decision making in the varying types of leadership. We invite you to be informed and to be innovative with your thinking—especially when it comes to facilitating the growth of secondary programs. Trust in the research that backs up dual language education and remember to be creative and courageous in your adventures. Here are some key links to books, articles, reports, and organizations to support your work as you *aim for the stars*:

Books

Collier, V. P., & Thomas, W. P. (2018). *Transforming secondary education: Middle and high school dual language programs.* Dual Language Education of New Mexico–Fuente Press.

Cooper, A. (2020). *And justice for ELs: A leaders' guide to creating and sustaining equitable schools.* Corwin.

España, C., & Herrera, L. Y. (2020). El communidad*: Lessons for centering the voices and experiences of bilingual Latinx students*. Heinemann.

Freeman, Y., & Freeman, D. (2018). *Dual language essentials for teachers and administrators* (2nd ed). Heinemann.

Gottlieb, M. (2021). *Classroom assessment in multiple languages: A handbook for teachers.* Corwin.

Guerrero, M., & Lachance, J. (2018). *The National Dual Language Education Teacher Preparation Standards.* Fuente Press.

Honigsfeld, A., & Dove, M. (2014). *Collaboration and co-teaching for English learners: A leader's guide.* Corwin.

Honigsfeld, A., & Nordmeyer, J. (2020). Better together: Evidence for co-teaching and collaboration in today's classrooms. *AAIE InterEd Journal, 48*(129). https://fliphtml5.com/zxih/ppib/basic

Reeves, D. (2020). *The learning leader: How to focus school improvement for better results.* ASCD.

Safir, S. (2017). *The listening leader: Creating the conditions for equitable school transformation.* Jossey-Bass.

Safir, S., & Dugan, J. (with Wilson, C.). (2021). *Street data: A next-generation model for equity, pedagogy, and school transformation.* Corwin.

Thomas, W. P., & Collier, V. P. (2017). *Why dual language schooling.* Dual Language Education of New Mexico–Fuente Press.

Tedick, D. J., & Lyster, R. (2020). *Scaffolding language development in immersion and dual language classrooms.* Routledge.

Web-Based Resources

Center for Applied Linguistics evaluation tool kit for two-way programs: https://www.cal.org/twi/EvalToolkit/index.htm

(Continued)

(Continued)

Dual Language Education of New Mexico programmatic support: www.dlenm.org/what-we-do/programmatic-support-and-resources/

DualLanguageSchools.org leadership guidance for increasing dual language programs, supporting families to access dual language, and facilitating communication between programs and the communities they serve: https://duallanguageschools.org/

Migration Policy Institute resources for research and initiatives as well as supportive publications:

- www.migrationpolicy.org/research/dual-language-learner-identification-procedures-policies
- www.migrationpolicy.org/events/are-states-recognizing-and-responding-needs-their-dual-language-learner-children
- U.S. Department of Health and Human Services administrative support for dual language learners: https://eclkc.ohs.acf.hhs.gov/culture-language/article/administrators-managers-support-dual-language-learners

COUNTDOWN TO LAUNCH

Since this is our final countdown, the following practical tips will support both your leadership practices (be it Teacher Leadership, Collaborative Leadership, or Administrative Leadership) and your advocacy work for impactful implementation of dual language programs.

10. Offer and accept coaching in kind, helpful, and honest ways.
9. Embrace lifelong learning at all stages of your profession as an educator—learning is an adventure.
8. Work from your heart—and stay open-minded so you make informed decisions.
7. Keep realistic and high expectations for yourself, your colleagues, and your students—and celebrate your progress.
6. Reach higher: The sky is the limit!
5. When something doesn't work well, change it up and try again.
4. Collaborate with agency and build your leadership skills.
3. Involve all stakeholders in all important decisions, especially the difficult ones.
2. Recognize your students as intellectual partners—and recognize them often!
1. Guide others by sharing your transformations with students' heart spaces and voices as the primary sources of success.

CAPTAIN'S LOG: FINAL ENTRY

Based on Chapter 6, identify your key takeaways as you aim for the stars with your next steps.

1. What from Chapter 6 is directly applicable to your context? What could be a stretch for you at the moment?

   _____
   _____
   _____
   _____

2. What are some future goals or steps you wish to take? What might be challenging for you to discuss with your leadership team? What might be your first change into action steps?

   _____
   _____
   _____
   _____

References

American Councils Research Center. (2021). *2021 canvass of dual language and immersion (DLI) programs in U.S. public schools*. American Councils for International Education. https://www.americancouncils.org/sites/default/files/documents/pages/2021-10/Canvass%20DLI%20-%20October%202021-2_ac.pdf

August, D. (2018). Educating English language learners: A review of the latest research. *American Educator, 42*(3). https://www.aft.org/ae/fall2018/august

Baker, D., Roberson, A., & Kim, H. (2018). Autism and dual immersion: Sorting through the questions. *Advances in Autism, 4*(4), 174–183.

Beeman, K., & Urow, C. (2013). *Teaching for biliteracy: Strengthening bridges between languages.* Caslon.

Beninghof, A. M. (2020). *Co-teaching that works: Structures and strategies for maximizing student learning* (2nd ed.). Jossey-Bass.

Brookfield, S. (2017). *Becoming a critically reflective teacher* (2nd ed.). Jossey-Bass.

Brown, B. (2021). *Atlas of the heart: Mapping meaningful connection and the language of human experience.* Random House.

Bunch, G. C., Walqui, A., & Kibler, A. (2015). Attending to language, engaging in practice: Scaffolding English language learners' apprenticeship into the Common Core English Language Arts Standards. In L. C. de Oliveira, M. Klassen, & M. Maune (Eds.), *The Common Core State Standards in English Language Arts for English language learners, Grades 6–12* (pp. 5–23). TESOL.

Calderón, M. E., Dove, M. G., Staehr Fenner, D., Gottlieb, M., Honigsfeld, A., Ward Singer, T., Slakk, S., Soto, I., & Zacarian, D. (2020). *Breaking down the wall: Essential shifts for English learners' success.* Corwin.

Calderón, M., Espino, G., & Slakk, S. (2019). *Integrating language, reading, writing, and content in English and Spanish.* Velázquez Press.

Center for Applied Linguistics. (2017). *National dual language forum: Dual language program directory.* http://www.cal.org/ndlf/directories/

Cervantes-Soon, C. G., Dorner, L., Palmer, D., Heiman, D., Schwerdtfeger, R., & Choi, J. (2017). Combating inequalities in two-way language immersion programs: Toward critical consciousness in bilingual education spaces. *Review of Research in Education, 41*, 403–427.

Collier, V. P., & Thomas, W. P. (2007). Predicting second language academic success in English using the Prism Model. In J. Cummins & C. Davison (Eds.), *International handbook of English language teaching, Part 1* (pp. 333–348). Springer.

Collier, V. P., & Thomas, W. P. (2009). *Educating English learners for a transformed world.* Fuente Press.

Collier, V. P., & Thomas, W. P. (2018). *Transforming secondary education: Middle and high school dual language programs.* Dual Language Education of New Mexico–Fuente Press.

Compton, T. N. (2018, May). *Access to culturally responsive teaching for English language learners: Mainstream teacher perceptions and practice on inclusion* (Paper 2949) [Doctoral dissertation, University of Louisville]. ThinkIR: Electronic Theses and Dissertations. https://doi.org/10.18297/etd/2949

Cooper, A. (2020). *And justice for ELs: A leaders' guide to creating and sustaining equitable schools.* Corwin.

Darling-Hammond, L., Hyler, M. E., & Gardner, M. (2017). *Effective teacher professional development.* Learning Policy Institute.

Davison, C. (2006). Collaboration between ESL and content teachers: How do we know when we are doing it right? *The International Journal of Bilingual Education and Bilingualism, 9*(4), 454–475.

de Jong, E., & Howard, E. (2009). Integration in two-way immersion: Equalizing linguistic benefits for all students. *International Journal of Bilingual Education and Bilingualism, 12*(1), 81–99.

DeFlaminis, J., Abdul-Jabar, M., & Yoak, E. (2016). *Distributed leadership in schools: A practical guide for learning and improvement.* Routledge.

Donohoo, J. (2017). *Collective efficacy: How educators' beliefs impact student learning.* Corwin.

Dove, M. G., & Honigsfeld, A. (2014). Analysis of the implementation of an ESL co-teaching model in a suburban elementary school. *NYS TESOL Journal, 1*(1), 62–67. http://journal.nystesol.org/jan2014/60dove.pdf

Dove, M. G., & Honigsfeld, A. (2018). *Co-teaching for English learners: A guide to collaborative planning, instruction, assessment, and reflection.* Corwin.

Dove, M. G., & Honigsfeld, A. (2020a). Is there magic in co-teaching? In M. G. Dove & A. Honigsfeld (Eds.), *Co-teaching for English learners: Evidence-based practices and research-informed outcomes* (pp. 61–78). Information Age.

Dove, M. G., & Honigsfeld, A. (Eds.). (2020b). *Co-teaching for English learners: Evidence-based practices and research-informed outcomes.* Information Age.

DuFour, R., & DuFour, R. (2012). *The school leader's guide to professional learning communities at work.* Solution Tree.

DuFour, R., DuFour, R., Eaker, R., & Many, T. W. (2016). *Learning by doing: A handbook for Professional Learning Communities at Work™* (3rd ed.). Solution Tree.

Edmondson, A. C. (2012). *Teaming: How organizations learn, innovate, and compete in the knowledge economy.* Jossey-Bass.

Escamilla, K., Hopewell, S., Butvilofsky, S., Sparrow, W., Soltero-González, L., Ruiz-Figueroa, O., & Escamilla, M. (2014). *Biliteracy from the start: Literacy Squared in action.* Caslon.

Escamilla, K., Olsen, L., & Slavik, J. (2022). *Toward comprehensive effective literacy policy and instruction for English learner/emergent bilingual students.* National Committee for Effective Literacy. https://secureservercdn.net/50.62.174.75/v5e.685.myftpupload.com/wp-content/uploads/2022/04/21018-NCEL-Effective-Literacy-White-Paper-FINAL_v2.0.pdf

España, C., & Herrera, L. Y. (2020). *El communidad: Lessons for centering the voices and experiences of bilingual Latinx students.* Heinemann.

Espinosa, L. M. (2013). *Pre-K–3rd: Challenging common myths about dual language learners.* Foundation for Child Development. https://www.fcd-us.org/assets/2016/04/Challenging-Common-Myths-Update.pdf

Fang, Z. (2012). Language correlates of disciplinary literacy. *Topics in Language Disorders, 32*(1), 19–34.

Fang, Z., & Robertson, D. A. (2020). Unpacking and operationalizing disciplinary literacy: A review of disciplinary literacy inquiry and instruction. *Journal of Adolescent and Adult Literacy, 64*(2), 240–242. https://doi.org/10.1002/jaal.1070

Feinauer, E., & Howard, E. R. (2014). Attending to the third goal: Cross cultural competence and identity development in two-way immersion programs. *Journal of Immersion and Content-Based Language Education, 2*(2), 257–272.

Fizell, S. G. (2018). *Best practices in co-teaching and collaboration: The HOW of co-teaching: Implementing the models.* Cogent Catalyst.

Foltos, L. (2018, January 29). Teachers learn better together. *Edutopia.* http://www.edutopia.org/article/teachers-learn-better-together

Fredricks, J. A. (2014). *Eight myths of student disengagement: Creating classrooms of deep learning.* Corwin.

Friend, M., & Cook, L. (2012). *Interactions: Collaboration skills for school professionals* (7th ed.). Allyn & Bacon.

Friend, M., & Cook, L. (2016). *Interactions: Collaboration skills for school professionals* (8th ed.). Pearson.

García, O. (2009). *Bilingual education in the 21st century: A global perspective.* Wiley-Blackwell.

García, O. (2014). Becoming bilingual and biliterate: Sociolinguistic and sociopolitical considerations. In C. A. Stone, E. R. Silliman, B. J. Ehren, & G. P. Wallach (Eds.), *Handbook of language and literacy: Development and disorders* (2nd ed., pp. 145–160). Guilford Press.

García, O. (2020). Translanguaging and Latinx bilingual readers. *The Reading Teacher, 73*(5), 557–562. https://doi.org/10.1002/trtr.1883

García, O., Ibarra-Johnson, S., & Seltzer, K. (2017). *The translanguaging classroom: Leveraging student bilingualism for learning.* Caslon.

García, O., & Wei, L. (2014). *Translanguaging: Language, bilingualism and education*. Springer.

García, O., & Woodley, H. H. (2015). Bilingual education. In M. Bigelow & J. Ennser-Kananen (Eds.), *The Routledge handbook of educational linguistics* (pp. 132–144). Routledge.

Genesee, F., & Lindholm-Leary, K. (2013). Two case studies of content-based language education. *Journal of Immersion and Content-Based Language Education*, (1), 3–33.

Genesee, F., Lindholm-Leary, K., & Christian, D. (2006). *Educating English language learners: A synthesis of research evidence*. Cambridge University Press.

Gibbons, P. (2015). *Scaffolding language scaffolding learning: Teaching English language learners in the mainstream classroom*. Heinemann.

Gottlieb, M. (2021). *Classroom assessment in multiple languages: A handbook for teachers*. Corwin.

Gottlieb, M. (2022). *Assessment in multiple languages: A handbook for school and district leaders*. Corwin.

Grapin, S. (2019). Multimodality in the new content standards era: Implications for English learners. *TESOL Quarterly*, *53*(1), 30–55.

Greenberg Motamedi, J., Vazquez, M., Gandhi, E., & Holmgren, M. (2019, March). *English language development minutes, models, and outcomes: Beaverton School District*. Education Northwest. https://educationnorthwest.org/resources/english-language-development-minutes-models-and-outcomes-beaverton-school-district

Guerrero, M., & Guerrero, M. (2017). Competing discourses of academic Spanish in the Texas-Mexico borderlands. *Bilingual Research Journal*, *40*(1), 5–19. https://doi.org/10.1080/15235882.2016.1273150

Guerrero, M., & Lachance, J. (2018). *The national dual language education teacher preparation standards*. Fuente Press.

Hamman-Ortiz, L., & Palmer, D. (2020, September 22). Identity and two-way bilingual education: Considering student perspectives: Introduction to the special issue. *International Journal of Bilingual Education and Bilingualism*. Advance online publication. https://doi.org/10.1080/13670050.2020.1819096

Hattie, J. (2015, June). *What works best in education: The politics of collaborative expertise*. Open Ideas at Pearson. https://www.pearson.com/content/dam/corporate/global/pearson-dot-com/files/hattie/150526_ExpertiseWEB_V1.pdf

Honigsfeld, A. & Dove, M. G. (2010). *Collaboration and co-teaching: Strategies for English learners*. Corwin.

Honigsfeld, A., & Dove, M. G. (Eds.). (2012a). *Co-teaching and other collaborative practices in the EFL/ESL classroom: Rationale, research, reflections, and recommendations*. Information Age.

Honigsfeld, A., & Dove, M. G. (Eds.). (2012b). Teacher collaboration in TESOL [Special issue]. *TESOL Journal*, *3*(3). https://onlinelibrary.wiley.com/toc/19493533/2012/3/3

Honigsfeld, A., & Dove, M. G. (2015). *Collaboration and co-teaching for English learners: A leader's guide*. Corwin.

Honigsfeld, A., & Dove, M. G. (2017). The co-teaching flow inside the classroom. In M. Dantas-Whitney & S. Rilling (Eds.), *TESOL voices: Insider accounts of classroom life, Secondary education* (pp. 107–114). TESOL International Association.

Honigsfeld, A., & Dove, M. G. (2019). *Collaborating for English learners: A foundational guide to integrated practices*. Corwin.

Honigsfeld, A., & Dove, M. G. (2022). *Co-planning: 5 essential practices to integrate curriculum and instruction for English learners*. Corwin.

Honigsfeld, A., & Nordmeyer, J. (2020). Better together: Evidence for co-teaching and collaboration in today's classrooms. *AAIE InterEd Journal*, *48*(129). https://fliphtml5.com/zxih/ppib/basic

Howard, E. R., Lindholm-Leary, K. J., Rogers, D., Olague, N., Medina, J., Kennedy, B., Sugarman, J., & Christian, D. (2018). *Guiding principles for dual language education* (3rd ed.). Center for Applied Linguistics.

Howard, E. R., & Simpson, S. (2016, Summer). Teaching in tandem: Coordinating instruction across languages. *Soleado: Promising Practices From the Field* [a publication of Dual Language Education of New Mexico]. https://cms.dlenm.org/uploads/FileLinks/e8cad80410274955bd-d342af00495387/2016.Summer.Soleado.pdf

Hunt, V. (2011). Learning from success stories: Leadership structures that support dual language programs over time in New York City. *International Journal of Bilingual Education and Bilingualism*, *14*(2), 187–206.

Kibler, A., Valdés, G., & Walqui, A. (Eds.). (2021). *Reconceptualizing the role of critical dialogue in

American classrooms: Promoting equity through dialogic education. Routledge.

Klein, A. (2021). 1,500 decisions a day (at least!): How teachers cope with a dizzying array of questions. *EdWeek.* https://www.edweek.org/teaching-learning/1-500-decisions-a-day-at-least-how-teachers-cope-with-a-dizzying-array-of-questions/2021/12

Lachance, J. (2020). Two brains are better than one! State-level professional development and teachers' descriptions of the benefits of co-teaching. In M. Dove & A. Honigsfeld (Eds.), *Co-teaching for English learners: Evidence-based practices and research-informed outcomes* (pp. 81–93). Information Age.

Levine, L. N., Lukens, L., & Smallwood, B. A. (2013). *The GO TO strategies: Scaffolding options for teachers of English language learners, K–12.* https://www.cal.org/what-we-do/projects/project-excell/the-go-to-strategies

Lindholm-Leary, K. (2012). Success and challenges in dual language education. *Theory Into Practice, 51*(4), 256–262.

Lindholm-Leary, K. (2016). Bilingualism and academic achievement in children in dual language programs. In E. Nicoladis & S. Montanari (Eds.), *Bilingualism across the lifespan: Factors moderating language proficiency* (pp. 203–223). American Psychological Association.

Martin-Beltrán, M., & Madigan Peercy, M. (2012). How can ESOL and mainstream teachers make the best of standards-based curriculum in order to collaborate? *TESOL Journal, 3,* 425–444.

Martin-Beltrán, M., & Madigan Peercy, M. (2014). Collaboration to teach English language learners: Opportunities for shared teacher learning. *Teachers and Teaching, 20,* 721–737.

Marzano, R. J., Warrick, P. B., Rains, C. L., & DuFour, R. (2018). *Leading a high-reliability school.* Solution Tree.

Massachusetts Department of Elementary and Secondary Education. (2019). *Collaboration tool.* http://www.doe.mass.edu/ell/curriculum.html

Mattos, M., Dufour, R., DuFour, R., Eaker, R., & Many, T. W. (2016). *Concise answers to frequently asked questions about Professional Learning Communities at Work™: Stronger relationships for better education leadership.* Solution Tree.

Menken, K. (2017). *Leadership in dual language bilingual education: A National Dual Language Forum white paper.* Center for Applied Linguistics.

Moje, E. B. (2015). Doing and teaching disciplinary literacy with adolescent learners: A social and cultural enterprise. *Harvard Educational Review, 85*(2), 254–278. https://doi.org/10.17763/0017-8055.85.2.254

Moll, L. C., Amanti, C., Neff, D., & Gonzalez, N. (1992). Funds of knowledge for teaching: Using a qualitative approach to connect homes and classrooms. *Theory Into Practice, 31,* 132–141.

Murawski, W. (2009). *Collaborative teaching in secondary schools: Making the co-teaching marriage work!* Corwin.

Murawski, W. W., & Lochner, W. W. (2017). *Beyond co-teaching basics: A data-driven, no-fail model for continuous improvement.* ASCD.

Nagle, J. F. (Ed.). (2013). *English learner instruction through collaboration and inquiry in teacher education.* Information Age.

National Clearinghouse for English Language Acquisition. (2022). *Benefits of multilingualism* [Infographic]. https://ncela.ed.gov/files/announcements/20200805-NCELAInfographic-508.pdf

New York State Education Department. (2018). *Program options for English language learners/Multilingual learners.* http://www.nysed.gov/bilingual-ed/program-options-english-language-learnersmultilingual-learners

Nolte, J., Garavito, D., & Reyna, V. F. (2019). Decision making. In R. J. Sternberg & J. Funke (Eds.), *Introduction to the psychology of human thought* (pp. 177–198). Heidelberg University Publishing.

Nordmeyer, J., Boals, T., MacDonald, R., & Westerlund, R. (2021). What does equity really mean for multilingual learners? *Educational Leadership, 78*(6), 60–65.

Norton, J. (2016, October). Successful coteaching: ESL teachers in the mainstream classroom. *TESOL Connections.* http://newsmanager.commpartners.com/tesolc/issues/2016-10-01/3.html

Palmer, D. K., Cervantes-Soon, C., Dorner, L., & Heiman, D. (2019). Bilingualism, biliteracy, biculturalism, and critical consciousness for all: Proposing a fourth fundamental goal for two-way dual language education. *Theory Into Practice, 58*(2), 121–133.

Park, M., Zong, J., & Batalova, J. (2018). *Growing superdiversity among young U.S. dual language learners and its implications.* Migration Policy Institute.

Pawan, F., & Ortloff, J. (2011). Sustaining collaboration: ESL and content area teachers. *Teaching and Teacher Education, 27,* 463–471.

Peercy, M. M., Ditter, M., & Destefano, M. (2017). "We need more consistency": Negotiating the division of labor in ESOL–mainstream teacher collaboration. *TESOL Journal*, *8*(1), 215–239. https://doi.org/10.1002/tesj.269

Peery, A. (2019). *The co-teacher's playbook: What it takes to make co-teaching work for everyone.* Corwin.

Perez, K. D. (2012). *The co-teaching book of lists.* Jossey-Bass.

Pérez, M. I. (2009). *My diary from here to there/Mi diario de aqui hasta alla* (1st paperback trade ed.). Children's Book Press.

Pryor, S. (2018). *To plan together or not to plan together: Why is that a question?* https://www.teachingforbiliteracy.com/to-plan-together-or-not-to-plan-together-why-is-that-a-question/

Reeves, D. (2020). *The learning leader: How to focus school improvement for better results.* ASCD.

Robertson, K., Honigsfeld, A., & Dove, M. G. (2022). Return to better: Post-pandemic collaboration practices. In A. Honigsfeld & M. G. Dove (Eds.), *Portraits of collaboration* (pp. 164–190). Seidlitz.

Roda, A., & Menken, K. (under review). A case of disregarded civil rights in gentrifying New York City schools: The conflation of dual language bilingual education with gifted programs. *Educational Evaluation and Policy Analysis*.

Safir, S. (2017). *The listening leader: Creating the conditions for equitable school transformation.* Jossey-Bass.

Safir, S., & Dugan, J. (with Wilson, C.). (2021). *Street data: A next-generation model for equity, pedagogy, and school transformation.* Corwin.

Santos, M., Darling-Hammond, L., & Cheuk, T. (2012). *Teacher development to support English language learners in the context of Common Core State Standards.* https://ul.stanford.edu/sites/default/files/resource/2021-12/10-Santos%20LDH%20Teacher%20Development%20FINAL.pdf

Scanlan, M., Frattura, E., Schneider, K. A., & Capper, C. A. (2012). Bilingual students with integrated comprehensive service: Collaborative strategies. In A. Honigsfeld & M. G. Dove (Eds.), *Co-teaching and other collaborative practices in the EFL/ESL classroom: Rationale, research, reflections, and recommendations* (pp. 3–13). Information Age.

Scanlan, M., & Johnson, L. (2021). Inclusive leadership on the social frontiers: Family and community engagement. In G. Theoharis & M. Scanlan (Eds.), *Leadership for increasingly diverse schools* (2nd ed., pp. 227–258). Routledge.

Schon, D. A. (1990). *Educating the reflective practitioner: Toward a new design for teaching and learning in the professions.* Jossey-Bass.

Shafer Willner, L. (2013). *Proficiency level descriptors for English language proficiency standards.* Council of Chief State School Officers.

Shanahan, C., & Shanahan, T. (2020). Disciplinary literacy. In J. Patterson (Ed.), *The SAT® suite and classroom practice: English language arts/literacy* (pp. 91–125). College Board.

Simpson, S., & Howard, E. (2021). *Planning for co-planning.* https://www.duallanguagetandemteaching.com/post/planning-for-co-planning

Sleeter, C. E., & Carmona, J. F. (2017). *Un-standardizing curriculum: Multicultural teaching in the standards-based classroom* (2nd ed.). Teachers College Press.

Solorza, C. R., Aponte, G. Y., Leverenz, T., Becker, T., & Frias, B. (with García, O., & Sánchez, M. T.). (2019). *Translanguaging in dual language bilingual education: A blueprint for planning units of study.* CUNY-NYS Initiative on Emergent Bilinguals. https://www.cuny-nysieb.org/wp-content/uploads/2019/09/Translanguaging-in-Dual-Language-Bilingual-Education-A-Blueprint-for-Planning-Units-of-Study-RSVD.pdf

Theoharis, G., & O'Toole, J. (2011). Leading inclusive ELL social justice leadership for English language learners. *Educational Administration Quarterly*, *47*(4), 646–688.

Thomas, W. P., & Collier, V. P. (2002). *A national study of school effectiveness for language minority students' long-term academic achievement.* Center for Research on Education, Diversity & Excellence, University of California–Santa Cruz. https://escholarship.org/content/qt65j213pt/qt65j213pt_noSplash_2e6e3e1b23afa60cf00da25f77178252.pdf?t=krnd6g

Thomas, W. P., & Collier, V. P. (2014). *Creating dual language schools for a transformed world: Administrators speak.* Fuente Press.

Thomas, W. P., & Collier, V. P. (2017). *Why dual language schooling.* Fuente Press.

Tyrrell, J. (2021, December 4). Herricks district's mission is to "prepare our students to become global citizens." *Newsday*. https://www.news

day.com/long-island/education/spanish-immersion-program-c59399

Villa, R. A., Thousand, J. S., & Nevin, A. I. (2013). *A guide to co-teaching: New lessons and strategies to facilitate student learning* (3rd ed.). Corwin.

Visual Learning. (2018). *Collective teacher efficacy (CTE) according to John Hattie.* https://visible-learning.org/2018/03/collective-teacher-efficacy-hattie

Vygotsky, L. (1978). *Mind in society: The development of higher psychological processes.* Harvard University Press.

Walqui, A., Koelsch, N., Hamburger, L., Garrder, D., Insaurralde, A., Schmida, M., & Weiss, S. (2010). *What are we doing to middle school English learners? Findings and recommendations for change from a study of California EL programs.* WestEd.

WIDA. (2020). *WIDA English language development standards framework, 2020 edition: Kindergarten—Grade 12.* https://wida.wisc.edu/sites/default/files/resource/WIDA-ELD-Standards-Framework-2020.pdf

Yoon, B. (2022). *Effective teacher collaboration for English language learners: Cross-curricular insights from K–12 settings.* Routledge.

Author Index

Abdul-Jabar, M.
   see DeFlaminis, J.
ACTFL (American Council on the Teaching of Foreign Languages), 60
Alarcon, Elia, 50*f*
Alavi, Sana, 44*f*
Aldrich, J., 140
Al Kurwai, H., 8*f*
Amanti, C.
   see Moll, L. C.
American Councils Research Center, 2
Aponte, G. Y.
   see Solorza, C. R.
Ascenzi-Moreno, L., 103
Association of Two-Way & Dual Language Education (ATDLE), 60
August, D., 94

Baker, D., 10
Batalova, J.
   see Park, M.
Becker, T.
   see Solorza, C. R.
Beeman, K., 60, 84, 174
Beninghof, A. M., 71, 117, 136
Boals, T.
   see Nordmeyer, J.
Brookfield, S., 164, 165, 171
Brooks, S., 114*f*
Brown, B., 186
Bunch, G. C., 93
Butvilofsky, S., 60, 103, 171
   see also Escamilla, K.

Calderón, M. E., 67, 106, 171
Capper, C. A.
   see Scanlan, M.

Carmona, J. F., 71
Center for Advanced Research on Language Acquisition (CARLA), 60
Center for Applied Linguistics, 15, 16, 61, 207
Cervantes-Soon, C. G., 18, 48, 51, 56
   see also Palmer, D. K.
Cheuk, T.
   see Santos, M.
Choi, J.
   see Cervantes-Soon, C. G.
Christian, D., 60, 103
   see also Genesee, F.; Howard, E. R.
Cloud, N., 60
Cohan, A., 136
Collier, V. P., 2, 9, 10, 11, 33, 41, 51, 56, 60, 72, 183, 196, 199, 207
Compton, T. N., 11
Cook, L., 71, 117
Cooper, A., 204, 205–206*f*, 207
Costa, B., 128*f*, 129*f*

Darling-Hammond, L., 190
   see also Santos, M.
Davison, C., 10, 11
DeFlaminis, J., 178
de Jong, E., 41, 51
Destefano, M.
   see Peercy, M. M.
Ditter, M.
   see Peercy, M. M.
Donohoo, J., 16
Dorner, L.
   see Cervantes-Soon, C. G.; Palmer, D. K.
Dove, M. G., 10, 15, 33, 44, 49, 68, 71, 88*f*, 94, 94*f*, 99*f*, 100–101*f*, 103, 117, 118, 136, 145, 171, 207
   see also Calderón, M. E.; Robertson, K.

Dual Language Education of New Mexico, 61, 207
DualLanguageSchools.org, 207
DuFour, Rebecca, 71
  see also DuFour, Richard; Mattos, M.
DuFour, Richard, 71
  see also Marzano, R. J.; Mattos, M.
Dugan, J., 145, 174, 181
Dyer, W., 64

Eaker, R.
  see DuFour, Richard; Mattos, M.
Edmondson, A. C., 108
Escamilla, K., 54, 60, 86, 89, 102, 103, 164, 171, 200*f*
Escamilla, M., 60, 103, 171
  see also Escamilla, K.
España, C., 51, 207
Espino, G.
  see Calderón, M. E.
Espinosa, L. M., 3
Espinoza, C., 103
Ewing, Jaclyn, 155*f*

Fang, Z., 87, 88
Feinauer, E., 51, 54
Fizell, S. G., 117
Foltos, L., 10, 171
Francis, Hartwell (Unega Tisidu), 17*f*
Frattura, E.
  see Scanlan, M.
Fredricks, J. A., 183
Freeman, J., 207
Freeman, Y., 207
Frias, B.
  see Solorza, C. R.
Friend, M., 71, 117

Gandhi, E.
  see Greenberg Motamedi, J.
Garavito, D.
  see Nolte, J.
García, O., 35, 36, 60, 65, 86
  see also Solorza, C. R.
Gardner, M.
  see Darling-Hammond, L.
Garrder, D.
  see Walqui, A.

Genesee, F., 33, 60, 127
Gibbons, P., 93, 94
Gonzalez, N.
  see Moll, L. C.
Gottlieb, M., 36, 60, 66, 143, 145, 146, 147*f*, 153, 167, 168–169*f*, 171, 196, 207
  see also Calderón, M. E.
Grapin, S., 83
Greenberg Motamedi, J., 10, 33, 127
Guerrero, M. C., 45
Guerrero, M. D., 11, 45, 183, 207

Hajdun, M., 76*f*
Hamayan, E., 60
Hamburger, L.
  see Walqui, A.
Hamman-Ortiz, L., 4, 109
Hattie, J., 14
Heiman, D.
  see Cervantes-Soon, C. G.; Palmer, D. K.
Hernandez, R., 8*f*, 159*f*
Herrera, L. Y., 51, 207
Hichwa, M., 8*f*
Holmgren, M.
  see Greenberg Motamedi, J.
Honigsfeld, A., 10, 15, 33, 44, 49, 68, 71, 88*f*, 94, 94*f*, 99*f*, 100–101*f*, 103, 117, 118, 136, 145, 171, 188, 188–189*f*, 207
  see also Calderón, M. E.; Robertson, K.
Hopewell, S., 60, 103, 171
  see also Escamilla, K.
Howard, E. R., 3, 9, 11, 18, 41, 42, 48, 49, 51, 52, 54, 60, 70, 86, 95, 103, 149, 170, 190
Hunt, V., 175
Hyler, M. E.
  see Darling-Hammond, L.

Ibarra-Johnson, S., 60
  see also García, O.
Insaurralde, A.
  see Walqui, A.

Johnson, L., 109

Kennedy, B., 60, 103
  see also Howard, E. R.
Kibler, A., 56, 89
  see also Bunch, G. C.
Kim, H.
  see Baker, D.
Klein, A., 180
Koelsch, N.
  see Walqui, A.
Al Kurwai, H., 8*f*

Lachance, J., 11, 41, 45, 183, 207
Ladson-Billings, G., 28
Leverenz, T.
  see Solorza, C. R.
Levine, L. N., 94
Lindholm-Leary, K. J., 41, 51, 60, 103, 127
  see also Genesee, F.; Howard, E. R.
Lochner, W. W., 71
Los Angeles Unified School District, 136
Lukens, L.
  see Levine, L. N.
Lyster, R., 207

MacDonald, R.
  see Nordmeyer, J.
Madigan Peercy, M., 10, 11
Manriquez, J., 128*f*, 129*f*
Many, T. W.
  see DuFour, Richard; Mattos, M.
Martin-Beltrán, M., 10, 11
Marzano, R. J., 71
Massachusetts Department of Education, 61
Massachusetts Department of Elementary and Secondary Education, 10, 103
Mattos, M., 71
Medina, J., 60, 103
  see also Howard, E. R.
Menken, K., 51, 178, 194
Migration Policy Institute, 61, 207
Moje, E. B., 84
Moll, L. C., 36
Multistate Association for Bilingual Education, Northeast, 61
Murawski, W. W., 71, 117

Nagle, J. F., 10
National Clearinghouse for English Language Acquisition, 2, 200*f*
Neff, D.
  see Moll, L. C.
Nevin, A. I.
  see Villa, R. A.
New America, 119*f*, 120*f*, 121*f*, 122*f*, 123*f*, 124*f*, 125*f*
New York State Education Department (NYSED), 10
Nolte, J., 180
Nordmeyer, J., 56, 92, 109, 188, 188–189*f*, 207
Norton, J., 10

Olague, N., 60, 103
  see also Howard, E. R.
Olsen, L.
  see Escamilla, K.
Olsen, S., 8*f*
Ortloff, J., 10
O'Toole, J., 11

Palmer, D. K., 4, 18, 48, 51, 56, 109
  see also Cervantes-Soon, C. G.
Park, M., 29
Paul H. Brookes Publishing, 171
Pawan, F., 10
Peercy, M. M., 10, 11
  see also Madigan Peercy, M.
Peery, A., 71
Pérez, A. I., 115
Perez, K. D., 117
Pryor, S., 80

Rahman, S., 85*f*
Rains, C. L.
  see Marzano, R. J.
Ramsey, B., 114*f*
Reeves, D., 182, 207
Reyna, V. F.
  see Nolte, J.
Roberson, A.
  see Baker, D.
Robertson, D. A., 87
Robertson, K., 144–145
Roda, A., 51

Rodriguez, D., 136
Rogers, D., 60, 103
   see also Howard, E. R.
Ruiz-Figueroa, O., 60, 103, 171
   see also Escamilla, K.

Safir, S., 11, 145, 174, 181, 186, 188
Sánchez, M. T.
   see Solorza, C. R.
Santos, M., 77
Scanlan, M., 11, 109
Schmida, M.
   see Walqui, A.
Schneider, K. A.
   see Scanlan, M.
Schon, D. A., 189*f*
Schwerdtfeger, R.
   see Cervantes-Soon, C. G.
Seltzer, K., 60
   see also García, O.
Shafer Willner, L., 23
Shanahan, C., 87
Shanahan, T., 87
Simpson, S., 70, 170
Slakk, S., 171
   see also Calderón, M. E.
Slavik, J.
   see also Escamilla, K.
Sleeter, C. E., 71
Smallwood, B. A.
   see Levine, L. N.
Smith, M., 45*f*
Solorza, C. R., 86
Soltero-González, L., 60, 103, 171
   see also Escamilla, K.
Soto, I., 171
   see also Calderón, M. E.
Sparrow, W., 60, 103, 171
   see also Escamilla, K.
Staehr Fenner, D., 171
   see also Calderón, M. E.
Sugarman, J., 60, 103
   see also Howard, E. R.

Tedick, D. J., 207
TESOL International, 61
Theoharis, G., 11
Thomas, W. P., 2, 9, 10, 11, 33, 41, 51, 56, 60, 72, 183, 196, 199, 207
Thousand, J. S.
   see Villa, R. A.
Tyrrell, J., 15

Urow, C., 60, 84, 174
U.S. Department of Health and Human Services, 207

Valdés, G.
   see Kibler, A.
Vazquez, M.
   see Greenberg Motamedi, J.
Villa, R. A., 71, 116
Visual Learning, 16
Vygotsky, L. S., 92

Walqui, A., 33
   see also Bunch, G. C.; Kibler, A.
Ward, K., 45*f*
Ward Singer, T., 171
   see also Calderón, M. E.
Warrick, P. B.
   see Marzano, R. J.
Wei, L., 86
Weiss, S.
   see Walqui, A.
Westerlund, R.
   see Nordmeyer, J.
WIDA, 66, 83, 94
Wilson, C., 207
Woodley, H. H., 35

Yoak, E.
   see DeFlaminis, J.
Yoon, B., 10, 71
Youtsey, María Cristina, 155*f*

Zacarian, D., 171
   see also Calderón, M. E.
Zong, J.
   see Park, M.
Zwiers, J., 103

Subject Index

Academic achievement
  see Grade-level academic achievement
ACTFL (American Council on the Teaching of Foreign Languages), 60
Additive/dynamic dual language education, 35, 41, 43
Administrative leadership, 175–176, 182, 182*f*, 193–194, 195*f*
Aguilera, Alejandra, 52–53
Ahmed, Dalal Ali, 90–91*f*
Alarcon, Elia, 49
Al Romaihi, Maha, 43–44
Alternative teaching model, 117
Anchoring activities, 49, 155
Arizona Proposition 203 (2000), 39–40*f*
Aspiazu, Vanessa, 70–71
Assessment and measurement processes
  actionable steps, 164–165, 166–167*f*
  authentic assessment, 140–143
  basic concepts, 145, 146, 164
  collaborative leadership and support, 181–182
  collaborative planning, 81, 92*f*, 99*f*
  cultural considerations, 145
  District 54 program, 159–160, 159*f*, 203, 203*f*
  EL ESPEJO Framework, 167, 168–169*f*, 170
  essential strategies framework, 150, 151*f*
  frequency, 149
  holistic programs, 196, 197–198*f*, 201*f*
  implementation tips, 171
  instructional cycle, 12–13, 13*f*, 110, 110*f*
  instructional partnerships, 144, 148, 157–158*f*
  key collaborative practices, 189*f*
  levels of assessment, 153–155, 154*f*, 156–158*f*, 196
  multidimensional classroom language, 146, 147*f*
  navigation systems, 153–155, 170
  practitioner feedback, 148
  professional learning communities (PLCs), 159–163, 170
  program resources, 171
  reflective practices, 146, 155, 164–165, 172
  research results, 143, 149
  scaffolding practices and support, 155, 155*f*
  student/teacher perspectives, 140–142
Assessment as learning, 153, 154*f*, 155, 156*f*, 166*f*, 168*f*, 196
Assessment for learning, 154–155, 154*f*, 157*f*, 166–167*f*, 168*f*, 196
Assessment of learning, 154–155, 154*f*, 158*f*, 167*f*, 168*f*, 196
Association of Two-Way & Dual Language Education (ATDLE), 60
Authentic assessment, 140–142
  see also Co-assessment

Basic dynamic biliteracy, 87, 88*f*
Belief and value systems, 56
Bilingualism and biliteracy
  basic concepts, 48–49
  co-agreements, 76, 76*f*
  collaborative assessment, 155
  collaborative leadership and support, 195*f*, 197*f*, 202
  collaborative planning, 73, 73*f*, 82–83, 86–89, 90–91*f*, 92, 95–98, 97*f*

collaborative practices and
   partnerships, 41, 48–49
co-planning agreements, 128–129,
   128f, 134
curricular and instructional decisions,
   95–98, 97f
EL ESPEJO Framework, 168–169f
essential strategies framework, 77
free-writing activity, 28, 29
pillars and priorities crosswalk grid, 75f
reflective practices, 164–165
shared visions and goals, 200–201f
see also Dual language programs;
   Language and literacy development;
   Multilingual learners (MLs)
Bilingual Multicultural Education Act
   (1973), 38–39f
Booster engines, 35
The Bridge instructional strategy,
   84–85, 85f, 174
Bridging
   collaborative assessment, 142, 154, 166f
   collaborative planning, 81, 84–87, 85f
   collaborative teaching, 46, 107, 111,
      112, 114–115, 119–126, 136
   language and literacy development, 88f
   self-assessment and reflection
      checklist, 92f
Brockton Public Schools
   (Massachusetts), 180
Brooks, Sarah, 113, 114f
Brown Station Elementary School
   (Maryland), 148

California Proposition 58 (2016), 39f
Capacity-building strategies, 54, 55f, 57
Captain's Log
   collaborative assessment,
      141–142, 143, 146, 153, 160, 163
   collaborative leadership and support,
      176, 180, 195
   collaborative planning, 68, 72, 81, 98
   collaborative practices and partnerships,
      33, 47, 53, 65
   collaborative teaching,
      107, 112, 117, 134
   critical thinking skills, 33

curricular and instructional
   decisions, 53, 98
dual language programs, 31, 42–43
four pillars of effective dual language
   education, 29, 52, 195
goals and objectives, 22
heart-centered conversations, 187, 187f
informed dynamic components, 55
language development, 65
legislative enactments and
   regulations, 40
student perceptions, 31
Captain's Log: Final Entry
   collaborative assessment, 172
   collaborative leadership
      and support, 209
   collaborative planning, 104
   collaborative teaching, 137
   educational challenges, 62
   equitable instruction, 57
   reflective feedback, 25
Castañeda v. Pickard (1981), 37f
Center for Advanced Research on
   Language Acquisition (CARLA), 60
Center for Applied Linguistics, 61
Charlotte-Mecklenburg Schools (North
   Carolina), 49, 202
Chen, Sami, 17
Cherokee language, 16–18, 17f
Cho, Gloria, 180–181
Cicero School District 99 (Illinois), 80
Civil Rights Act (1964), 36–37f
Classroom design, 134, 135f
Co-assessment
   actionable steps, 164–165, 166–167f
   authentic assessment, 140–143
   basic concepts, 145, 146, 164
   collaborative leadership and support,
      181–182
   cultural considerations, 145
   District 54 program, 159–160, 159f,
      203, 203f
   EL ESPEJO Framework, 167,
      168–169f, 170
   essential strategies framework,
      150, 151f
   frequency, 149

holistic programs, 196, 197–198f, 201f
implementation tips, 171
instructional cycle, 12–13,
    13f, 110, 110f
instructional partnerships, 144, 148,
    157–158f
key collaborative practices, 189f
levels of assessment, 153–155, 154f,
    156–158f, 196
multidimensional classroom language,
    146, 147f
navigation systems, 153–155, 170
practitioner feedback, 148
professional learning communities
    (PLCs), 159–163, 170
program resources, 171
reflective practices, 146, 155,
    164–165, 172
research results, 143, 149
scaffolding practices and
    support, 155, 155f
student/teacher perspectives, 140–142
Co-delivery, 12, 13f
Cognates, 85, 147f
Co-instruction
  see Collaborative leadership;
    Collaborative teaching; Teaching
    partnerships
Collaborative leadership
  The Bridge instructional strategy, 174
  decision-making practices, 180–184,
    184–186f, 186–188, 190–191,
    191–193f, 193–194
  discussion prompts, 191–192f
  educator/administrator perspectives,
    174–176
  four pillars of effective dual language
    education, 182f, 183, 195f
  guiding questions, 205–206f
  implementation tips, 208
  key collaborative practices, 188–189f
  leadership styles, 182–184, 182f,
    187–188, 190–191, 193–194, 195f
  navigation systems, 199, 200–201f
  practitioner feedback, 180–181,
    193, 194
  program resources, 207–208

  real-world examples, 202–203, 203f
  research results, 175, 178, 188,
    190, 199
  roles and responsibilities,
    178–180, 179f
  self-assessment and reflection, 181–182
  stakeholder dialogues, 174–176,
    177f, 193–194
  trusting relationships,
    186, 187f, 188, 190
  see also Curricular and
    instructional decisions
Collaborative scaffolding, 94f, 101f
Collaborative teaching
  beliefs and objectives, 126–127
  classroom design, 134, 135f
  collaborative assessment,
    144, 148, 157–158f
  collaborative planning, 19, 67, 71–72
  co-planning agreements, 76, 76f,
    128–129, 128f, 134
  curricular and instructional decisions,
    52–53
  daily lessons/routines, 129f, 130–131
  definition, 109, 116
  dual language programs, 44–47,
    45f, 112–115, 114f, 127–133,
    128f, 129f
  implementation tips, 61, 126–127,
    136–137
  instructional cycle, 12, 13f
  instructional models, 116–124, 119f,
    120f, 121f, 122f, 123f, 124f,
    125f, 135f
  key collaborative practices, 188–189f
  navigation systems, 117–126
  practitioner feedback, 111, 113, 116
  program resources, 60–61, 136
  real-world examples, 127–133
  research results, 10, 108, 109, 127
  student/teacher perspectives, 106–108
  two-way dual language programs,
    112–115, 114f
  see also Collaborative leadership
Collier, Virginia, 9, 33–34, 56
Collinswood Language Academy, 49
Columbus School (Colombia), 76, 76f

Commitment
  see Shared goals; Team norms
Common understandings, 200–201f
Complementary co-teaching model, 116
Content-integrated biliteracy approach, 95–97, 97f, 98
Conversations from the heart, 186, 187, 187f
Co-planning
  anchoring strategies, 80
  basic concepts, 68–69
  basic tools and resources, 98, 99–102f, 102
  benefits, 71–72, 74
  The Bridge instructional strategy, 84–85, 85f
  co-agreements, 76, 76f, 128–129, 128f, 134
  curricular and instructional decisions, 95–98, 97f
  dual language programs, 12, 13f, 34, 43–44, 128–129, 128f
  EL ESPEJO Framework, 167, 168–169f, 170
  essential strategies framework, 76–77, 78–79f
  four-dimensional planning framework, 73–74, 73f
  implementation tips, 82, 103
  importance, 64–66
  instructional cycle, 12, 13f, 110, 110f
  instructional partnerships, 19, 67, 71–72
  key collaborative practices, 188–189f
  key instructional practices, 82–83
  language and literacy development, 86–89, 88f, 90–91f, 92
  logistical concerns, 69
  multilingual/multimodal/multilevel practices and resources, 83–84
  navigation systems, 76–77, 78–79f, 80–81
  pillars and priorities crosswalk grid, 75f
  practitioner feedback, 70–73
  program resources, 103
  real-world examples, 95–97
  refinement strategies, 80–81
  research results, 66, 83–84
  scaffolding practices and support, 92–95, 94f, 98, 100–101f
  self-assessment and reflection checklist, 92f
  student/teacher perspectives, 64–66
  translanguaging, 86–87
Core Beliefs
  collaborative assessment, 164
  collaborative leadership and support, 204
  collaborative planning, 82
  collaborative teaching, 126
  dynamic multilingualism, 23
  equitable instruction, 56
  purpose, 23
Co-reflection
  collaborative assessment, 146, 155, 164–165, 170, 172
  collaborative conversations, 58–59f, 110f
  collaborative planning, 92f, 128f, 129
  collaborative teaching, 131–133
  four-lens approach, 165
  instructional cycle, 13, 13f, 110, 110f
  key collaborative practices, 189f
Costa, Bridget, 127–133, 128f
Countdown to Launch
  collaborative assessment, 171
  collaborative leadership and support, 208
  collaborative planning, 103
  collaborative teaching, 61, 136–137
  purpose, 24
Critical consciousness
  basic concepts, 52
  collaborative leadership and support, 195f, 198f
  collaborative planning, 73, 73f, 82, 89, 95, 97f
  collaborative practices and partnerships, 52
  curricular and instructional decisions, 95, 97f
  EL ESPEJO Framework, 168–169f
  equitable instruction, 56

essential strategies framework, 77, 79f, 152f
free-writing activity, 29
pillars and priorities crosswalk grid, 75f
scaffolding practices and support, 94f, 100f
Critical conversations, 183
Critical thinking skills, 33
Cultural identity, 50–51
Curricular and instructional decisions
collaborative leadership and support, 183–184, 184–186f, 190–191, 191–193f, 193–194
collaborative planning, 95–98, 97f
collaborative teaching, 52–53
discussion prompts, 184–186f, 191–193f
dual language programs, 48–49, 50f, 52–53
EL ESPEJO Framework, 168–169f
equitable instruction, 56
Curriculum mapping, 108, 110f

Digital scaffolding, 94f, 100f
Disciplinary literacy, 87–89, 88f
Discourse, 147f
Discussion prompts
collaborative leadership and support, 191–192f
curricular and instructional decisions, 184–186f, 191–193f
District 54 program, 159–160, 159f, 203, 203f
Dual Language Education of New Mexico, 61
Dual language programs
basic concepts, 3–4
benefits, 16, 33–35, 54, 56–57
classroom design, 134, 135f
collaborative conversations, 57, 58–59f, 110f
collaborative planning, 12, 13f, 34, 43–44, 128–129, 128f
collaborative practices and partnerships, 10, 19, 41–47, 45f, 65

collaborative teaching, 44–47, 45f, 112–115, 114f, 127–133, 128f, 129f
core premises, 18
curricular and instructional decisions, 48–49, 50f, 52–53
educational challenges, 62
effectiveness, 10–11
EL ESPEJO Framework, 167, 168–169f, 170
equitable instruction, 9, 11, 35, 51, 56–57
facts versus myths, 14
foundational elements, 28–29, 48–52
guiding questions, 205–206f
historical perspective, 35–36, 36–40f, 40
immersion programs, 41–42
implementation practices, 41–43
importance, 9, 16–18, 33–35
inclusivity, 10, 71
informed dynamic components, 54, 55f
instructional cycle, 12–13, 13f, 110, 110f
practitioner feedback, 11–12, 15, 33–34, 43–44
prevalence, 2, 10
program options, 8f
program resources, 60–61, 103
research results, 10, 14, 56, 108, 109, 127
shared visions and goals, 200–201f
student/teacher perspectives, 29–32
terminology, 4–5
transitional bilingual education (TBE) programs, 30–31
see also Bilingualism and biliteracy; Co-assessment; Collaborative leadership; Co-planning; Four pillars of effective dual language education; Language and literacy development; Multilingual learners (MLs)
Dynamic bilingualism, 18, 35
Dynamic biliteracy, 87, 88f
Dynamic Lived Experiences, 54, 55f
Dynamic multilingualism, 23, 200f

Eastern Band of Cherokee
    Indians (EBCI), 16–18
Educator perspectives
    collaborative assessment, 142
    collaborative leadership and
        support, 174–175
    collaborative planning, 65–66
    collaborative teaching, 107–108
    dual language programs, 31–32
    purpose, 22
Elder Speakers, 17
Elementary classrooms, 114–115
EL ESPEJO Framework, 167,
    168–169*f*, 170
Embedded Language Expectations for
    Systemic Planning, Enacting, and
    Justifying Outcomes (EL ESPEJO)
    framework
    see EL ESPEJO Framework
English as a foreign language (EFL), 10
English as an additional
    language (EAL), 10
English as a second language (ESL), 5,
    6–7*f*, 10, 32, 39–40*f*
English-dominant groups, 41
English language development (ELD)
    collaborative assessment, 144
    collaborative teaching, 67, 71, 109, 115
    definition, 5
    dual language programs, 6–7*f*
    legislative enactments and
        regulations, 38*f*, 40*f*
    real-world examples, 29–32
    research results, 127
    see also Bilingualism and biliteracy;
        Language and literacy development
English learners (ELs), 5, 6–7*f*, 10,
    36–40*f*, 127
    see also Multilingual learners (MLs)
English-only instruction, 35–36, 39–40*f*
Environmental scaffolding, 94*f*, 100*f*
Equitable practices
    collaborative assessment, 92, 145, 146,
        150, 152*f*, 155, 164, 170
    collaborative leadership and support,
        181, 198*f*, 200–201*f*, 204, 207
    collaborative planning, 68, 71–72, 74,
        76*f*, 77, 79*f*, 86, 92

collaborative teaching, 61, 106, 135*f*, 143
curricular and instructional
    decisions, 56
decision-making practices, 181
dual language programs, 7*f*, 9, 11,
    14, 35, 48, 51, 56–57
EL ESPEJO Framework, 168–169*f*
four pillars of effective dual language
    education, 51, 52
goals and objectives, 23
guiding questions, 205–206*f*
home languages, 5
practitioner feedback, 33–34, 194
reflective questions, 58*f*
research results, 109, 143
scaffolding practices and support, 94,
    95, 100–101*f*
Essential mindsets, 76, 76*f*
Every Student Succeeds Act (ESSA,
    2015), 38*f*
Ewing, Jaclyn, 155
Exploration
    collaborative assessment,
        140–146, 148–150, 153
    collaborative leadership and support,
        174–196
    collaborative planning, 64–74, 76
    collaborative teaching, 106–117
    dual language programs, 29–36,
        41–42, 44–51
    purpose, 21

Federal legislation enactments and
    regulations, 37–38*f*, 40
Five Objects Categories, 17, 17*f*
Formative assessment, 154, 163, 197*f*
Foster, Julianne, 148
Four-dimensional planning framework,
    73–74, 73*f*
Four-lens reflective approach, 165
Four pillars of effective dual language
    education
    basic concepts, 48–52
    collaborative leadership and support,
        182*f*, 183, 195*f*, 197–198*f*
    collaborative teaching, 125–126
    equitable instruction, 56
    free-writing activity, 28–29

Fourteenth Amendment (U.S. Constitution), 36–37f
Francis, Hartwell (Unega Tisidu), 16–18
Fratto, Francesco L., 15
Freeport Public Schools (New York), 34
Free-writing activities, 28–29

Gear Up!
  collaborative assessment, 165–170
  collaborative conversations, 58–59f
  collaborative leadership and support, 204
  collaborative planning, 98, 99–102f, 102
  collaborative teaching, 134, 135f
  foundational resources, 57
  purpose, 24
Goals, shared, 71, 74, 160–161, 190, 200–201f
González, Claribel, 11, 20, 21
Grade-level academic achievement
  anchoring activities, 49, 50f
  basic concepts, 49
  collaborative leadership and support, 195f
  collaborative planning, 73, 73f, 82, 89, 95, 97f
  curricular and instructional decisions, 95, 97f
  EL ESPEJO Framework, 168–169f
  essential strategies framework, 77
  free-writing activity, 28, 29
  pillars and priorities crosswalk grid, 75f
Gradual Release of Responsibility (GRR) Model, 80–81
Grajeda, Liliana, 52–53
Grammar, 85
Graphic scaffolding, 94f, 100f

Haaland, Mats, 72
Hackman, Richard, 108
Hajdun, Matt, 76
Heart-centered conversations, 186, 187, 187f
Henking School (Illinois), 111
Heritage language programs, 7f, 16–18, 17f
Hernandez, Rocio, 159, 160, 203, 203f

Hernandez v. Texas (1954), 36f
Herricks Union Free School District (New York), 15
Holistic programs, 196, 197–198f, 201f
Home language
  benefits, 33
  collaborative teaching, 115
  definition, 5
  dual language programs, 3, 7f, 9
  historical perspective, 35
  legislative enactments and regulations, 36f, 39f
Horizontal program planning, 44, 113, 114, 189f, 190, 192f, 200–201f
Hybrid teaching models, 70–71

Immersion language programs, 41–42
Indigenous languages, 16–18, 17f
Individualized education programs (IEPs), 81
Informed dynamic components, 54, 55f
Instructional co-teaching models, 116–126, 119–125f, 135f
Instructional partnerships
  see Collaborative leadership; Collaborative teaching; Teaching partnerships
Instructional scaffolding
  collaborative assessment, 150, 151f, 155f
  collaborative planning, 92–95, 94f, 98, 100–101f
Integrated curricular frameworks, 95–97, 97f, 168–169f
Integrated ELD programs, 6f
Interactive scaffolding, 94f, 101f
Intermediate literacy, 87, 88, 88f
International Baccalaureate programs, 42, 43–44, 44f

Jackson, Gilliam, 17
Jefferson County School District 251 (Idaho), 45
John F. Kennedy Elementary School (New York), 52

Kauffman, David, 194
Kennedy, Sean, 70–71

Kindergarten classrooms, 114
Kittilsen, Vanessa, 116
Kobari, Seika, 203, 203f

La Beach, Keisha, 11–12
Language and literacy development
   collaborative assessment, 150, 170
   collaborative leadership and support, 170, 177f
   collaborative planning, 74, 81–84, 86–89, 88f, 90–91f, 92, 108
   curricular and instructional decisions, 95–98, 97f
   dual language programs, 5–6, 6–7f, 42, 87–88
   essential strategies framework, 77
   multilevel discourse, 84
   navigation systems, 200–201f
   research results, 190
   scaffolding practices and support, 94f, 95
   see also Bilingualism and biliteracy; Multilingual learners (MLs)
Language Opportunity for Our Kids (LOOK) Act (2018), 38f
Language progressions, 77, 78f, 150, 151f
Language scaffolds, 77, 78f, 150, 151f, 155, 155f
Language supports, 77, 79f, 150, 152f
Launched Missions
   collaborative assessment, 159–163
   collaborative leadership and support, 202–203, 203f
   collaborative planning, 95–97, 97f
   collaborative teaching, 52–53, 127–133, 128f
   curricular and instructional decisions, 95–97, 97f
   purpose, 23
   real-world examples, 52–53
Lau v. Nichols (1974), 36–37f
Leadership
   see Collaborative leadership
Leadership Commitment, 54, 55f
"Let's Agree" Statements
   collaborative assessment, 164
   collaborative leadership and support, 204

   collaborative planning, 82
   collaborative teaching, 56–57, 126–127
   purpose, 23
Levels of assessment, 153–155, 154f, 156–158f, 196
Linguistic expectations and opportunities, 77, 78f, 150, 151f, 197f
Linguistic scaffolding, 94f, 101f
Literacy Squared biliteracy model, 96
LoPresti, Sarah, 203, 203f

Macro-scaffolding, 93
Manriquez, Jessica, 127–133, 128f
Massachusetts Department of Education, 61
Massachusetts state legislation, 38f
Mathematics skills, 49, 50f
McNally, Caitlyn, 111
Mechanics Grove Elementary School (Illinois), 155
Meso-scaffolding, 93
Metalinguistic awareness
   collaborative assessment, 141, 147f, 148, 156f
   collaborative planning, 66, 84, 86
   daily lessons/routines, 129f
   scaffolding practices and support, 93
   student perceptions, 65
Micro-scaffolding, 93
Migration Policy Institute, 61
Mindfulness practices, 145
Mission Control
   collaborative assessment, 140
   collaborative leadership and support, 174
   collaborative planning, 64
   collaborative teaching, 106
   four pillars of effective dual language education, 28–29
   purpose, 21
Monolingualism, 35–36
Montgomery County Public Schools (Maryland), 148
Morphology, 85
Mosquera, Amy, 95
Multidimensional classroom language, 146, 147f

Multidimensional teaching
　　and learning, 183
Multilevel practices and resources, 84
Multilingual learners (MLs)
　　academic achievement, 49, 54
　　collaborative assessment, 146, 147*f*,
　　　　153–155, 158*f*
　　collaborative conversations, 58–59*f*
　　collaborative leadership and support,
　　　　178–179, 179*f*, 190, 199,
　　　　200–201*f*, 203, 203*f*
　　collaborative planning, 83–84
　　collaborative practices and
　　　　partnerships, 10, 54
　　critical consciousness, 51
　　critical thinking skills, 54
　　dual language programs, 29, 33, 41, 42
　　EL ESPEJO Framework, 168–169*f*
　　equitable instruction, 56
　　language and literacy development,
　　　　86–89, 88*f*, 90–91*f*, 92
　　legislative enactments and
　　　　regulations, 39–40*f*
　　prevalence, 2
　　shared visions and goals, 200–201*f*
　　sociocultural competence, 51
　　state legislation and regulations, 35
　　teaching partnerships, 19
　　see also Collaborative leadership;
　　　　Curricular and instructional
　　　　decisions
Multilingual scaffolding, 94*f*, 101*f*
Multimodality, 83–84
Multimodal scaffolding, 94*f*, 101*f*
Multisensory scaffolding, 94*f*, 101*f*
Multistate Association for Bilingual
　　Education, Northeast, 61

Navigation Systems
　　capacity-building strategies, 54, 55*f*
　　collaborative assessment, 153–155, 170
　　collaborative leadership and support,
　　　　199, 200–201*f*
　　collaborative planning, 76–77,
　　　　78–79*f*, 80–81
　　collaborative teaching, 117–126
　　purpose, 22
New Mexico state legislation, 38–39*f*

New York State Association of
　　World Language Administrators
　　(NYSAWLA), 15
New York State Education Department
　　(NYSED), 15
No Child Left Behind Act (NCLB,
　　2001), 37–38*f*
Norms, team, 160

One-way dual language programs, 7*f*,
　　41–43

Paired literacy approach, 95–97,
　　97*f*, 102, 102*f*
Parallel co-teaching model, 116
Parallel monolingualism, 18
Paraprofessionals, 47
Partner languages
　　collaborative assessment,
　　　　147*f*, 156–158*f*
　　collaborative planning, 83
　　collaborative teaching, 119–125, 136
　　curricular and instructional
　　　　decisions, 97*f*
　　definition, 5, 41
　　dual language programs, 3
　　paired literacy units, 97*f*
Partnerships, collaborative
　　see Collaborative leadership;
　　　　Collaborative teaching; Teaching
　　　　partnerships
Partnership teaching
　　see Collaborative leadership;
　　　　Collaborative teaching;
　　　　Teaching partnerships
Patchogue-Medford Union Free School
　　District (New York), 111
Phonemic awareness, 85
Phrases/words, 147*f*
Pillars and priorities crosswalk grid, 75*f*
Planning, collaborative
　　see Co-planning
Plyler v. Doe (1982), 37*f*
Pohl, Natalie, 181
Port Chester Public Schools
　　(New York), 70
Practitioner feedback
　　collaborative assessment, 148

collaborative leadership and support, 180–181, 193, 194
collaborative planning, 70–73
collaborative practices and partnerships, 11–12, 33–34
collaborative teaching, 111
dual language programs, 11–12, 15, 33–34, 43–44
partnership teaching, 116
Practitioner Learning, 54, 55f
Pragmatics, 85
Primary language, 3, 6f, 41
Problem-solving skills, 49
Professional learning communities (PLCs)
collaborative assessment, 149, 159–163, 170
collaborative leadership and support, 175, 183
collaborative planning, 71
curricular and instructional decisions, 184–186f, 192f
Program languages, 5, 49, 89, 92
Program resources
collaborative assessment, 171
collaborative leadership and support, 207–208
collaborative planning, 103
collaborative practices and partnerships, 60–61
collaborative teaching, 136
Protocols, collaborative, 110f, 155, 156–158f, 170
Pryor, Susan, 80

Qatar Academy Doha Primary School, 43–44, 44f

Ramsey, Blake, 113, 114f
Raymondville Independent School District (Texas), 37f
Reflective practices
collaborative assessment, 146, 155, 164–165, 170, 172
collaborative conversations, 58–59f, 110f
collaborative planning, 92f, 128f, 129
collaborative teaching, 131–133

four-lens approach, 165
instructional cycle, 13, 13f, 110, 110f
key collaborative practices, 189f
Relational trust, 186, 187f, 188, 190
Research Findings
collaborative assessment, 143, 149
collaborative leadership and support, 175, 178, 188, 190, 199
collaborative planning, 66, 83–84
collaborative practices and partnerships, 14, 56
collaborative teaching, 108, 109, 127
informed dynamic components, 54, 55f
multilingual/multimodal/multilevel practices and resources, 83–84
Rocha, Alma G., 34
Rodd, Carol, 202
Rodríguez, Michael, 193
Al Romaihi, Maha, 43–44

Scaffolding practices and support
collaborative assessment, 150, 151f, 155f
collaborative planning, 92–95, 94f, 98, 100–101f
translanguaging, 101f
Schaumburg School District 54 (Illinois), 159–160, 163
see also District 54 program
Secondary classrooms, 115
Self-assessment and reflection
bridging strategies, 92f
collaborative assessment, 155
collaborative leadership and support, 181–182
collaborative planning, 92f
translanguaging, 92f
Semantics, 85
Sentence structure, 85, 147f
Shared goals, 71, 74, 160–161, 190, 200–201f
Shared visions, 161–162, 200–201f
Smith, Katie, 203, 203f
Smith, Megan, 45, 45f
Social-emotional scaffolding, 94f, 101f
Sociocultural competence
basic concepts, 50–51

collaboration and co-teaching
practices, 50–51
collaborative leadership and
support, 195*f*, 197–198*f*
collaborative planning, 73, 73*f*,
82, 89, 95, 97*f*
curricular and instructional
decisions, 95, 97*f*
EL ESPEJO Framework, 168–169*f*
essential strategies framework,
77, 79*f*, 152*f*
free-writing activity, 29
pillars and priorities crosswalk grid, 75*f*
scaffolding practices and
support, 94*f*, 100*f*
Sound systems, 85
Stand-alone English language
development (ELD) programs, 6*f*
State legislation enactments and
regulations, 38–40*f*, 40
Station teaching model, 117
Staying the Course
collaborative assessment, 164–165
collaborative leadership and support, 204
collaborative planning, 82–89, 92–95
collaborative teaching, 126–127
equitable instruction, 56
purpose, 23
Student assessments, 170
Student perspectives
collaborative assessment, 140–142
collaborative planning, 64–65
collaborative teaching, 106–107
purpose, 22
transitional bilingual education (TBE)
programs, 30–31
Students with disabilities, 10, 71
Summative assessment, 154, 197*f*
Supportive co-teaching model, 116
Supportive practices
see Collaborative leadership
Supreme Court decisions, 36–37*f*
Syntax, 85, 147*f*

Tariq Bin Ziad school (Qatar), 89, 90–91*f*
Teacher leadership, 182, 182*f*,
183–184, 195*f*

Teaching partnerships
beliefs and objectives, 126–127
classroom design, 134, 135*f*
collaborative assessment,
144, 148, 157–158*f*
collaborative planning, 19, 67, 71–72
co-planning agreements, 76, 76*f*,
128–129, 128*f*, 134
curricular and instructional decisions,
52–53
daily lessons/routines, 129*f*, 130–131
definition, 109
dual language programs, 44–47, 45*f*,
112–115, 114*f*, 127–133, 128*f*,
129*f*
implementation tips, 126–127,
136–137
instructional cycle, 12, 13*f*
key collaborative practices, 188–189*f*
practitioner feedback, 111, 113, 116
program resources, 136
real-world examples, 127–133
research results, 10, 108, 109, 127
student/teacher perspectives, 106–108
two-way dual language programs,
112–115, 114*f*
see also Collaborative leadership
Team norms, 160
Team teaching model, 116
TESOL International, 61
Texas House Bill 3 (2019), 39*f*
Thomas, Wayne, 9, 33–34, 56
Transitional bilingual education (TBE)
programs, 6*f*, 30–31, 35
Translanguaging
collaborative assessment,
147*f*, 148, 156*f*
collaborative planning, 86–87
collaborative teaching, 107, 109,
119, 123, 124, 130–132
daily lessons/routines, 129*f*
implementation practices, 42
scaffolding practices and support, 101*f*
self-assessment and reflection
checklist, 92*f*
Trusting relationships, 186, 187*f*,
188, 190

Tune In!
    collaborative assessment, 171
    collaborative leadership and
        support, 207–208
    collaborative planning, 103
    collaborative teaching, 60–61, 136
    purpose, 24
Two-way bilingual education (TWBE)
    classrooms, 109
Two-way dual language programs, 4, 6*f*,
    41–43, 112–115, 114*f*

Unega Tisidu
    see Francis, Hartwell (Unega Tisidu)

Vaz-Correia, Nidia, 116
Vertical program planning, 44, 113, 114,
    177*f*, 189*f*, 190, 200–201*f*
Virtual teaching models, 70–71
Visions, shared, 161–162, 200–201*f*
Vygotsky, Lev, 92–93

Ward, Keri, 45, 45*f*
Washington State Transitional
    Bilingual Instruction
    Program, 39*f*
Web-based resources
    see Program resources
Week-at-a-Glance
    Tool, 99*f*
WIDA Consortium, 43
Wilson, Chelsea, 72, 73
Worcester Public Schools
    (Massachusetts), 127
Word formation, 85, 147*f*
World language programs, 7*f*

Xiong, Ruiyan, 203, 203*f*

Youtsey, María Cristina, 155

Zone of proximal
    development (ZPD), 92

A SAGE Publishing Company

Helping educators make the greatest impact

CORWIN HAS ONE MISSION: to enhance education through intentional professional learning.

We build long-term relationships with our authors, educators, clients, and associations who partner with us to develop and continuously improve the best evidence-based practices that establish and support lifelong learning.

Collaborate with us!

Joan Lachance

Empowerment, active engagement, and equitable access to multilingual education are at the heart of Joan Lachance's scholarly work and educational consulting. She is an associate professor in the Cato College of Education at the University of North Carolina at Charlotte. She is the co-author of the National Dual Language Education Teacher Preparation Standards©.

Dr. Lachance offers research-based and highly interactive virtual and on-site professional learning sessions for teachers, administrators, and others involved with teaching and learning. Additional services to support multilingualism include:

- Classroom visits and collaborative coaching
- Guidance for multilingual learners
- Dual language program development and expansion
- Professional learning institutes

Learn more at **https://cloverseedseducation.com**

Andrea Honigsfeld

Andrea Honigsfeld offers professional learning and leadership support for educators working with multilingual learners. Dr. Honigsfeld is a professor in the School of Education and Human Services at Molloy University, Rockville Centre, New York, where she teaches graduate courses related to cultural and linguistic diversity, language and literacy development, and equity.

Dr. Honigsfeld offers virtual and on-site professional learning opportunities primarily focusing on effective differentiated strategies and collaborative practices for ELD/ELL specialists and general education teachers. All training opportunities can be customized to schools' and districts' specific needs. Sample topics include:

- Collaboration and co-teaching for English language learners
- Effective literacy strategies for multilingual learners
- Leadership support

Learn more at **https://andreahonigsfeld.com**